PROMISED LAND

Anthony Clavane

Promised Land

The Reinvention of Leeds United

YELLOW JERSEY PRESS
LONDON

Published by Yellow Jersey Press 2010

2 4 6 8 10 9 7 5 3 1

Copyright © Anthony Clavane 2010

Anthony Clavane has asserted his right under the Copyright,
Designs and Patents Act 1988 to be identified as the author of this work

First published in Great Britain in 2010 by
Yellow Jersey Press
Random House, 20 Vauxhall Bridge Road,
London SW1V 2SA

www.rbooks.co.uk

Addresses for companies within The Random House Group
Limited can be found at:
www.randomhouse.co.uk/offices.htm

The Random House Group Limited Reg. No. 954009

A CIP catalogue record for this book
is available from the British Library

ISBN 9780224082631

The Random House Group Limited supports The Forest Stewardship Council
(FSC), the leading international forest certification organisation. All our titles
that are printed on Greenpeace approved FSC certified paper carry the
FSC logo. Our paper procurement policy can be found at
www.rbooks.co.uk/environment

Mixed Sources
Product group from well-managed
forests and other controlled sources
www.fsc.org Cert no. TT-COC-2139
© 1996 Forest Stewardship Council
FSC

Typeset in Bembo by Palimpsest Book Production Limited,
Falkirk, Stirlingshire
Printed and bound in Great Britain by
CPI Mackays, Chatham ME5 8TD

To Alison, Rosa, Miriam and Matthew
Sorry – and thanks

Contents

Illustrations

Section 1

1. Leeds winning the 1973-4 championship
2. The European Cup final (1975)
3. Solomon Saipe and customers in Leeds Market (c. 1905)l
4. Harry Clavane
5. Elaine and Emile Clavane
6. Keith Waterhouse, outside the Queen's Hotel
7. The Leylands: the Jewish ghetto of Leeds
8. Herbert Chapman
9. John Charles
10. Jewish Gazette article on author (1975)
11. Don Revie signs for Leeds United (November 1958)
12. Don Revie outside Elland Road (December 1969)
13. Don Revie and his Leeds squad, at a training session before the 1972 FA Cup Final
14. The Leeds United board in 1964
15. Albert Jonanneson
16. Leeds United with the 1969 League Championship

'[My dream is to] find the name of Leeds inscribed indelibly on the rolls of the Football Association as the city which passed through fire, was cleansed, and given a fair and sporting chance to rehabilitate itself' – Alf Masser, co-founder of Leeds United, 1920

'We are going to become a Real Madrid. One day, this club will rule in Europe' – Don Revie, 1961

'We lived the dream. We enjoyed the dream' – Peter Ridsdale, 2002

'We're not famous, we're not famous, we're not famous any more' – Leeds United fans, 2004–2010

Prologue

Alan: 'Look, what happened when Leeds lost to Bayern Munich, hey? Your smile slipped a bit then – you threw a bottle at the telly!'
Rigsby: 'That was different wasn't it? We were, we were robbed, definitely robbed – at the last gasp. And just after our valiant-hearted lads had run themselves into the ground. My God, did you see their faces? They were drained. I hadn't seen expressions like that since Dunkirk.'

Rising Damp, 1975

28 May 1975. Bayern Munich v Leeds. The European Cup Final. Giles to Madeley, Madely to Hunter, Hunter blasts over. Lorimer's shot just fizzes wide. Clarke is hacked down by Beckenbauer. Everyone knows it's a penalty; except the referee. 'It looks like a definite penalty to me,' says Don Revie, who is sitting alongside David Coleman in the TV gantry. 'Clarke was through and he's pulled the right leg from underneath Clarke.' In the second half Leeds continue to dominate possession. They have six attempts on goal to Bayern's none. Then: Giles to Madeley, who heads back to Lorimer. '1-0!'

screams Coleman. 'And while you're watching this there's bedlam on the field. Lorimer put it away and Bremner may have been offside. And the referee, who's seemed to have had his problems, has now given a goal.' And Revie was right. Leeds United are, finally, about to become European champions, the new Real Madrid, the greatest team in football the world has ever seen. Paris will be the defining moment in the club's history. It will be frozen in time and enshrined at the heart of all the stories Loiners tell about themselves for years to come. Stories passed on to each new generation of Leeds, Leeds, Leeds. 'But what's this?' says Coleman. Beckenbauer has persuaded the referee to consult the linesman, who is at the halfway line for the Bayern kick-off. 'The referee hasn't given a goal. Total confusion. He's given offside.'

On the morning of 4 September 2009, as my dad was giving me a lift to Leeds railway station, we heard on the car radio that the journalist and novelist Keith Waterhouse had died. Dad immediately started telling me about the Mecca, the dance hall he took Mum to when they started courting. It was now a fancy shop, he said, in one of those swanky Victorian arcades. When the DJ Jimmy Savile took over as assistant manager in 1959 – the year Waterhouse's great novel Billy Liar was published – you had to shave your sideburns off if you wanted to get in. Savile used to let the Leeds United players in for free but when Revie became manager all that stopped. My dad, who was born in the same year as Waterhouse, explained that the Mecca was the inspiration for the Roxy, the venue where Billy and Liz, his free-spirited girlfriend, planned their great escape to London. My favourite moment in the film, which appeared in 1963, is when Liz – portrayed by Julie Christie as an irresistible force, a harbinger of an exciting future, a portent of the deliverance to come – skips through the half-demolished streets of her smoky old city towards a new, dynamic, classless, handbag-swinging, white-heat meritocracy.

I've always associated Waterhouse's classic tale of an upwardly mobile, inwardly anxious Northern Man with the story of Leeds. The writer was born and brought up on an estate near Elland Road. The fantasy war sequences in Billy's mythical world of Ambrosia were filmed on the Headrow, the steps of Leeds town hall and an area off Wellington Road. The book was written in the late 1950s, when the city was on the cusp of a great transformation. Its big issue – its narrative hinge – is whether our anti-hero would dare to act on his fantasies and actually cross the threshold. 'It's easy,' Liz tells him. 'You get on a train and, four hours later, there you are in London.'

After Dad dropped me off that morning, I walked through the station's shiny concourse and looked up at its huge vaulted ceilings. As I watched the birds flying around in crazy circles, I remembered a sign that had once hung there and which bore the legend: 'Leeds, the Promised Land delivered.' Like most signs it could be read in a number of different ways. Many visitors must have thought it typical of the smug Yorkshire chauvinism they had heard so much about. Those more intimately acquainted with the self-capital of God's Own Country will have chuckled knowingly at its irony, taking a quiet pride in yet another example of the city's endless capacity for self-mockery. I always saw it as a sign of the times. In its blunt, no-nonsense, Yorkshire-plain-talking-tek-as-you-find kind of way, it let the world know exactly what Leeds thought of itself. It was a sign of hope and optimism. A prophecy. And then, one day, it was no longer there.

In the half-hour wait for the London train I worked out – or at least convinced myself – that the sign must have come down on 29 May 1975. The day after Paris. I certainly can't remember seeing it at all in the late seventies, when I first started catching the southbound train. The European Cup Final at the Parc des Princes was the closest Leeds United have ever come to reaching the promised land. They won the League in 1992 and were Champions League semi-finalists in 2001. But it was in Paris, in 1975, that they caught a glimpse of footballing immortality. If they had beaten Bayern Munich, as all neutral observers agreed they deserved to, their place in history would have been assured. Their legacy wouldn't have been tainted. Their fans wouldn't have rioted. People would have stopped blathering on about Dirty Leeds and started recognising the great-ness of Super Leeds. Paris could have, should have, would have been the greatest day in the club's – the city's – history. An epiphany, not a requiem.

Paris is not the only time Leeds have failed to cross the threshold. Before Paris, before Leeds United, there was Leeds City, a team that blossomed during the Edwardian era but, crippled by controversial payments and a mountainous debt, imploded at the end of the First World War. After Paris there were Wilkinson's Wonders, who won the title – and then were almost almost relegated the following season. At the end of

4

the 1990s, the club experienced the infamous living-the-dream era. It should have been the climax to an epic psychodrama. The end of the grand narrative. Leeds United would act on their fantasies, Billy Liar would get on that train, the Israelites would cross over into the promised land.

Everyone knows what happened next: controversial payments, a mountainous debt and a decade of shame and humiliation.

Throughout that decade, Leeds fans continually took refuge in the Events of May '75. We'll always have Paris. It is burned into our psyche, hardwired into our biology; it symbolises our fate. The referee turned down a cast-iron penalty, Lorimer had what appeared to be a good goal scrubbed for offside and Roth and Muller picked us off with two predatory strikes. After Paris, decline set in; apart from the 1992 title, all forms of success have eluded the club. To some supporters, Paris is an everlasting reminder of the club's cursed existence, the moment they were cheated out of glory, their rightful place in history. The dice has always been loaded against Leeds. It is because of Paris that, even during their three seasons in the third tier of English football, fans continued to chant: 'We are the champions, the champions of Europe.' Paris encapsulates the two contradictory narratives of Leeds, Leeds, Leeds: one, that we have a manifest destiny to triumph, and, two, that we never do triumph. For we are Leeds and, for the last fifty years, we have suffered the slings and arrows of outrageous offside decisions, disciplinary reports, gypsy curses, ground closures, points deductions, tropical goldfish, financial meltdowns and winding-up orders.

I, too, am Leeds. But I have no time for conspiracy theories. It is true that, at crucial moments in our history, important decisions have gone against us. But every football fan could tell you the same story. We are not really the Damned United. Thinking we are, however, is part of the problem.

Introduction

January 3rd, 2010. Manchester United v Leeds. The FA Cup third round. Naylor nicks the ball off Berbatov and Howson hits a 50-yard pass over the defence. Beckford's first touch is terrible. But he outruns Brown and, with his second touch, clips the ball past Kuszczak. Ferguson appears in the technical area, his eyes burning holes in his players. He sends on Giggs, Valencia and Owen. But Leeds keep passing and pressing. The fourth official signals five minutes of Fergie Time. Owen throws himself to the floor; no penalty. Johnson goes into a tackle with a diving header. Kisnorbo, his headband an emblem of defiance, wipes the blood away from his nose.

May 8th, 2010. Leeds v Bristol Rovers. The final game of the League One season. Almost an hour gone and Leeds are down to ten men and a goal behind. Once again, they are staring at the abyss. A fourth successive season in the lower half of the Football League beckons. Grayson sends on Howson, a local lad who once stood in the Kop. Howson curls a 20-yard shot past the goalkeeper. Three minutes later, Beckford smashes in the winner. When the referee blows his whistle, the Tannoy announcer pleads with fans to keep off the pitch. But the green turf quickly disappears beneath a sea of delirious white. And history rushes towards us, making us feel lightheaded.

For a brief, but glorious, moment at the beginning of 2010, the team that disappeared reappeared. To paraphrase Sam Tyler, the time-travelling Life On Mars detective played by Leeds-born actor John Simm, it was as if we had all taken leave of our senses – or gone back in time. After watching Simon Grayson's belligerent, in-your-face upstarts overcome Manchester United, and then draw at Spurs, Leeds fans began reminiscing about the halcyon days of yore, when Bremner and Giles patrolled the central midfield – just like Kilkenny and Doyle – and the swaggering Clarke sniffed out goals – just like Beckford – and Big Jack Charlton took no prisoners – just like Kisnorbo.

Many of the ecstatic, high-fiving, furiously-texting Leeds supporters who spilled out of Old Trafford will have been given The Damned United DVD for Christmas. The film, a fictionalised account of Brian Clough's disastrous spell at Elland Road in the mid-1970s, had been a huge hit. 'Leeds United,' it announced in its opening titles, 'is the dominant force in British football.' The blue-and-white Leeds United AFC sign of the Revie era had been recreated by a local metalworker and hoisted, once more, above Elland Road. The training pitch opposite the West Stand, converted into a car park 20 years earlier, had been re-turfed. The Glory Days alumni popped up to tell the nation where they were now in various where-are-they-now TV shows. The top floor of Leeds City Museum became a shrine to the sock tags, Smiley badges and purple tracksuits of the Glory Days. The local branch of Waterstone's put on a celebratory promotion. Three main books were on display: *The Damned Utd*, *The Unforgiven: The Story Of Don Revie's Leeds United* and *Service Crew: The Inside Story Of Leeds United's Hooligan Gangs*.

Then came the inevitable wobble. And, like DCI Tyler, we awoke from our nostalgia-induced coma to discover that it had all been a dream. The runaway League One leaders, having toppled the English champions and forced a replay in the next round against Tottenham, lost to Carlisle United in the northern area final of the Johnstone's Paint Trophy. They then won only eight out of their next 23 games. Their last victory at Old Trafford had been 29 years ago. In terms of glamour, success and finance, the two clubs were light years apart. At the beginning of the millennium, David O'Leary's side had attempted to supplant Ferguson's as British football's dominant force. They had made a fevered dash for glory, over-reached themselves and disappeared into the wilderness. Manchester United had gone on to win another 11 major trophies, including a hat-trick of league titles and the Champions League.

Appearing and disappearing tends to be the Leeds way. The insular industrial city was conspicuous by its absence at the birth of British football in the latter half of the nineteenth century. Holbeck Rugby Club, the first occupants of Elland Road, vanished suddenly in 1904. Leeds City Football Club, who had moved into the ground, disappeared fifteen years later. Leeds United then appeared – but spent their first forty years shuffling inconsequentially between the top two divisions.

Howard Wilkinson's first act on becoming manager, in 1988, was to banish the ghosts of Revie's Leeds, taking all their pictures off the walls. His title winners were then airbrushed from history by the O'Leary regime, which itself went up in a puff of smoke following the infamous meltdown at the turn of the millennium.

Nothing lasts forever. No team has a divine right to enter, or stay in, the promised land. Several clubs have dramatically risen and fallen in modern times. Nottingham Forest, for example, who in a three-year spell under Brian Clough won promotion, the First Division title and the European Cup. And Wimbledon, who clattered up the divisions and then crashed straight back down them again. Last season, Leeds pitted their wits against the likes of Norwich, Southampton and Charlton – all teams who, in recent years, have experienced a fall from grace. During the noughties, three other big clubs from the great northern industrial cities slipped off the radar – Sheffield Wednesday, Newcastle United and Bradford City. But such disappearances tell us, I would argue, something important about how both football and life have changed in Britain over the past half century.

Leeds United are the football story of our times. The club have always represented, to me, an exhilarating escape from a benighted past. But it seemed significant that, in the week they returned to the second tier of English football – the same division they were struggling in when Revie became manager – the privately-educated, Home Counties establishment returned to the heart of government. A young man born in 1958, the year Revie made his Elland Road debut, is likely to have a better job than his father; a young man born in 1970, who grew up under successive Thatcher governments, is less likely to. This downward spiral of mobility continued throughout the noughties, a decade in which Britain underwent the biggest growth in inequality since Victorian times.

United's peaks and troughs over the past fifty years have coincided with the peaks and troughs not only of the game itself, but also of the city of Leeds and its Jewish community. The Leeds United story is intertwined, in my mind at least, with these other two stories. All three came of age together. All three felt the world was theirs for the taking and the shaping. And all three, in recent times, have turned inwards.

The central strand of this book examines Leeds United's fifty-year quest to turn outwards, to transcend their origins, to reinvent themselves. Leeds is unique among England's major cities in having only one football club. They are fanatically supported, play in a big stadium and train at a state-of-the-art, purpose-built, multi-million-pound complex. And yet, before Revie arrived, they were – even in the eyes of their own supporters – a music-hall joke: 'Leeds Urinals'. Under The Don, they made a gigantic leap forward from provincial backwater to European superpower. After he left the empire crumbled. Their fortunes were revived in the 1990s – winning the last of the old-style league titles – but, in their desperation to join the rich men at football's top table, they crashed and burned.

The second strand concerns the city's parallel attempt to transform its image from a dirty, northern industrial town into 'the Barcelona of northern England'. In the 1960s it concreted over its grimy past, burst its boundaries and became a metropolitan super-region. In the 1980s, like the rest of the north, it took a big Thatcherite hit before emerging as a hub of commerce and business. It rode the crest of the nineties' speculative boom, rebranding itself as a modern, diverse, cultural powerhouse. Today it is a dual city, polarised between affluence and squalor. Perhaps it always has been. But, when I was growing up in the sixties and early seventies, it felt like a New Jerusalem was being built. There was a fluidity between the classes, races and religions. Aspirations were being fulfilled and potential was being realised. There was a feeling that anything was possible.

The third strand delves into an overlooked aspect of the Leeds United story: Leeds Jewry's climb from the squalid slums of the inner-city to the clean air of the northern suburbs. My great-grandparents, refugees from the antisemitic pogroms that broke out throughout Russia at the end of the nineteenth century, simply wanted to survive. My grandparents, who lived through two world wars, great poverty and a depression, wanted to belong. My parents' generation were the first to be given a real chance to escape the ghetto. Leeds United gave them that chance. Through their involvement with the club they were able, at long last, to engage with the outside world; to prove themselves and find new identity in an alien society.

A few months before Paris, while standing in the Kop watching the European Cup quarter-final first leg against Anderlecht – 3-0: Jordan, McQueen and Lorimer – I was asked whether I 'was Leeds'. My interrogators clearly didn't accept my answer; so much so that one of them decided to punch me in the face. But I was then, and remain to this day, an unrepentant, card-carrying member of Yorkshire's Republican Army. When my children were very young they thought that being Jewish and being Leeds were the same thing. This was because they would be driven up to their grandparents' house every school holiday, usually arriving in time for the traditional Friday-night meal of chicken soup and noodles. Then, the following day – nominally one of rest – they would be whisked off to Elland Road. We still spend our Easters in Leeds 17; after removing all leavened products from the house, we gather around the passover table to read from the haggada, a book of prayer which literally means 'telling the story'. Then we stay up all night eating, drinking and singing from a wide, if somewhat dated, repertoire of Hebrew dirges, Yiddish musical hall numbers, contemporary pop ballads and Leeds United anthems.

When I was young, I too equated Jewishness with Leedsness. At the passover meal we always drink four cups of wine, which represent the four movements from slavery to freedom: bring out, deliver, redeem, take. For me, these phases form the narrative arc of the Book of Leeds. During the industrial revolution, the dirty old town was 'brought out' of its prickly isolation. In the go-getting, upwardly mobile sixties, Revie's Leeds 'delivered' it from its decaying industrial heartland. In the fizzy, flashy nineties, after the dark years of the post-Paris exile, the club were 'redeemed', re-invented as a swashbuckling, vibrant force of nature; the apotheosis of the shiny, post-industrial, postmodern city. At the dawn of the millennium, as the Premier League went stratospheric and the football economy lost all inhibitions about debt, there was a hubristic, last-ditch attempt to turn the club into a global brand. I am fully aware, of course, that presenting Dirty Leeds as avatars of a fifty-year quest for self-actualisation will, for some people, border on heresy. But they were, undeniably, part of a shift in power, a challenge to the old order, a northernisation of culture; part of a sweeping panorama of social evolution that reinvigorated old Blighty and, more specifically and enduringly, helped transform football from a parochial, working-class entertainment into a global obsession.

When, in 2007, the team became victims of that transformation and dropped into League One, the anti-Leeds brigade rubbed their hands with glee. The latest disappearing act was presented as a modern parable. Ambition's debt had been paid. The deluded upstarts had risen from obscurity, cheated their way to the Top and had now been returned to obscurity. Good riddance to bad rubbish. The dirty-cheating-northern-bastards had been punished for their crimes against the beautiful game. This is the dominant narrative, the cliche of Dirty Leeds. In the lexicon of modern footballing abuse 'doing a Leeds' has become shorthand for chasing the dream and going into a nightmarish freefall through the divisions.

I can remember a time when 'doing a Leeds' meant a thrilling, rags-to-riches rise; coming from nowhere to challenge – even topple – the establishment. Leeds United AFC were the product of, and helped shape, English football's evolution. They aspired to great

Introduction

heights and attempted to consign the old-boy network to history. Now that the old-boy network appears to be making a comeback, it seemed like a good time to examine what went wrong.

1. Bring Out

'Two of the many passengers by a certain late Sunday evening train, Mr Thomas Idle and Mr Francis Goodchild, yielded up their tickets at a little rotten platform (converted into artificial touchwood by smoke and ashes), deep in the manufacturing bosom of Yorkshire . . . Thus, Thomas and Francis got to Leeds; of which enterprising and important commercial centre it may be observed with delicacy, that you must either like it very much or not at all.'

Charles Dickens,
The Lazy Tour of Two Idle Apprentices, 1858

1900. My great-grandfather disembarks at Hull. He sits in the Paragon railway station with all the other refugees, some of whom look ill after their rough voyage across the North Sea. He feels all alone in the world, a stranger in a strange land, and he is easy prey for the innkeepers and railway officials and ticket agents. Some charge extortionate room rates, steal baggage, sell dud tickets. But his ticket is real: a one-way ticket to the promised land. On board the SS Leeds, disease was rife. Some passengers, mainly youngsters, died on the journey. But he has made it, he is here, at last, at the threshold of a new life, a new beginning, a new world across the ocean. He puts his hand into his pocket and pulls out a piece of paper. On it is written one word. 'Leeds'.

Dirty Leeds

Leeds is a schizophrenic city. A city with two parallel existences. To the outside world it often appears as brash and overconfident, a little too much in love with itself. Promised Land Delivered, indeed. Such apparent self-satisfaction often masks a gnawing insecurity about its grimy, provincial roots. 'Leeds is usually a dull, spiritless and inert town,' complained the *Leeds Times* back in 1843. 'It is awanting in social as well as political activity and energy. It is an inert mass always difficult to be moved. It wants the enthusiasm of Manchester, the enterprise of Glasgow, the volatile gaiety of Liverpool, the intense feeling of Birmingham and the power of London.'

Before it became a city, which was as late as 1893, it was a small river crossing, a village, a township, a hamlet and a market town. Victorian industrialists transformed its landscape, turned muck into brass and invested their newfound riches in such grandiose monuments as Tower Works and the reconstruction of Giotto's campanile at the Duomo in Florence. They littered the dirty old town with slums and satanic mills, but they also fostered a new civic pride which found its expression in three monumental buildings, all designed by the Hull-born architect Cuthbert Brodrick: Leeds Town

Hall, the Corn Exchange and the Mechanics Institute.

I grew up in the 1960s, so my Leeds – or my idea of Leeds – is a place of mobility, transformation, escape. An irresistible force, a harbinger of an exciting future, a portent of the deliverance to come. As the train pulls into the station, and the glittering sets of residential towers lining the river come into view, I only have eyes for the brooding town hall and the cantilevered football stadium, the city's two great monuments to metamorphosis. They both symbolise for me Leeds' desire to cross the threshold, to breach the narrow confines of its rough, isolated world. Up until the Industrial Revolution it had been largely landlocked, surrounded by dense forest.

In times of crisis, the city burdens itself with a chippy isolationism, retreating into the worst of itself, a perverse mixture of fear – usually of the foreigner – and brutality. 'Every late-twentieth century slur on Pakistanis,' reflected the Leeds-born writer Martin Wainwright, writing about his hometown, 'has its early-twentieth-century equivalent about the Jews ("filthy, dirty, the lowest and worst sort") or the nineteenth-century Irish, whose supposedly inbred slumminess led to typhus being nicknamed the Irish disease. Both of those groups reacted to racism by rioting. In the Jewish and Irish cases that actually led to deaths.' At its best, however, usually in booming economic times, Leeds tries to break boundaries, extend the parameters of the possible, turn the world upside down. This is the Leeds I love. We are Leeds and we are always trying to escape the inescapable, embrace the exotic, worship the Other – a Michael Marks, a Montague Burton, an Albert Johanneson, a Lucas Radebe. Which is why, as the railway curves around the football stadium, my heart always lifts.

And, as a low sea of industrial units parts to allow the vast monolith to rear up out of its pitiless heartland, I feel that I'm home, back where I started, on the threshold of possibility.

If Leeds was a person, it would be a combination of Brodrick and Revie. Just as Fortress Elland Road is a monument to Revie's legacy, so the palatial town hall will always be associated with Brodrick's ambition. The visionary young architect helped invent industrial Leeds in the same way the visionary young manager would, in the 1960s, reinvent the city for the white-hot, techno-logical age. His opus, with its Corinthian columns and imperious stone lions, catapulted the dirty old town into the national consciousness, announcing its arrival as an economic force. It was described by Sir Charles Barry, who, with A. W. N. Pugin, designed the Houses of Parliament, as 'the most perfect architectural gem outside London'. Yet it was the product of an inferior-ity complex. In 1847, at a packed talk at the Mechanics Institute, Charles Dickens denounced Leeds as 'a beastly place'. His view was endorsed by several of his contem-poraries during their adventurous forays into the new metropolis. This was a great age of exploration and, just as Victorian archaeologists were unearthing ancient cities in the old mysterious East, so their less intrepid literary counterparts were discovering hidden, menacing worlds in the new industrial north. Most of them considered Leeds to be, as Dickens put it, the most menacing of them all. Lord Shaftesbury even likened it to Sodom. Coal, the railways, engineering, engine-making and tailoring – the five pillars of the thrusting town's commercial success – had sucked in a rag-bag of migrant tribes, a collection of shifting, disconnected identities, their bodies blackened by smoke and exploited by wage-slavery, their souls polluted by an inhumane existence. Dirty Leeds.

Industrialisation triggered a mass exodus from the land to the new towns and cities, creating a poverty-stricken workforce. But it also spawned a manufacturing elite keen to build monuments to its grandeur. The enlightened mill owners and ambitious aldermen who ran the newly formed Corporation were determined to challenge the citadels of Manchester and Liverpool. In the nineteenth century, towns and cities competed with each other to construct the largest town halls. Leeds became the first English town to commission a building which incorporated council chambers, town clerk's offices, mayoral parlour, assize courts, assembly rooms and concert halls. The Leeds Improvement Society argued that it would put Leeds on the map, draw people from all over the world, 'attracting to our town the visits of strangers and dilettante tourists . . . from distant places'. One of the society's maxims, 'Industry overcomes all things', was inscribed on the frieze of the lavish Victoria Hall. It was inspired by Samuel Smiles' self-help lectures at the Mechanics Institute. Smiles' maxim was: any man, no matter how low his rank, can rise to the Top. 'Even,' he insisted, 'a tailor.'

A steady stream of strangers and dilettantes were, indeed, attracted to the newly aspirational, outward-looking town. They came, they saw, they inhaled its soot – and then they wrote up their parables of greed, gluttony and beastliness. Some of them denounced Brodrick's 'grand folly': the clock tower which had been added to the town hall at great expense. It was, declared one critic, a deranged architectural enterprise. According to another, it was an outsized, out-of-control plaything determined to swallow the world. The young architect, rejecting the fashion for neo-medievalism, had insisted on using gritstone, informally known as millstone grit, from seventeen local quarries. Due to excessive pollution the stone soon became covered in a rich, sooty, black coating – the grime of Leeds. A belligerent group of aldermen attacked the tower as a complete waste of money. Shortly after building the Grand Hotel at Scarborough, Brodrick bolted to France, seeing out his remaining years in self-imposed exile with the wife of a solicitor seven years his senior. The Grand had bankrupted the consortium which commissioned it and the town hall had become a byword for profligacy, costing four times the original budget. Dirty, greedy, hubristic, reckless Leeds.

Mir Zanen Do

My paternal great-grandfather, Phillip Clavanski, arrived in the city in the first year of the twentieth century. He was one of two million Jews who fled the Russian Empire following the assassination of Tsar Alexander II. He came over in 1900 – his wife Maria following him a year later – sharing his boat with cattle which needed constant mucking-out. On his arrival at Leeds station, he was taken on a handcart to the Jewish ghetto. His 'driver' was a kind Irish boxer called Jimmy Gilmour who, when drunk, was known to fight lamp-posts with his bare fists. As they approached the ghetto, Jimmy – who spoke a bit of Yiddish – called out '*Mir zanen do*', which means 'We are here'. Phillip said that those were the three best words he'd ever heard.

Like the vast majority of first-generation immigrants, he was a tailor and an orthodox Jew. He died in his thirties and his son, Harry Clavane, a tailor and an atheist, became head of the family. Everyone loved Harry. I knew him as a sweet-natured, if somewhat reserved, old man. Towards the end of his life, when I was a teenager, he began to open up and tell me stories about his past. These stories powerfully affected my imagination. He told me about his childhood in the ghetto, about working as a young tailor in his uncle Abe's attic, about the large – and larger-than-life – ladies whose dresses and coats he made. He told me about the Yiddish boxers who had fought the anti-Semites and the communist ramblers who had whisked him up the bleak hills for fresh air, recreation and indoctrination; in the 1930s, half the Party's Leeds branch were Jewish. He told me about his wife's brother, Myer Tompowski, who went to 'cheder' – the Hebrew word for prison – for beating up an anti-Semite. He never mentioned the old country: the Heym. Looking up meant not looking down. Looking forward meant not looking back. Harry was a great believer in integration. He wanted to belong. He wanted his tribe to be accepted. He had lived through two world wars and the Great Depression. 'Never again,' he told me. 'No going back.'

In the late 1970s, a few months before he died, he
revealed that the only religious story he had any time
for was the exodus. Like the rest of his generation –
whether communists or capitalists, Zionists or interna-
tionalists, orthodox or reform – he was inspired by the
great escape from Egypt. It was seared into his, and
every Jew's, consciousness. It is hardwired into our
DNA. Bring out, deliver, redeem, take. The day before
I left for university, he finally recounted the story of
his father's own great escape. Leeds, said Harry, had
been shaped by such stories. Jews docking in Hull en
route to the United States were lured to the city, hearing
tales of it being an 'earthly paradise'. It was built on
the sweat of strangers: Jewish, Scottish, Irish, rural
Yorkshire sweat. It was a community of communities;
a giant factory fuelled by migrant labour from the
Dales, the most deprived parts of Scotland, the famine
areas of Ireland and the shtetls of Eastern Europe.
Factory hands, cobblers, flax-workers and tailors were
all thrown together into one great big melting pot. My
three great-grandfathers (the fourth settled in Glasgow)
– Phillip, Chaim Tompowski and Solomon Saipe –
hadn't been allowed to integrate. As long as they
confined themselves to the ghetto, however, they were,
on the whole, left in peace. This was a classic Leeds
trade-off; the goyim believed in 'live and let live' and
the Jews believed in not upsetting the goyim.

Sometimes though, said Harry, the goyim would get
upset for no reason. Sometimes there would be raids
by bands of hooligans armed with clubs and knives.
Which is why the second generation – his generation
– decided to fight back, stand up for themselves, defend

their right to stay in Leeds; their right to belong. There were quite a few tough lads back then. Some went on to become famous fighters, others famous rugby players. One lad – a hard-as-nails defender called Leslie Goldberg – even broke into the Leeds United side for a couple of years.

Going Going Gone:
The 1919 Choke

1903. Colonel Harding unveils the Black Prince statue in the new City Square in front of the station. He tells the crowd that Leeds must 'rise above the sordid, and rejoice in the beautiful'. Football, he argues, is the sport of the future, rugby league the sport of the past. Leeds must be ambitious and outward-looking and engage with, become part of, the modern world.

Leeds was conspicuous by its absence at the birth of association football. The Football Association was formed in 1863, followed by the Football League in 1888, but Leeds City didn't emerge until 1904. 'This city is built to support top-flight football,' their manager Herbert Chapman proclaimed in 1914. 'It has to happen at some point soon.' It would in fact, be another ten years before it happened. City's successors, Leeds United, were promoted to the old First Division as comparatively recently in the game's history as 1924. By this time both Liverpool and Manchester had two strong, well-supported teams; the City–United derby drew 53,000 Mancunians – as against just 17,000 for comparable rugby matches.

Like the town hall, Leeds City represented a belated attempt by the city fathers to take Leeds out of its self-willed isolation. After only fifteen years of existence, however, they were dissolved. United, their successors, then languished in the wilderness for almost forty years until Revie – and revolution – arrived. Being a deeply superstitious man, Revie had his own theory about this failure to become part of the new order of northern football city-states. Like all those near misses during his own reign, it could be explained by the 'curse' Romany gypsies had put on Elland Road.

There is another, far more rational, reason: an unwillingness to become part of the mainstream of national life. When football opened its gates in the north of England, the West Riding of Yorkshire stubbornly refused to play ball – or at least round ball. The region remained rugby territory, preferring the parochial oval-ball game, with its unlimited opportunities for on-field thuggery, to the emerging 'namby-pamby' football. Folk football had been around in Britain since the sixteenth century, when it was denounced by puritan preachers as a vehicle for 'beastly fury and extreme violence'. Industrial Britain's new, religious middle class was determined to refine the manners of the 'brutish, backward' working classes. Christian missionaries invaded northern slums, forming

character-building, church football teams such as
Everton, Manchester City and Bolton Wanderers. The
citizens of Leeds – known as Loiners – had no intention of being civilised by gentlemanly Corinthians
intent on reinventing folk football. They had always
been partial to a bit of beastliness and violence. They
still are.

In the late nineteenth century, during the great flower-
ing of soon-to-be-professional football clubs, it was
Leeds Rugby who led the sporting charge in the city.
In 1895 they were part of a dissenting cabal which
broke away to form the Northern Union. Crowds
quickly rose, the rugby clubs made big profits and almost
all the West Riding's football teams folded. The Football
League was split between Lancashire and the Midlands;
by 1892, when all twenty-eight clubs were from the
north-west, the north-east or the Midlands, Leeds was
home to five big rugby league teams: Leeds RL, Hunslet,
Bramley, Holbeck – who were based at Elland Road –
and Leeds Parish Church.

Loiners have always been known for their fierce in-
dependence. Boycotting the new national game was
their way of refusing to bow to authority. During the
Edwardian period, with local trade at record levels,
the Football League made several overtures to the city
fathers, desperate to extend their influence to this
densely populated outpost of Britain's expanding industrial empire. In 1903, at the grand opening of City
Square, which Colonel T.W Harding had commissioned to celebrate the granting of city status, the indus-
trialist argued that rugby league was now a minority
sport, a barrier against the city's ambition. An associa-

tion football team, he argued, was long overdue. Leeds was at the epicentre of change and a city-wide football club would be the start of a bright new era. It must, like every other northern city, be represented at the national level by a football team. The really big provincial metropolises with which it was compared – Manchester, Liverpool and Birmingham – had, for many years, embraced the game. So why not the fourth largest city outside London? '[Rugby league] has had a good run,' noted the *Leeds Mercury*, 'but the public want a national game rather than a code peculiar to a circumscribed area . . . the Association game is national in scope and influence, and is yearly becoming more powerful and more popular.' To ambitious aldermen like Harding, the team's formation was as significant a leap forward as the unveiling of the Black Prince in City Square. It symbolised Leeds' coming of age.

Leeds City, however, flowered and then withered, establishing a rise-and-fall narrative that was to become all too familiar in the second half of the century. Elected League members in 1905, they had great difficulty drawing crowds into the ramshackle Elland Road, the lure of the more successful rugby sides being too strong. Facing re-election seven years later, the bankers called in the club's £7,000 overdraft. Chairman Norris Hepworth's £15,000 investment kept them afloat and, following Chapman's arrival, their fortunes improved. Under him, they finished sixth in Division Two – centre forward Billy McLeod scoring twenty-seven goals – and gates at Headingley, home of Leeds RL, halved.

Chapman was football's first great innovator. He

would go on to win the FA Cup and two League Championships at Huddersfield Town, followed by three successive titles at Arsenal. In his first couple of seasons at Elland Road he built a strong team. In the 1913–14 campaign they rose to fourth. His innovations included salt baths, golf breaks and team talks. He even – shock horror – consulted players over tactics. Just as City looked certainties for promotion, war broke out. Normal competition was suspended and, after enlisting the support of famous guest players like Charlie Buchan, Billy Hampson and Fanny Walden, Chapman's reinvigorated side won the unofficial championship of England. However, in 1919, after being grassed up by an ex-player, they were kicked out of the League for making illegal payments to their guests. 'We will have no nonsense,' the League chairman declared. 'The football stable must be cleansed.'

City were dissolved and forced to sell off all their players in a humiliating, week-long cattle auction at the plush Metropole Hotel. The *Daily Mail*'s report of the auction was headlined: 'Going Going Gone'. Thirty clubs haggled over the squad, who fetched a total of £10,000. Billy Kirton, who ended the season scoring Aston Villa's extra-time winner in the FA Cup Final, went under the hammer at £250. Ordered to produce documents for inspection or face expulsion, Chapman was accused of, literally, cooking the books – burning them at his home before resigning. He had done his best to keep the side together during the war while working as chief storekeeper at a munitions factory in east Leeds. All clubs employed guest players during the conflict, paying them more than just expenses; the League simply turned a blind eye to the practice. But when they decided to make an example of City and summon Chapman to Manchester to answer charges, he received no backing from either the board or the fans. He was, in effect, hung out to dry – and banned from football for life.

A few years later, his ban was overturned after he proved he was working at the factory when the payments were made. At Highbury – he joined Arsenal in 1925 – he came up with several innovations, including a white ball, numbers on shirts, rubber studs, European competition and floodlights. Before Chapman arrived, the Gunners had never won a major trophy. By the time he left they were the most famous club in the world. Typical Leeds.

There are three Jewish cemeteries clustered together at the top of one of the millstone-grit hills that overlook Elland Road. The only one of my ancestors not buried at the top of this steep upland is Myer Tompowski. He served in the West Yorkshire Rifles during the Great War. In a desperate attempt to stop him returning to the front, his young sister Gertie poured boiling water over his feet. Her attempt failed – and Myer returned to France, where he was killed in action.

Although Myer was awarded a posthumous medal for attempting to rescue his commanding officer, this was a time when young Jewish men were being accused of unpatriotic leanings. In an article headlined 'The Jews of Leeds and the Army – Are They Doing Their Share?' the *Yorkshire Post* referred to the parade of flashily dressed young Jews 'swaggering' along Briggate, by then the main shopping street of Leeds. Meanwhile 'our brave boys' were meeting their deaths in the trenches in France. In fact, in Leeds a greater proportion of Jews than non-Jews had joined up. The *Post* article provoked a mini-pogrom. In June 1917, there were two days of rioting in the Leylands. A three-thousand-strong mob rampaged through the cramped, terraced streets causing widespread damage. Jewish properties were vandalised and looted.

My great-grandparents' generation lacked the means to better themselves, to escape the shtetl, to climb over the wall at the bottom of the Leylands ghetto. They squeezed into the square mile of dark courtyards, hovels, dangerous passageways, narrow, cobbled streets and unsanitary back-to-backs. Leeds councillors had opposed Julius Friend's appointment as the Corporation's medical officer on the grounds that 'it would be a standing disgrace to the city if a member of that race were appointed'. In 1909 the vicar of Leeds observed: 'There is hardly a Christian firm in Leeds that will employ Jews.' Jewish weavers, spinners, dyers and blacksmiths all tried to get jobs outside the Leylands, but were greeted with signs reading 'No Jews Need Apply'. So they, too, became tailors. To the early immigrants, the world was neatly divided into Them and Us; the goyim and the Yiddishers. They took great pride in their foreignness, their otherness, their ghettoisation.

The second-generation Jews, however, cast around for something to belong to, and settled on the city's number one sport: rugby league. At the beginning of the century they enthusiastically attached themselves to the Leeds Parish Church rugby league team. The side was set up, in 1901, to be muscular Christianity's flagship in the West Riding. They attracted crowds of 10,000 and regularly upstaged Leeds, their richer rivals from the northern suburb of Headingley. Their players were accused of roughness, tripping and generally playing 'in a pugilistic manner'. Jeering, stone-throwing and general intimidation of referees was so bad that they had difficulty attracting officials for home games. Their ground was closed in 1891 after fans attacked the referee. Even more mortifying for local clergy was the passionate support of the local Jewish community. Church fans had even become known by the anti-Semitic epithet 'sheenies'. This was the final straw; the club was closed down and all the players were offloaded to Headingley.

When Jewish rugby fans transferred their affections to Headingley, the community elders became outraged. They preached the classic, conservative, Anglo-Jewish strategy of 'work hard, heads down and don't upset the goyim'. Every other Saturday, Selig Brodetsky, who was president of the Board of Deputies, watched hundreds of his non-yarmulked co-religionists walking past his house on their way to the match. Not only were they breaking shabbat, the day of rest, they were drawing attention to themselves, going meshugah on the terraces, singing Yiddish songs and even gambling. My great-uncle Louis, who edited a Jewish newspaper, and was a founder member of the Council for Christians and Jews, countered that sport was a pathway to integration. It helped liberate us from the bigotry of anti-Semitism. Supporting Leeds RL, he argued, helped us make a place

for ourselves in the city. He pointed out that a succes-
sion of high-profile boxing and rugby triumphs had
done more than cartloads of oratory and writing to
combat anti-Semitism. Between the wars, social snob-
bery and racist prejudice were still rife. Jacob Kramer's
Day of Atonement was unveiled in the art gallery to a
storm of anti-Semitic protest. Most law firms and golf
clubs, as well as institutions like the General Infirmary
and the Leeds Club, operated an unofficial ban on Jews.
According to the *Yorkshire Post*'s golf correspondent, Jews
and Gentiles 'just don't mix'. My great-auntie Millie
claimed she had once been kicked out of the Queen's
Hotel for being a 'scruffy Jew'. The story might be apocryphal as she also claimed to have been there at Louis
Armstrong's behest. The hotel manager, who had waived
the colour bar for the world's greatest entertainer, was
– apparently – flabbergasted when Satchmo himself
appeared in the foyer demanding Millie's readmittance.
More sinisterly, swastika posters were plastered on Jewish-
owned shops when Oswald Mosley's blackshirts rallied
on Holbeck Moor in front of 30,000 people.

Rugby league was a parochial sport, but it gave Louis'
and Harry's generation a sense of pride and belonging.
They were English-born and had grown up differently
from their Yiddish-speaking parents. They were fluent
in English; some of them had even changed their names
to get jobs outside tailoring. They had moved out of
the Leylands, taking their loaded pantechnicons up the
hill to Chapeltown. They were desperate to assimilate
into the host culture, even if the host culture seemed
unwilling to accept them. The migration to Chapeltown
was described in a 1930s' book by Leeds novelist Gordon

Stowell as a 'stealthy, insidious advance . . . they seem to be making an attack in force . . . bringing with them swarms of children and grandchildren'. Stowell's attitude was not uncommon. Even thirty years later, not long after Hyman Morris had become Leeds' first Jewish Lord Mayor, a local newspaper columnist felt compelled to question 'Little Israel's' loyalty to its adopted city. The Jews of Chapeltown, the writer argued, remained 'an outpost of an ancient civilisation, loyal to the age-old doctrines, precepts, customs and beliefs of the race'. Estate agents blamed upwardly mobile Jews for bringing down property prices. One councillor admitted turning them away from the Conservative Club. 'There are no longer any street fights as there were sometimes in the early days of this century,' concluded an early fifties feature in *Picture Post*, the prestigious national photo-news magazine, 'but the gulf, though both sides turn a blind eye to it, is still there.'

The Nearly City

From the opening of City Square in the 1890s to the great slum clearance of the early sixties, civic visionaries tried – and mostly failed – to reverse the image of a grimy, industrial mill town, the eternal Victorian city. Every now and then, this 'inert mass always difficult to be moved' made a great leap forward, galvanised by big men with big ideas: idealistic dreamers whose plans tended to be sneered at, both locally and nationally, as utopian and, more often than not, failed to bear fruit.

Brodrick and Harding had attempted to reinvent modern industrial Leeds as a powerful, outward-looking city, but the former's town hall tower and the latter's Black Prince statue were both ridiculed as emblems of excess; delusions of grandeur. Charles Wilson, the self-styled Sultan of Leeds, dreamed of a progressive, modernising metropolis, sweeping eastwards from the Pennines to the sea. His plans were rejected by Parliament. The outside world still viewed Leeds as the ugly child of the Industrial Revolution, a breeding ground for dirt. Following in the footsteps of those Victorian writers who had trekked north to witness the ruination of their Eden, the Edwardian literati poured scorn on Leeds' abysmal weather, slag heaps and grimy landscape. George Bernard Shaw advocated burning it down.

It was not all doom and gloom. Two new department stores opened in the 'hungry thirties': Lewis's, with its snazzy escalators and American soda fountain, and Marks and Spencer's flagship store, faced in polished black granite. And Burton's enormous tailoring factory, the largest in the world, was completed in 1934. It produced more than 100,000 garments a week, clothed one in five English males and provided work for most of the Clavanes. My dad was particularly taken with the startling whiteness of new buildings like Civic Hall, the Bus Station and the stylish Queen's Hotel. They were a stark contrast to the slum dwellings he'd grown up in, and which were being vigorously pulled down by Charles Jenkinson.

Jenkinson was a utopian-minded council leader who housed over 34,000 people between 1933 and 1940. He had been to Paris, seen the future – Europe's first ever skyscrapers – and it worked. He commissioned two flagship estates: the Quarry Hill flats and the Gipton. My dad's family were rehoused in the latter, which was presented as a New Jerusalem, a 'garden city set on a hill'. And yet, when *Picture Post* hired Marc Riboud to photograph these estates in the mid-fifties, the young Frenchman discovered a drab and dismal city; one still blighted by pollution and littered by darkened factories. One hundred and fifty years of burning pure coal to power mills and factories had left the city's buildings with a distinctive matt black finish. Robert Capa's protégé saw no imprint of the new Elizabethan age on his month-long trawl of the city. Riboud's pictures of grimy street urchins and washing slung across back-to-back terraces confirmed the magazine's thesis about 'Black Leeds'. Riboud liked to get up early in the morning to capture the 'beautiful mist' over the city, only realising later that it was the pollution spewed out by the local power station. Leeds had got off lightly during the war; nine bombing raids, intended for the mills and factories of Hunslet and Kirkstall, had caused only minor destruction. And yet his scenes of rubble-filled dereliction made it look like post-war wastelands.

Despite the urban improvers' heroic efforts, there were still 90,000 unfit homes – 56,000 of them back-to-backs – out of a total of 156,000 houses. By the end of the fifties, Quarry Hill had become obsolete and the Gipton was one of the roughest areas in the city. The smoke continued to cast a pall of wintry bleakness over Leeds. Twenty-five tons of soot fell every month on every square mile of the city south of the River Aire. Try as it might, Leeds still could not erase its ugliness, scrub off the muck of ages, escape the shadow of its grimy, parochial past.

The Nearly Team

'If you come from the South, thinking that Leeds' only claim to fame is that Test Matches are played there,' warned Gordon Watkins, in the article accompanying Riboud's photographs, 'it is as well to keep your ignorance under your hat.' The *Picture Post* writer explained that Loiners enjoyed several other traditionally popular sports apart from cricket, such as rugby league and horse racing. There was no mention whatsoever of association football. This was because, nearly a hundred years after a group of public school boys had codified its rules, football had still not made any inroads into rugby's fan base. The city had doggedly remained a rugby league town, resisting the lure of 'namby-pamby' football.

In their first forty years of existence – apart from a second division title in 1924 – Leeds United won nothing, existing in a twilight zone between the top two leagues.

The only thing that stopped the new club going under was a £35,000 loan from former Huddersfield Town chairman Hilton Crowther; at one point the increasingly desperate Crowther offered to move his old club 'lock, stock and barrel' to Elland Road – such was the lack of interest in United. The team dropped out of the First Division three years after promotion, and then simply dropped off the radar altogether. Their managers were either bland nonentities like Billy Hampson, famous faces like Dick Ray or eccentric has-beens like Major Frank Buckley. Football in Leeds – until Revie's arrival – was considered a bit of a joke.

For United fans, the 1953–4 season is always cited as the most memorable one of the 'wilderness years' simply because they witnessed one of the world's greatest players at the peak of his powers. John Charles scored forty-two goals in thirty-nine games, a club record. For most of the fifties, Leeds were known as John Charles United. Even with their Gentle Giant leading from the front, they struggled to compete with three rugby league rivals. Rugby pitches still out-numbered football pitches. Between them, Leeds RL, Hunslet and Bramley clocked up gates of over 20,000. When United, who often attracted crowds of around 15,000, returned to the top flight after a nine-year absence in 1956 – mainly thanks to Charles' twenty-nine goals – their opening match of the new campaign warranted only a couple of paragraphs in the *Yorkshire Post*.

Charles came to Leeds from Swansea and lived in a club house in Middleton, another of Jenkinson's brave new council estates. In 1957, he travelled by bus to the

Queen's Hotel to meet the Italian millionaire Umberto Agnelli. There, in room 223, the Juventus president wrote out two cheques: one to Leeds United for £65,000 – a world-record transfer fee – and another to the Welshman for £10,000. The previous year, the club's West Stand had been destroyed by fire, causing £100,000 of damage – about £1.7 million in today's money. To pay for a new stand, the board decided to cash in on their most famous player of the pre-Revie era. Charles was, in fact, the club's *only* famous player of the pre-Revie era. As one fan complained in the local paper, the city had lost 'its greatest attraction since the Town Hall was built'.

Charles went on to make a huge impact in Turin, helping Juventus to three Italian Championship titles and being voted footballer of the year. His old team, meanwhile, continued to wallow in obscurity. Despite manager Raich Carter being given half the Charles transfer money to spend on new players, they only just avoided relegation. Carter was sacked and his replacement, Bill Lambton, lasted a mere ten months. Lambton had made his reputation as a fitness trainer for British boxers. 'He made a fool of himself in front of us,' remembered Jack Charlton. 'I didn't take him seriously as a football man.' The next man in was Jack Taylor, the club's sixth post-war manager – and the board's sixth choice for the job; even non-League boss Arthur Turner had turned them down. Training under Taylor consisted of long runs, at the end of which players arrived back with lollies in their hands. Before one vital away game, they stopped at a café near the ground and ate beans on toast as a pre-match meal.

When Taylor left Leeds – and with the club seemingly destined for the Third Division – Ronald Crowther, a crusading local journalist who had been banished from Elland Road for criticising the board, advised directors to appoint their club captain as boss. United might have a shambolic team, argued Crowther, but this intelligent, visionary player was part of an emerging new breed; a group of ambitious young men who were about to break through into football management and give the game a good shake-up. 'Banned from the ground,' an obituary of the *Yorkshire Evening News* sports editor would later recall, 'Crowther paid at the turnstile, balanced his type-writer on a crash barrier, and carried on attacking until Don Revie and revolution arrived.'

2. Deliver

'This is *This Is Your Life* . . . Tonight we're in the north of England inside a hotel where a celebration dinner is about to begin. Although there are many famous faces, the man I'm after is only just about to arrive because he is the guest of honour of the Variety Club here at Leeds. Now, he's so respected and so well known that stars from many fields have come here to pay tribute . . . There's *Man at the Top* Kenneth Haigh, soccer manager Joe Mercer, television personality Michael Parkinson, playwright and actor Colin Welland, that great character of showjumping Harvey Smith, cricketer Freddie Trueman, footballer Derek Dougan, the Super Leeds United team . . . I've got to move very quickly because he's on his way in now, and make sure I'm right behind him and his host Marshall Bellow as he's welcomed into that dining room.'

Eamonn Andrews, *This Is Your Life,* 1974

1963. On the set of Billy Liar, *the General is taking the salute at the victory parade. He has brought his people out of isolation, with a strong hand and an outstretched arm; with great terror, and with signs and wonders. But he has forgotten to post his mother's request for* Housewives' Choice. *As the camera zooms in over the Leeds rooftops, to the noisy accompaniment of an early-morning radio programme of record requests, we get a panoramic view of a dirty, Victorian city on the cusp of a momentous, once-in-a-lifetime change. And now, says the radio announcer, for a special request for Mrs Betty Bullock. But the announcer doesn't know Mrs Bullock's address. As the camera arrives at her house, we see it being demolished amid a deafening chorus of pneumatic drills. On a demolition site off Wellington Road, General Fisher is smiling and waving at his people. The women are throwing flowers at him and the soldiers are cheering. Goggled and jack-booted, carrying binoculars and a revolver, the triumphant hero salutes his troops as they march past the grime-coated town hall. 'We will rebuild,' says the General. 'Battalions of craftsmen will change the face of our cities. We will build towers.'*

The Rise of Northern Man

Liz: 'It's easy. You get on a train and, four hours later, there you are in London.'

I had the good fortune to be born in 1960 and to grow up in a decade touched by a perfect storm of opportunity and talent. A decade in which Leeds United, the city of Leeds and the Jewish community, all moved from the margins to the epicentre of a re-energised new Britain forged in the white heat of the technological revolution. The world appeared to be theirs — ours — for the taking and the shaping A spirit of emancipation was in the air. This was a golden age of social mobility, working-class aspiration and northern writing. 'Growing up in Leeds,' wrote the novelist Caryl Phillips — who came to the city as a young child from the Caribbean island of St Kitts — 'was like every black-and-white British film you ever saw from the sixties, starring Tom Courtenay or Albert Finney and set in these dirty, cobbled northern streets, with the hero ending up on a train platform with a one-way ticket to London.'

A new kind of man sprang into the public imagination during these years. A working-class iconoclast and provincial braggart. Northern Man. In novels, the theatre, television and the cinema, he suddenly became the subject of ground-breaking kitchen-sink dramas. He found his way into the glare of the spotlight via his writing ability, photography, acting talent, musicianship and football skills. His brash, truculent film persona was an antidote to both the upper-middle class tweediness portrayed by Dirk Bogarde and Kenneth More and the warm-hearted proletarian stereotypes offered up, in a previous era, by Gracie Fields and George Formby. Before the 1950s, 'the north' had been reconstructed on London film sets; in the classic Fields vehicle *Sing As We Go*, for example, the streets of her home town were rebuilt in the Ealing Studios. Filmed on location on the backstreets of Leeds, Bradford, Nottingham and Salford, the New Wave brought a new vitality to British cinema.

The West Riding battalion of the New Wave was a crack force: Waterhouse, John Braine and David Storey. In 1960, their trinity of anti-heroes exploded on to the scene. *Billy Liar* was a hit in the West End, *Room at the Top* won ten Oscar nominations and *This Sporting Life* was hailed as one of the best books ever written about sport. Billy Fisher, Joe Lampton and Frank Machin spoke to a generation of edgy provincials determined to barge through the privileged ranks of the elite. John Schlesinger's 1963 screen version of *Billy Liar* cut from naturalistic depictions of everyday life to the surreal scenes of Billy's own imagination. One minute, Courtenay's fantasist imagines himself to be the powerful dictator of a small country, the next a scriptwriter for a popular TV comedian. His girlfriend

Liz offers him a clear route out of his drab existence, the one real chance he'll get to leave the past behind. Waterhouse, like my dad, was born in 1929 in a two-up-two-down back-to-back in inner-city Leeds. His comic masterpiece appeared at the moment Leeds, like the rest of the north, was on the cusp of change – and Northern Man was about to reap the benefits of the new social mobility. It had been a long gestation period but, after nearly a century of slow-baked, stop-start, class-ridden evolution – including two world wars and a depression – the working classes were finally going to be 'delivered' from their grinding conditions.

Post-industrial Leeds began to look for a new identity. Its manufacturing base was eroding and the new economic, social and cultural forces provided an opportunity finally to throw off the cloak of a dirty Victorian city and cultivate the image of a thrusting, modern metropolis; a booming super-region threaded with a vast network of orbital and radial roads. Arnold Ziff opened the Merrion Centre, the first shopping mall in Europe. The council's demolition man, Karl Cohen, razed the last of the slums, replacing them with concrete tower blocks. Regional accents were suddenly in vogue. Northern actors, writers, comedians, trade union leaders and football managers became overnight TV stars. There was a big expansion of middle-class and professional jobs, allowing many lower-income males to climb the ladder. Like the rest of the country, Leeds began to move from a blue-collar to a white-collar society. Thousands of its sons and daughters studied at college and university. Only one man in three had the same social status as his father. Between 1951 and 1975, the purchasing power of a manual worker's wage increased by three-quarters.

The city's changing skyline reflected its new civic pride. The back-to-backs and factories were flattened to make way for the M1, an inner ring road and brutalist buildings like the *Yorkshire Post* complex and John Poulson's International Pool. '[Leeds] was stirring out of its pre-war, post-Edwardian sleep,' wrote Waterhouse. 'There was a civic restlessness about, a growing clamour for clearing away the old.' A working-class anti-hero was something to be. Northern Man invaded the capital, storming the citadels of literature, film, pop music, television, photography and sport. His success was symbolised by the meteoric ascent of the Beatles, the footballing resurgence of Liverpool and Manchester and the rise to power of Harold Wilson, the first prime minister to keep a photograph of a West Riding football club – Huddersfield Town – in his wallet.

Revie and Revolution

Billy: 'I wish life was something you could tear up and start again. You know, like starting a new page in an exercise book.'

1961. The Don is sitting in the communal bath at Elland Road next to Jack Charlton. He tells Big Jack that he lacks discipline. And that he puts himself before the team. And that he could start an argument in a Trappist monastery. And that if he, Revie, were ever manager, he'd be straight out that door, no mistake. Big Jack says that if Revie ever became manager – which wouldn't happen in a million years – he'd hand in his cards, no mistake. Two weeks later, the Leeds director Harry Reynolds calls a players' meeting. Reynolds says that Bournemouth had wanted Revie to be their manager. But in the middle of writing the reference, the retired steel magnate had a flash of revelation and tore up the letter. 'Gentlemen,' smiles Reynolds, 'I'd like to introduce you to the new manager.' And Revie walks in.

Although Revie's Leeds are not often lumped together with Billy Liar, the Beatles, David Hockney, the New Wave writers, the Liverpool poets, Granada TV and uncle Harold Wilson and all, they were just as much a part of the vital transfusion that re-energised sixties' Britain with new northern blood. Revie's time at Elland Road spanned the era some historians have labelled the Long Sixties. When he took over as manager in 1961, more than a hundred years after Dickens' idle apprentices ventured deep into the manufacturing bosom of Yorkshire, Leeds was still a byword for muck and misery. Its football team were a laughing stock. When he departed, in 1974, they were the most feared team in Europe.

His appointment coincided with the start of both a new era in football – the maximum wage had just been abolished – and a new age of upward mobility. It came as Leeds was tearing up its industrial roots, cleaning its air of soot and telling a different story about itself.

Revie was born in a 'respectable slum' close to Middlesbrough's Ayresome Park ground in 1927. His memories of hardship produced an enduring distaste for conspicuous consumption and a dread of personal debt. His father was frequently unemployed. His mother, a washerwoman, died of cancer when he was twelve and he became a latch-key kid, obsessively kicking a ball of rags around a cobbled alley in a pair of Wellingtons for hours on end. He left school at fourteen to begin an apprenticeship as a bricklayer, joining Leicester City two years later. He spent half a day lugging bricks and the other half training at Filbert Street. He was so keen to learn that he would often burst into tears. Football was his way out of the darkness, his escape route from poverty.

He rose to prominence at Manchester City after a short spell at Hull. His finest hour and a half was his eponymous Plan, implemented during the 1956 FA Cup Final. Typically, he devoted twenty pages of his autobiography, *Soccer's Happy Wanderer*, to explaining it. It involved him playing as a deep-lying centre forward – a role adopted by Nándor Hidegkuti in Hungary's humiliation of England three years earlier – roaming about the Wembley pitch as a free agent. That 6–3 defeat by the Magnificent Magyars was a watershed for English football. It had the same effect on Revie as Hillary and Tenzing Norgay's ascent of Everest had on mountain climbers and Roger Bannister's four-minute mile had on middle-distance runners. The Hungarian revolution exposed the FA's failure to adapt to the spread of football as a world game. It convinced Revie that you could turn the world upside down, reorder the universe, kick evolution's arse. And that brilliant teamwork, technical skill and tactical intelligence were all as important as physical courage, the traditional mainstay of the English game. Above all, you had to have a set of rules, a team ethos, a code.

In March 1961, two and a half years after signing for United as a player, Revie applied to become manager of Bournemouth and asked Harry Reynolds to write him a reference. The self-made millionaire, who still lived in a two-up, two-down terraced house, tore up his letter of recommendation and offered his captain Jack Taylor's job. Revie told Reynolds he was determined to overhaul a culture of low expectations. There were so many wrongs at the club that needed putting right. Leeds United were badly supported, had a dilapidated stadium and primitive training facilities – and were struggling to survive in what was still considered a rugby league stronghold. On his first day as manager, Revie called all the players together and told them United were 'a dead club'. There was lousy discipline, primitive training methods and a happy-go-lucky, slap-happy attitude. Hence the lousy results. Half of them looked like they didn't want to be there, so he was showing them the door. For the rest it was time to wipe the slate clean and make a fresh start. Training, he promised, would become much more enjoyable – and innovative – with the worst trainer being given a yellow jersey with a wooden spoon sewn into it. Revie made them a pledge: stick with him, do it his way and Leeds would become the new Real Madrid. A film of Real's 7–3 thrashing of Eintracht Frankfurt in the 1960 European Cup Final was shown to every apprentice as part of their induction programme; even more than the Hungarian hammering of England, this was the game – possibly the greatest exhibition of football of all time – that had turned his head.

One of his great managerial gifts was an ability to spot and nurture young talent. But teenagers like Billy Bremner, Paul Reaney, Gary Sprake, Norman Hunter, Peter Lorimer and Terry Cooper would all need time to develop. In his first two years, as he ruthlessly purged the squad of twenty-seven players, the team struggled. At the end of his second season, battling relegation, he barely slept. United only avoided the drop after a final-day win at Newcastle. During the following campaign, they flirted with bankruptcy and crowds dropped to 8,000 – drawn from a population of half a million. After one defeat, chairman Sam Bolton called the rookie boss into his office. 'You must do better if we want to keep soccer in Leeds,' he warned Revie.

The three great managers of the sixties – Revie, Matt Busby and Bill Shankly – all had their own maxims. Busby's was: find a red shirt. Shankly's was: back up the man with the ball. And Revie's? Keep fighting. He erected a sign emblazoned with this mantra outside the home dressing room. He instructed his charges to play with vigour and intensity, to refuse to give quarter, to ruthlessly exploit their opponents' weaknesses. In an era when pre-match preparation consisted of a quick chat before the game, his famously long briefings on such topics as a striker's favourite foot and the opposition's free-kicks were revolutionary. Nothing was left to chance. All three Leeds teams, first, reserve and youth, studied obsessively compiled dossiers – a

The Leeds United squad celebrate winning the 1974 championship in front
of the Elland Road Kop.

Peter Lorimer 'scores' against Bayern Munich in the 1975 European Cup final.
'But what's this?' screams David Coleman. 'The referee hasn't given a goal.
Total confusion. He's given offside.'

My maternal great-grandfather Solomon Saipe at his stall in Leeds Market, circa 1905. According to family folklore, he set up a trestle table next to Michael Marks' penny bazaar. Sadly, Thomas Spencer got to Marks first.

My grandad Harry Clavane: master tailor, atheist and strong advocate of Jewish integration.

My mum and dad, pictured on Blackpool Pier - where they first met.

Keith Waterhouse, pictured outside the Queen's Hotel, was born and brought up on an estate near Elland Road football ground. I've always associated his comic masterpiece, *Billy Liar* - a classic tale of an upwardly-mobile, inwardly-anxious Northern Man - with the story of Leeds.

My dad was born in The Leylands. By the turn of the 20th Century, 8,000 east European immigrants were living in this Jewish ghetto, squeezed into a square mile of dark courtyards, hovels, dangerous passageways, narrow cobbled streets and insanitary back-to-backs.

Leeds City manager Herbert Chapman was banned from football for life after the team were kicked out of the league for making illegal payments during the First World War. After the ban was overturned Chapman went on to great things with Huddersfield Town and Arsenal.

John Charles was the only famous Leeds player of the pre-Revie era. During the mid-1950s, the team were known as John Charles United.

ANTHONY'S MORE THAN JUST A DREAMER

ANTHONY CLAVANE, aged 14, put his dream of being the star of the Leeds United side in the European Cup Final down on paper and earned himself several columns in print in the junior section of the "Evening Post".

I was given a write-up in the *Jewish Gazette* after my *Billy Liar*-esque story about scoring the winner for Leeds in the 1975 European Cup final was published in the *Yorkshire Evening Post*.

Revie and revolution came to Leeds in
November 1958. Here, the Don signs as a player
for United, watched by (*left to right*):
Harold Marjason (director), Cyril Williamson
(secretary) and Bill Lambton (manager).

Revie, pictured outside Elland Road
in December 1969, turned an obscure
club into European giants.

Revie and The Lads at a training session before the 1972 FA Cup Final.
No stars, no egos, no prima donnas. Side before self every time.

The Leeds United board in 1964. *Left to right*: Robert Roberts, Percy Woodward, Sydney Simon, Harry Reynolds, Sam Bolton, Albert Morris and Manny Cussins. As David Peace wrote in *The Damned United*: 'Half Gentile, half Jew; a last, lost tribe of self-made Yorkshiremen and Israelites. In search of the promised land; of public recognition, of acceptance and of gratitude.'

Albert Johanneson, the first black player to play in an FA Cup Final, lit up Elland Road during Revie's early years.

The breakthrough. Revie and The Lads with their first championship in 1969 - which they won with a record number of points and only two defeats.

'And Leeds will go mad,' predicts Barry Davies on *Match Of The Day*, 'and they've every right to go mad.' Referee Ray Tinkler is mobbed by United players after allowing the controversial West Brom goal which 'cheated' the club out of the 1971 title.

Davies again: 'And poor Southampton just don't know what day it is.' As this programme of the 7-0 massacre reveals, it was Saturday, March 4th, 1972.

Nº 19256

Official Programme 5p

LEEDS UNITED A.F.C. TOKEN

SOUTHAMPTON 23 1971-72

LEEDS UNITED
versus SOUTHAMPTON

Saturday, 4th March, 1972   Kick-off 3 p.m.   at ELLAND ROAD

Photo by Jack Hickes, Leeds

Leeds United
Colours
WHITE SHIRTS, WHITE SHORTS
1. GARY SPRAKE
2. PAUL MADELEY
3. TERRY COOPER
4. BILLY BREMNER
5. JACK CHARLTON
6. NORMAN HUNTER
7. PETER LORIMER
8. ALLAN CLARKE
9. MICK JONES
10. JOHNNY GILES
11. EDDIE GRAY

Sub.

Southampton
Colours
RED & WHITE SHIRTS, BLACK SHORTS
1. ERIC MARTIN
2. BOB McCARTHY
3. ROGER FRY
4. JIM STEELE
5. JIMMY GABRIEL
6. TONY BYRNE
7. TERRY PAINE
8. MIKE CHANNON
9. RON DAVIES
10. GERRY O'BRIEN
11. BOBBY STOKES

Sub.

Referee : Mr. D. CORBETT, Wolverhampton.
Linesmen : Mr. A. GORTON, Macclesfield (Red Flag)
Mr. P. BIRCHALL, Bolton (Yellow Flag)

Super Leeds parade
the 1972 FA Cup in an
open-top bus through
the city centre.

A Leeds hooligan
is escorted out of the
ground by a policeman
during trouble at
Coventry City in 1983.

The gates of Elland Road are draped with fans' scarves as a tribute to
Revie after his death in 1989.

kind of pre-computer version of the widely respected Prozone – which analysed every opposing team's strengths and weaknesses. Revie pinned up a list of eighty referees on his office wall, scrawling comments such as 'gives a penalty for anything' and 'don't show any dissent' beside their names. He would go to any lengths to gain an edge. Before one FA Cup tie at Bristol City, the referee was presented with an envelope stuffed full of newspaper cuttings, all on the subject of the home side's bad behaviour. Second Division football, said Revie, was more of a physical contest than an art exhibition; it was certainly not an egg-and-spoon race in which the nicest team always won. The season was a slog. Pitches soon became mud heaps and, when the temperature dropped, players skated around on frozen surfaces. It was do or die, conquer or be conquered.

Revie's holistic approach is now acknowledged, grudgingly in many quarters, as a precursor of Arsène Wenger's revolution at Arsenal. But at the beginning of his reign he was dismissed as a deluded fantasist. Like Billy Liar, and a long line of city visionaries, his dreams of self-improvement invited widespread ridicule. When his young team first ran out in their new, spotlessly-white kit – a homage to the five-times-European Cup-winning Real side – they were greeted with wolf whistles by their own fans. When he introduced a new club song, 'Leeds United Calypso', some wags altered the last word of the title to 'collapso'. As Hunter would later write, 'you could almost hear the laughter ringing throughout English football'.

The Don acted like a father to Big Norm and all

his other rookies, bringing them up as a family and trying to keep them all together. He found houses and jobs for their parents. Ultimately, he promised them, they would all play for their countries. Off the pitch, just as much as on it, they were expected to look after themselves and each other; all for one and one for all. They were required to dress smartly – no long (or even facial) hair, no jeans; ties and grey suits to be worn on match days – to be polite at all times and behave as though they were the city's ambassadors; a perching owl, taken from the city's coat of arms, was added to the pristine white strip. They were taught about bank accounts, table manners and sex. They had access to a club doctor, a club padre and a club educationalist. Revie advised them to settle down quickly and 'not get caught with loose girls'. Their wives were sent flowers on their birthdays. He hired ballet dancers to give the players lessons on balance and imposed dietary and nutritional standards. Everyone, from the directors to the cleaning ladies, was a valued member of the Family. Wage differentials were abolished – which upset Charlton – the players were put up in the best hotels – which upset the directors – and they were kitted out in smart new tracksuits and light, comfortable boots, both provided by local Jewish businesses.

In his first year of management, there was a new spirit abroad, an optimism brought by prosperity. For the next four years, unemployment in Leeds stood at less than 1 per cent and job vacancies exceeded numbers employed. In the country as a whole, white-collar workers formed 36 per cent of the population, compared to 23 per cent before the war. Twenty per cent of fifteen-to eighteen-year-olds were still in education, which was 14 per cent up on 1931. Suburban housing estates were popping up all over the country. Private home-ownership had increased from 25,000 in 1951 to 150,000. Washing machines, vacuum cleaners and fridges were all available on hire purchase. New flats and houses had baths. Car ownership had increased to eight million. Most of us, as Prime Minister Harold Macmillan reflected, had never had it so good.

And yet, as Harold Wilson was quick to point out, we were still 'governed by an Edwardian establishment mentality'. Macmillan's cabinet included six lords and a duke. In 1963, when the grammar school-educated, Huddersfield Town-supporting, HP Sauce-loving Wilson became Leader of the Opposition, Supermac was replaced as Prime Minister by Sir Alec Douglas-Home, a grouse-hunting Old Etonian. In football there was still a huge divide between the corporal class which ran the game and the industrial communities in which it thrived. Spotting Jimmy Greaves having something to eat at the airport before an England game abroad, FA secretary Stanley Rous barked, 'Greaves, put that cake down this instant. You will be fed on the plane.' The desk-bound, time-serving men in waistcoats, who continued to cling to the Corinthians' maxim of 'play up, play up and play the game', were appalled by Revie's uncompromising, win-at-all-costs ethos. They considered his attempt to develop a ruthless, fiercely competitive, hard-hearted winning machine to be, at best, ungentlemanly. At worst, they claimed, it heralded the game's loss of innocence.

The Great Escape

Billy: 'Today's a day of big decisions – going to start writing me novel – two thousand words every day, going to start getting up in the morning.'

1963. My first ever memory of Leeds. I am getting scrubbed up to go to York with my dad. I am going to his new work, wearing a new suede coat, with a fur collar, and my hair is slicked back. I am going on a train, for the first time. Always the station, always the train. On my way to the station I pass my dad's old work, the Queen's Hotel, white underneath its filthy, blackened coating. 'The Ritz of Leeds' he calls it. I didn't know it then – although maybe I sensed it, felt it – but this was his first big job, his big break, his new beginning. As soon as the train pulls out of the station, Dad points out the giant spaceship which appears to have crash-landed on the edge of the city. Just before we depart, he reads aloud the new 'Promised Land Delivered' sign. I have no idea what he is saying, or what the words mean. I just know that we are going on some kind of an adventure.

The romantic in me would like to think that the Promised Land sign went up in 1963 – between the end of the *Chatterley* ban and the Beatles' first LP.

The moment Leeds United, like the sixties, caught fire. The moment Julie Christie caught the train to London, leaving behind her weak-willed boyfriend, Victorian parochialism and northern insularity. The moment the Profumo affair brought down the Macmillan government, Wilson promised to deliver Britain into a new age, Dr Beeching announced the modernisation of the railways and traffic engineers built a new motorway in Leeds. Year Zero. Martin Luther King had a dream, the film *The Great Escape* was released and Larkin's poem, 'Annus Mirabilis', captured the mood of an era in which anything was possible and nothing was safe; a time when the established order was being challenged, subverted and ultimately buried.

In the 1963–4 season, Revie's rookies began their youthful ascent, displaying the form that would result in a decade-long domination of the English game. Albert 'Hurry Hurry' Johanneson, the Don's first signing, scored one of the best goals ever seen at Elland Road, skipping past three Newcastle players after being boxed in near the halfway line. Our Albert lit up the stadium during Revie's early years, offering fans a glimpse of what lay ahead once Dirty Leeds had been delivered from Egypt. He scored fifteen League and Cup goals in the promotion-winning season, a post-war club record for a winger, as United finally drew a line under the failures of the past. The most recent failure had been the return of John Charles, who was clearly ill equipped for the team's new hard-running, hi-tempo, hustling style. The Gentle Giant had little appetite for the grind of second-tier football, scoring only three times in eleven games. After he was returned to sender – the far more suitable Italian top flight – Revie rebuilt Leeds around two players who knew how to handle themselves: Bobby Collins and Johnny Giles, a £33,000 buy from Manchester United. They gave his team a lot more bite. Another key signing – centre forward Alan Peacock – gave them a lot more goals. A Peacock brace and a Giles strike secured the 3–0 win at Swansea that clinched promotion to the First Division. Revie's scrappers ended up as Second Division champions, shattering the league's records for most points in a season, most away victories and fewest defeats. Home attendances rose to almost 30,000.

In 1963, I travelled with my dad from Leeds to York. When we arrived at the Lyons frozen foods depot there, he introduced me to 'Houdini', one of his 'ding-dong men'. I found out later that the man's real name was John. Houdini would often disappear in Dad's small carpeted office and then reappear a few minutes later in the Mister Softee ice-cream van parked outside. He reminded me of my great-uncle Louis, who was always doing card tricks and waving magic wands around and producing coins from behind his ears. Dad had been the first Clavane not to go into tailoring. His Lithuanian grandfather had slaved away in the ghetto to keep his family above the poverty line. His father had made suits in uncle Abe's attic in the Camp Road district, the bleak area photographed by Riboud for the 'Black Leeds' *Picture Post* feature – and his brother would eventually go on to manage a clothing factory owned by the Leeds United chairman, Manny Cussins. Dad left school at fourteen to work, very briefly, at the big Burton factory. But he was ambitious. He didn't want to get stuck in a dead-end job, so he applied for a job at the Queen's. He made quick progress, learning about wine, food, accounts and invoices. After a couple of years, though, the hotel let him go; he was told he lacked the 'correct background' to become a trainee manager. So he went to work for the country's biggest catering company, which had been founded by the Gluckstein brothers and Barnett Salmon in the 1890s and was about to increase massively its market share of the ice-cream business. Lyons had a depot in Beeston, a stone's throw away from Elland Road. Dad started off as a clerk, worked his way up to chief clerk and was then moved to York, where he was put in charge of van drivers, salesmen, cold-store operatives and disappearing ding-dong men.

When we returned from our great adventure in York, just before the train pulled into the new station, he again pointed out the 'spaceship', a football stadium which looked as if it had fallen out of the sky – or at least off the top of Beeston Hill. In the 1990s a huge, steel-grey, multimillion-pound cantilevered stand was grafted on to one of its sides, making it flood the skyline. But it still looked as if it had fallen off the top of the hill. It was soon to become my entrance into an exciting new world: the grand, shared, collective narrative of Leeds, Leeds, Leeds.

Do Unto Others

Councillor Duxbury: 'You're a young man. You've got a long way to go. But you can't do it by yourself. Think on.'

1963. Richard Harris, who is playing Frank Machin in This Sporting Life, *is ploughing through a muddy no man's land, a war zone where men are men and 'great apes' can become sporting heroes. He has been acting the Big Movie Star, shocking everyone with his casual swearing. He's been hailed as the next Brando and has just finished filming* Mutiny on the Bounty, *starring the great American mumbler. Suddenly, the Wakefield Trinity captain comes round the blind side and cops him a real 'un, a right bloody handful, giving him a broken nose. Harris is carried off the pitch, his teeth in pieces. But that's football, son. It's a rough old game; he'll have to learn, he'll have to pay something for his ambition.*

Revie was an enigma, a man of contrasts, both cynic and idealist. His cynicism dominated the first phase of his revolution, 1963 to 1968: the kitchen-sink years. He was desperate to bring the Lads, as he always referred to them, out of the darkness — by whatever means necessary. If this meant battering the opposition into submission, then so be it. It wasn't pretty but it established Leeds as a top four side. His idealism, which has been strangely ignored by both critics and fans – the latter, at times, preferring to revel in the unreconstructed thuggishness of Dirty Leeds – emerged during the second phase, when he took the brakes off, allowing his charges to play the kind of free-flowing, Real Madrid-style football he had always coveted.

I often think of that first phase when I reread *This Sporting Life*. Eye for an eye, conquer or be conquered, get your retaliation in first. Kick or be kicked, kill or be killed. No stars, no egos, no prima donnas. Do unto others before they do unto you. Side before self every time. In my first week at Sussex University, while working my way through the social-realist canon, I met a beautiful science student who told me her grandfather had worked down a Yorkshire pit. What a coincidence, I lied; my grandfather had also been a horny-handed son of the West Riding. After we'd been going out for a few weeks, she saw me reading *This Sporting Life* and revealed that she was David Storey's daughter.

Our relationship was doomed. Kate was an earnest, upper-middle-class Londoner, a bit like I imagined Margaret, the heroine of her dad's second novel – *Flight into Camden* – might have turned out. And I was a lower-middle-class Jewish fantasist from Leeds. Our pillow talk, however, has stayed with me all these years. She told me how her dad used to get down on his hands and knees and scrub the kitchen floor in the middle of the night to the sound of John Lennon's primal screaming. How he spent eight hours at his writing desk every day in imitation of the rhythm of a working-class routine. How he used to climb to the top of a hill just outside Wakefield to get a glimpse of the bright blue sky partly obscured by the drifting smoke of mill chimneys. How he had written his great novel on the train from King's Cross to Leeds. And when I went home I told my dad about my new girl-friend and her famous father. And he said of course he'd heard of David Storey. 'Played for Leeds Rugby, didn't he? Didn't know he was a writer, though.'

In the fifties, Storey had used his wages from the Headingley club to pay his way through Slade School of Art. Machin, his fictional alter ego, was a gifted athlete – but he also watched his back and, in a phrase which is forever seared into my memory, took great delight in throwing his opponents 'neatly over the touchline and against the concrete balustrade'. He was, in short, a brutal bastard. 'Stars?' he sneered, 'there are no stars in this game. Just men like me.' Whenever I watch Lindsay Anderson's film of the great novel, which is quite often, I think of the snarling, keep fighting, us-against-the-world defiance of the early-to-mid-sixties Leeds. I think of the hard-as-nails young Revieites being given a once-in-a-lifetime chance to escape the squalor of their childhoods. They were an aggressive, unsentimental bunch, ruthless in the tackle, unadorned by frills and refinements. A team with something to prove, brimming with talent.

Storey's theory was that there were three kinds of athlete: the scientific, the nervous and the animal. In the sixties, every team had its allotted 'animal', the hatchet man who would clatter anyone who showed the slightest bit of skill. Liverpool had Tommy Smith, Manchester United had Nobby Stiles, Arsenal had Peter Storey and Chelsea had Ron Harris. Leeds had Collins, Hunter, Bremner, Reaney and Charlton – to name but five. Up until 1968, they were a real bastard of a team, their 'ultra-professionalism' lifting them out of the Second Division relegation zone – and near bankruptcy – and into the European elite. Those early European games left an indelible mark on Revie's rookies. After one brutal encounter, a group of players visited Bobby Collins in hospital. Their captain, who had been taken out by a Torino defender, threw off his blanket to reveal a bolt through his leg. Gray, who eventually replaced Johanneson as the token flair player, was initially shocked by his team-mates' penchant for brutality. Yet he understood where they were coming from. He remembered Bremner's eye blowing up like a tennis ball during a Scotland–Brazil game. 'When nobody was looking,' he recalled, 'Pele had stuck the nut on him. There was blood all over the place. He'd been headbutted by the great Pele, but things like that happened.'

Frank Machin's story could be lifted from any one of the the Lads' autobiographies. There's Little Billy, arms spread wide in an apparent plea for mercy, being lifted clean off his feet by Dave Mackay following a late tackle on the Spurs captain. There's Big Jack and Denis Law punching and wrestling one another to the ground. There's Joe 'Dracula' Jordan emerging, like Storey's anti-hero, with his front teeth missing following a clash with a defender. There's Charlton threatening to knock Hunter's block off as a Leeds fan shouts: 'Go arn, Norman, 'ave a go at him.' There's Big Jack chasing a Valencia defender round the pitch after the Spaniard had punched him. There's Little Billy, described by Michael Parkinson as 'ten stone of barbed wire', hurling his shirt to the ground after scrapping with Keegan at Wembley. There's Bites Yer Legs decking Frannie Lee after another dive by the Derby striker. There's Sprakey decking a lad at the Mecca after being accused of eyeing up the lad's bird. There's a tearful David Harvey telling his unsympathetic team-mates how his pet monkey had switched on the oven and gassed himself. There's the entire Leeds team goading George Best, who had just been caught in bed with a girl in the team hotel, asking him repeatedly 'What kind of professional are you?' There's Revie giving his players their wages in readies 'so you can go straight to the bookies'. There's coach Les Cocker telling his defenders to go in hard with the first tackle, the one the referee never books you for.

The London press jumped on Dirty Leeds' gamesmanship, particularly their tactics of stealing yards at free-kicks and throw-ins and running down the clock when the points had been won. 'We picked it up from the continentals,' admitted Bremner. 'They would just walk out to take a corner, or if the game was getting a bit heated, someone would feign an injury.' But these habits had been formed long before their heads were turned by Italian cynicism. Even before 1964's Battle of Goodison, when the referee threatened to stop the Everton–Leeds match unless the players stopped kicking each other. During the previous season, in a ferocious game at Preston, the referee had halted play and lectured both teams about their behaviour. A Football Association newsletter revealed that Leeds received more bookings, suspensions and fines than any other team in the country. Lancaster Gate's eagerness to publicise these findings produced the first accusations of conspiracy. Outraged directors wrote a letter of complaint, alleging 'victimisation'. Outraged fans accused the FA of doctoring the records. But the damage had been done.

The emergence of Northern Man, and more generally the post-war regeneration of the north, coincided with the rise of the three big-city, powerhouse clubs: Manchester United, Liverpool and Leeds. Busby, the game's elder statesman and the first man Revie turned to for advice after getting the Leeds job, had taken over at Old Trafford in 1945 with the club bankrupt and the stadium a bombsite. By 1968, when the Reds became the first English team to win the European Cup, they were a national institution. In the sixties and early seventies, Shankly, like Revie, transformed a second-rate Second Division club into one of the most powerful teams of their generation. If Busby's new babes were defined by the Holy Trinity − Best, Law and Charlton − and Shankly's Scousers were identified with the Fab Four, then Revie's rookies were the Dirty Dozen. Each player, as in Lee Marvin's platoon, had a specific job, was rigorously prepared and was drilled in the art of protecting themselves, and their team-mates, from the many dangers that stalked their brutal world.

Football was extremely violent in the sixties. Foul play was routine. Revie felt the team had to 'earn the right to play' by being the hardest in the league. The Dirty Leeds label did some of the hard work, putting the fear of God into their opponents. The only time Best ever wore shin pads was at Elland Road. 'I hated playing against them,' he said. 'They had a hell of a lot of skill, but they were a bloody nightmare.' Given their lack of footballing history and culture, they needed an edge. A gritty, keep-fighting-till-the-end, don't-let-the-bastards-grind-you-down kind of edge which came from being a hybrid bunch of rough-and-ready, provincial outsiders. Lacking financial backing or a conveyor belt of home-grown talent – his plan for a youth academy would only be realised some thirty years later – Revie had to lure the best young players in Britain to Elland Road. They came to Leeds from Scotland, Wales and the north-east of England. Johanneson came all the way from Soweto in South Africa. The Don's persistence in recruiting his disciples was legendary, but his stalking of Scottish talent bordered on the pathological. At one stage he had seventeen Scots on his books. He befriended Lorimer's family for almost three years in a bid to win over the teenager's parents. Then he drove non-stop to Dundee at five in the morning – at one point being pulled over by police for speeding – to beat both Manchester United and Chelsea to his signature. Both of his skippers were hard and intimidating Celts; Bremner, his warrior king, took over from Collins, his pocket Napoleon. Revie enjoyed pairing the wee men together in mock Scotland–England matches at the training ground. Even Big Jack felt intimidated. 'I got on all right with Bobby,' admitted Charlton. 'But I didn't like playing against him. He'd kill his mother to get a result. When you were playing five-a-side, you never knew what he was liable to do.'

Harvey, frustrated after spending ten months on the transfer list, once made the mistake of telling Revie 'This is no bloody use to me'. The Scotland goalkeeper was seized by the throat and hung up by his collar on a coat hook. The gaffer later apologised. He thought Harvey had said 'This *club* is no bloody use to me'. Before Scotland–England internationals, Revie warned his players not to injure any of their Leeds team-mates. The only way to get to the Top, he told them, was to stick together, stick to the Revie code and stick two fingers up at the establishment. Tribe before country – side before self – every time.

The Four Sons

Mr Fisher (to Billy): 'It's a chance we never had.'

The Haggadah speaks of 'four sons'. And each of these sons asks: 'What is the meaning of this service?' And each one is answered: 'With a strong hand the Almighty led us out from Egypt, from the house of bondage.'

As I approached my fiftieth year, I began to have a recurring dream. Keith Waterhouse, Alan Bennett, Tony Harrison and David Storey were all sitting in the Jazz Age bar of the Queen's Hotel, which is built into Leeds station. They were all in their late-forties, wearing yarmulkes and tuxedos and appeared to be guests at my bar mitzvah. As they talked to Don Revie, trying to distract his attention away from some mysterious event that was about to happen, my dad walked in smoking a cigar. In some versions of the dream, Louis Armstrong and my great-auntie Millie strolled in, arm in arm. The dream always ended the same way. The oak double doors swung open and Variety Club host Marshall Bellow, who used to sit behind my mum's family in shul, suddenly appeared. He was quickly followed by Eamonn Andrews. And, just as Andrews was about to say 'Tonight, Don Revie, this is your life' – I woke up.

Waterhouse, Bennett, Harrison and Storey are my literary heroes. This is not just because they were responsible for four of the books – *Billy Liar*, *Talking Heads*, *V* and *This Sporting Life* – I would take to my desert island. They were cultural pathfinders, the Leeds-based wing of the New Wave movement. Like Revie and my dad, they were born in a period described as the 'Morbid Age' by historian Richard Overy, a time associated with poverty, unemployment, the slump and the rise of fascism. Their breakthrough into the big time coincided with both the rise of the Revieites and the city of Leeds. True, they all got out of the city at the earliest possible opportunity. But they were made in the West Riding. The perching owl of Leeds, emblazoned on the Dirty Dozen's pristine white shirts, had been imprinted on Bennett's schoolbooks. 'At every turn,' he wrote, 'there was this reminder that you were a son or daughter of Leeds.' When going up to Oxford, he felt himself to be an ambassador of the city.

Waterhouse, Bennett and Harrison all grew up near Elland Road in a settled working-class culture that was at once supportive and suffocating. It was described in Richard Hoggart's *The Uses of Literacy*, which was published in 1957, as the apotheosis of indifference. Storey was born in the nearby textile town of Wakefield and came to Leeds as a teenager, signing a fourteen-year-contract to play for the rugby team. It is surprising to discover how many of the writers and actors who 'made it' in the sixties and early seventies were brought up in the run-down, red-brick hinterland that surrounds the United stadium. It is less surprising, perhaps, to discover how few of them actually ventured into the ramshackle Old Peacock ground in their youth. Courtenay became friendly with Revie for a while. And Bennett, as he recorded in his diaries, once succumbed to a bit of star-ogling after spotting the Don at the Queen's Hotel kitchen waiting for some takeaway food. But only the actor Kenneth Haigh – the original Jimmy Porter in John Osborne's ground breaking play *Look Back in Anger* – was a fan.

Like the romantic novelist Barbara Taylor Bradford, Bennett came from Armley. Harrison was from Beeston. Waterhouse, like his sometime co-writer Willis Hall and Peter O'Toole, lived on one of the tram-rattling arteries running from the city centre. These inner-city districts – and others, just north of the river, which spawned the likes of Haigh, Jack Higgins and Malcolm McDowell – had once formed the engine room of the Industrial Revolution. The Four Sons, propelled by scholarships to grammar schools, traineeships on local papers and places at art colleges – all one-way tickets out of a life of provincial drudgery and confinement – reaped the benefits of the post-war economic and social consensus. Bennett was educated at Leeds Modern, a state grammar school which in the 1940s and 1950s regularly sent boys to Leeds University. He bucked the trend by going to Oxford. 'We grammar school boys were the interlopers,' he wrote. 'These [public school] slobs, as they seemed to me, the party in possession.'

Like Billy Fisher, Waterhouse had started out as a clerk in an undertaker's office – but he did get on the London train after making his mark at the *Yorkshire Evening Post*. Other Leeds interlopers included Frankie 'Give Me the Moonlight' Vaughan (whose sister went to school with my mum), Jack 'The Eagle Has Landed' Higgins and Peter 'Lawrence of Arabia' O'Toole. O'Toole had won a scholarship to study at RADA, in the same year as Harris, Finney and Alan Bates. The Royal Court gave him his big break in *The Long and the Short and the Tall*, written by Hall. When O'Toole became a Hollywood pin-up after starring in David Lean's epic, *Time* magazine put him on their front cover and called him 'Lawrence of Leeds'.

After being mentored by Waterhouse, Barbara Taylor Bradford worked her way up from the *YEP* typing pool to woman's editor and then she, too, caught the train. She went on to write an international bestseller about Emma Harte, a working-class girl from Leeds who became a business tycoon. The *YEP*'s upmarket rival, the *Yorkshire Evening News*, was also a breeding ground for talented writers. O'Toole had, very briefly, been its theatre critic. Ronald Crowther, before becoming a *Daily Mail* columnist, reported on Leeds United for the paper. At about the same time, Eddie Waring, his up-and-coming colleague, was recruited by the BBC to commentate on live rugby league matches.

There were some dark mutterings about the stampede south, but most Loiners were proud of their upwardly mobile sons and daughters. They were all, as Joe Lampton insisted, 'going to the Top'. So good luck to Harold Wilson's adviser Gerald Kaufman, comedy writer Barry Cryer, Mecca DJ Jimmy Savile and pools winner Viv Nicholson. Nicholson had hopped on the train the moment her eight score draws came up. At King's Cross station, Bruce Forsyth presented her with a cheque for £152,300, 18 shillings and 8 pence, worth about £3 million in today's money. When asked by reporters what she planned to do with it, she replied: 'Spend, spend, spend!' Good luck to them all: the long and the short and the tall.

The Switch

General Fisher: 'We have fought long and hard. Now, at last, our struggle has been rewarded.'

1965. Another Inter Cities Fairs Cup night. Another exotic sounding European team – a Torino or a Leipzig – at Elland Road. As I walk down the hill to the stadium clutching my father's hand, marvelling at the way the new floodlights illuminate the sky, he rhapsodises about the other teams in the competition: Valencia, Ujpest Dozsa and Real Zaragoza. After a long period of inertia, of confinement, the glacial pace of progress has suddenly accelerated – and a lingering sense of inferiority has exploded in an instant of euphoria. The past no longer casts its shadow over the present. An old world disappears and a new one emerges to fill the gap; a new tribe, a new generation, gets its chance. And a journey that has taken generations feels as though it has occurred in a moment.

In April 1974, the beaming Eamonn Andrews quietly made his way along the Queen's red-carpeted corridors to spring his big red book on a startled Revie. At the end of the programme, he asked Busby to sum up his first impressions of the young player-manager. 'I thought here was a man bursting to succeed, bursting

72

to build a great side,' said Sir Matt. 'And this, the world knows, Don Revie has done.' As Revie told the *This Is Your Life* presenter, there had been no dramatic ascendancy. It had taken him four years to build the beginnings of one of the greatest sides in English football. But by 1965, with the exception of strikers Mick Jones and Allan Clarke, the legendary Leeds team was in place. Over the next ten years they would win two First Division championships, two European trophies, an FA Cup and a League Cup. And they would never drop out of the top four.

Nineteen sixty-five was the year Leeds stopped being a parochial oval-ball town and started challenging the football establishment. In their first year in the First Division, Revie's rookies, incredibly, almost won the Double – losing the title to Manchester United, on goal average, and the FA Cup Final to Liverpool in extra time. The city now had 174 football pitches as opposed to forty rugby league ones – clear evidence that it had, at last, broken out of its insular West Riding mindset. Further confirmation came when an estimated 200,000 Loiners lined the streets to hail the Lads at the end of the 1964–5 season. Standing on the balcony of Brodrick's town hall, Revie talked about his dream of emulating Real Madrid – and this time nobody laughed. The rapturous civic reception marked Leeds' long-delayed arrival as a European city. True, they had lost out on two major trophies. But they had qualified for European competition for the first time – and just getting to the world-famous Wembley had been an extraordinary achievement. This was a time when the Cup Final was one of the few live games on TV, broadcast simultaneously on BBC and ITV – and all around the world. For the first time in their history, the city had been represented at the globe's greatest sporting venue. They had never previously got anywhere near the hallowed turf; in fact, in each of their previous ten seasons they had been knocked out in the third round. They were not yet Real Madrid, but the provincial no-hopers from rugby league land were now a nationally recognised, if not nationally admired, football team. It didn't matter that they had no history. As far as TV viewers were concerned, you could have been born, or formed, yesterday. Before televised matches, before *Match of the Day*, there was no history. *MOTD* was first screened on BBC2 in 1964, but as the channel was only available in London, only 20,000 watched the Liverpool–Arsenal game. When new transmitters were opened in the Midlands and the north the audience soared and the show moved to BBC1. Leeds United were finally introduced to the nation on 20 March 1965 when they thrashed Everton 4-1 at Elland Road.

United came out of the cold just as English football was about to come of age. In 1965, the year before Alf Ramsey's World Cup winners finally lifted the game out of its post-Hungary gloom, the club's programme notes explained to fans how to pronounce the names of teams like Ujpest Dozsa, Real Zaragoza and Hadjuk Split – and where exactly in Europe they were located. And it was around this time that Jewish Loiners, whose grandparents had escaped the strange sounding shtetls of Eastern Europe, also emerged from their narrow, insular world. They had left Chapeltown in their droves and had begun to play a key role in the city's economic and political resurgence. Ziff, whose father had fled the Russian pogroms at the turn of the century, kick-started the retail revolution when he opened the Merrion Centre. Cohen, the demolition man, knocked down 9,000 slums and built 11,427 new dwellings. Irwin Bellow, Marshall's brother, became the first Jewish leader of the council. The second gener- ation had moved out of the Leylands only to create a 'Little Israel' in Chapeltown. In the post-war period the third generation climbed out of the ghetto and into the northern heights of leafy Moortown and Alwoodley. Their arrival as a local force had not gone unnoticed. 'The language has changed,' lamented the traditionalist *Jewish Chronicle*. 'Yiddish is rarely heard and hardly ever spoken at public meetings. Its sons speak with pride of Leeds' prowess on the football field . . .'

A previously nonconformist, and at times maverick, community was finally assimilating into the host culture. 'Anti-Semitism is practically non-existent,' my uncle Louis assured Mordechai Richler in a 1965 *Sunday Times* profile. The fact that such a prestigious national news- paper had devoted several pages of its new colour supplement to Leeds Jewry was, in itself, proof of the community's advance. It had spawned influential polit- icians such as Cohen, Bellow and Kaufman. It had produced household names like Marks and Spencer, Burton and Barratts. It had even sent Frankie Vaughan to Hollywood. And, through the likes of John Collier and March the Tailor, it continued to dominate the tailoring industry. As Richler reflected, however, this rags-to-riches rise had required a trade-off. The people he interviewed seemed 'more inhibited-Yorkshire-in-

miniature than exuberantly Jewish'. Most of the younger
generation, he discovered, had abandoned the old
Yiddisher culture. Some of them had even abandoned
their ancestral and communal ties. My uncle took a
more positive view. In his father's day, he pointed out,
it had been dangerous to leave the Leylands. 'I speak
a lot here and there. Fifteen years ago I'd be asked:
"What's the difference between a Jew and an
Englishman?" But not today. As an Englishman I'd be
insulted . . . Today we have the same problems as non-
Jews. We shouldn't pretend to be special . . . Today,
the Jew is no longer treated like a neighbour. He is a
neighbour.'

Several of my neighbours were acting out my
fantasies, every other Saturday, inside the giant spaceship south of the river. Playing for Leeds United was
a clear breach of sabbath rules. Not being allowed to
kick a football on the Day of Rest had clearly put paid
to my own 'brilliant' career. In the orthodox community I grew up in it was as unacceptable an activity as
driving to the synagogue, lighting a fire or answering
the phone. So, the next best thing to playing for the
Revie-ites was supporting them. Or living next door
to them. Or selling rolls of cloth to them; one of my
uncles used to give Big Jack his bag of 'leftovers' – cut-
offs and seconds – to sell to his team-mates. Bill
Fotherby, a (non-Jewish) director, told me 'there would
be no Leeds United without the Jews'. This, coming
from a man who once claimed Maradona was bound
for Elland Road, should probably be taken with a large
bucket of salt. But there is no doubt that Jewish financial backing played a big part in the Revie revolution.

The relationship went far deeper than finance, of course. It was based on the community's need to prove themselves and find new identity in an alien society.

My own relationship with the club began one wet afternoon in April 1965, when I stood on the rain-lashed concrete terraces for the first time, watching a 1-0 defeat to Manchester United. I say watching but, until Dad lifted me on to his shoulders for the final few minutes, I couldn't actually see a thing. I can remember though, in those last few minutes, shouting out the names of a few players I recognised. They lived near us in Moortown. Revie himself lived just across the road for a while before moving into Manny Cussins' big house in Alwoodley. Cussins had made his fortune in the furniture retail business. As a thirteen-year-old he had sold chairs and tables from a handcart. He built up a chain of stores, which he sold for £1 million, and then founded John Peters, which controlled over a hundred retail outlets by 1975. I didn't know the Leeds United director but he could often be spotted in my synagogue, on the morning of a match, in a row reserved for local worthies. And I was on fairly intimate terms with his old house. I frequently climbed up the big hill to Three Chimneys to ask its new occupant – 'Mr Revie', as he insisted on being called – for an autograph. Mr Revie's new house had central heating, a sun lounge, two bathrooms, a four-car garage block, spacious drawing and dining rooms, a playroom and a kitchen and an adjoining annex with separate living accommodation. In the hallway there was a huge framed picture of him and Bill Shankly leading their teams out for the

1965 FA Cup Final. And, fastened to the outside wall, there was a big Star of David.

Albert Johanneson, David Harvey, Mick Jones and Peter Lorimer all lived in terraced and semi-detached club houses in the Chapeltown–Moortown area, a district classified by the sociologist Ernest Krausz as lower-middle class. This was only a few years after the abolition of a salary cap and, according to my friend Leon Apfel, whose dad was Albert's lawyer, the players earned between £5,000 and £10,000 a year, more than twice the average working wage. Johanneson was sometimes at Leon's when I called round and I once barged in on Bites Yer Legs Hunter when he was having tea at another mate's house. And there was a period when I kept bumping into bored-looking Leeds stars at Jewish charity events and coffee mornings.

Leeds United are no more a Jewish club than Manchester United are a Catholic one. But in the mid-sixties, just as a tide of cloth was washing through Old Trafford – in return for player tip-offs, Busby invited priests to games – the community attached itself to Elland Road with a fervour unknown in more established football cities. And just as the Edwards family began to create a Catholic dynasty – Busby would be succeeded by Wilf McGuinness, Frank O'Farrell, Tommy Docherty and Dave Sexton – so Cussins, Sydney Simon and Albert Morris established a strong Jewish influence in the Leeds boardroom. Switching codes – from rugby to Revie – was a bit like abandoning Yiddish for English or klezmer for jazz. In 1965, virtually en masse, the community transferred its dynamism and energy from Headingley to Elland Road.

It was at Elland Road, not Headingley, where you could hear songs praising a Jewish doctor for giving out sick notes every other Saturday ('Samuel, got me well, I was so delighted. When you're ill just take a pill and follow Leeds United'). It was at Elland Road where fans would now be taunted with the refrain 'Does your rabbi know your here?'. And it was at Elland Road that I would, over the years, hymn the praises of revered gentiles – Imre Varadi and Tony Yeboah immediately spring to mind – to the strains of the Hebrew folk song 'Hava Nagila'.

After losing to Liverpool at Wembley, my uncle – in his *Jewish Gazette* column – detected 'an air of bereavement in the Day Centre Discussion Group. It was suggested we should all rise for a two-minute silence. In one Jewish place of worship younger congregants whispered "Don, we wish you long life" instead of the Loyal Prayer.' Some members of the community were in a position to do a lot more than just pray. In 1961, with the club on the brink of bankruptcy, Cussins and wallpaper magnate Morris had responded to a desperate SOS from the board. On becoming directors they had each made interest-free loans of £10,000. A few years earlier, after the old West Stand burned down, the 100 Club had been formed to forge stronger ties with local business. This was one of the earliest examples of corporate sponsorship; Cussins, Morris, Ziff, Howard Levison, Bobby Caplin, Martin Goldman and many other wealthy Jews – and non-Jews – all paid £100 to watch games from a club room incorporated within the new West Stand. Although the motive was financial rather than enlightened, United had inadvertently become the first English football club to open its doors to a tribe previously barred from the city's sporting establishment. Revie made a point of joining a Jewish golf club and holidaying with local businessmen like Leslie Silver and Gabby Harris. Sidney Rose joined the Manchester City board in the sixties and, in 1981, Jack Dunnett became the first Jewish president of the Football League. But before the eighties the Football League, as its historian Simon Inglis noted, 'had been very much a bastion of Anglo-Saxon Protestantism'. Spurs fans might call themselves 'yiddos' but there were no Jews on the White Hart Lane board until the 1980s.

Just before the 1965 final, Shankly had invited comedian Jimmy Tarbuck into the dressing room to crack some jokes. When the laughter subsided he drew his players' attention to the silence in the Leeds dressing room. 'They're shitting themselves,' he said. This got Revie, a good friend of Shankly's, thinking. To relax his own players before big games, he brought in a local jeweller, part-time market seller and all-round-entertainer called Herbert Warner. Herbert had made Don laugh a lot after becoming his golfing partner at the Moor Allerton club. After introducing the Lads to the joys of bingo, carpet bowls and dominoes, he became their licensed court jester, providing much-needed light relief before big games. Herbert travelled all over Europe with the players. Hanging around hotel pools, they would amuse themselves by throwing his wig into the water. He would challenge much younger coach drivers to running races. Revie would be giving the players their ceremonial Thursday morning soap massages when Herbert would walk in and do his spiel, making them all crack up. And if you wanted a nice ring for your girlfriend – the gaffer insisted his players got married at the earliest possible opportunity – Jock the jeweller would see you right. I remember my dad excitedly returning from the wedding of one of Herbert's sons, having spotted a yarmulked Revie in the congregation. 'Don,' the rabbi had begun his sermon, 'believe it or not, you and I have a lot in common. We share congregations. I have them on Saturday morning, you have them in the afternoon.'

Off the Leash

Billy Fisher: 'It was a big day for us. We had won the war in Ambrosia. Democracy was back once more in our beloved country.'

1969. I am lying on my bed, communing with BBC Radio Leeds, on tenterhooks as I listen to Doug Lupton's bulletins from Anfield. Every time the presenter, John Helm, says, 'And now over to Doug Lupton at Anfield' I die a thousand deaths. All we need is a draw – and then the long wait will be over. Doug tells us about another Liverpool attack, another chance gone begging. Leeds are clinging on, but for how long? Every time John goes over to Doug for 'the latest news from Anfield' I am convinced Doug will report a Liverpool goal. In that split second before Doug speaks, I hear the roar of the Anfield

Kop. My heart skips a beat. Elation or despair? Triumph or disaster? Conquer or be conquered?

Between 1965 and 1968, Leeds became known as English football's 'nearly men'. After just missing out on the Double, they had just missed out on another two trophies – finishing runners-up in the league and losing an Inter Cities Fairs Cup Final – and reached two FA Cup semi-finals. When his rookies finally delivered, winning the League Cup and Fairs Cup in the same season, Revie's sense of relief was palpable. At a civic reception outside the town hall, he told fans that this was a watershed in their history. The following year they went one better, winning the First Division title with a record number of points and only two defeats. No major trophies for fifty years, then three arrive at once. They were on the cusp of footballing immortality, about to project their provincial shadow on to the global screen. Now they could embark on the second phase of the revolution. It was time for the brakes to come off.

After the goalless draw at Anfield which clinched the title, 27,000 Liverpool Kopites graciously hailed the new champions. Bremner and the players were at first shocked – but then spent twenty glorious minutes basking in the adulation. 'Being cheered by a rival crowd – any crowd – was a new experience for us,' Gray recalled. 'This was a turning point for Leeds.' A psychological weight had been lifted. Revie had taken the biggest also-rans in the British game to the Top. They had not just won the League title, they had finally won the respect, if not the admiration, of the nation. Now the

Lads could let their hair down, let themselves go, express themselves more.

Both cup victories had been won as a result of a trademark Dirty Leeds tactic: Jack Charlton standing on the opposition goal-line, directly in front of the keeper, waiting for the inswinging corner. In the League Cup Final against Arsenal in 1968 Big Jack had knocked Gray's cross down for Cooper to volley in. Against Ferencváros he had flicked on Lorimer's corner for Jones to score the Fairs Cup winner. Although they won the title with an unprecedented number of points, their goals tally was pitifully low. The distinguished football writer Brian Glanville called them 'deserving rather than popular champions'. At the end of the 1968–9 season, Revie promised to introduce more invention and creativity into their play. They would attack more. Their ruggedly defensive system would be replaced by a more expansive approach, spearheaded by their new £165,000 striker Allan 'Sniffer' Clarke, one of the deadliest finishers in football. They would shed their reputation for gamesmanship, time-wasting and rough play. He had been particularly stung by a Bobby Moore column which described Leeds as 'the most unpopular team to leave the county of cloth caps and racing pigeons to come south'. Down south, they were still only grudgingly accepted as part of the elite. It was time, he now acknowledged, to let the Lads off the leash.

Four Minutes to Go

Billy: 'The idea of being in London next Saturday, put down on paper and staring me in the face, filled my bowels with quick-flushing terror.'

1970. A new decade, a new era. The sixties are over: The Beatles break up, England fail to defend the World Cup, Wilson is kicked out of office. Busby retires, Bestie is burned out and Liverpool are in the middle of a trophy drought. Leeds, the champions of England, the north's last hope, are going for an unprecedented Treble. For invincibility. They have had seven players called up into the England squad. All their Scottish, Welsh and Irish players are full internationals. They are playing a more open, exhilirating brand of football. Revie says he won't be satisfied until his team have landed the European Cup – followed by the world club championship.

The 1965 Cup Final had been Leeds' first high-profile appearance in the nation's living rooms. And they had frozen, gone missing, choked. Five years later, now a central presence in the small-screen universe, Revie's new, improved team lined up opposite Chelsea for the most talked-about final in years. Leeds and Chelsea were both, in their different ways, archetypal sixties teams; models of social mobility, footballing arrivistes who had come from nowhere to challenge the stuffy, effete, complacent old-boy network. They had both given youth its head and were brimming with ambition.

'And the Cup,' says Kenneth Wolstenholme, 'is finally bound for Leeds.' Mick Jones has just put Leeds 2-1 up with six minutes to go. I've got a terrible headache from all the tension. I've had a headache throughout a TV lead-up which seems to have lasted all day. There was a special It's A Knockout *with Eddie Waring and Stuart Hall, then* Introducing The Teams, *then* Cup Final Question Of Sport. *And so on and so on. I'd seen a few live matches at Elland Road now, standing in the Lowfields section of Elland Road with my dad. But this was different. This was the FA Cup Final on our new colour telly with Dad, Grandad, my little brother and all my uncles. And, with four minutes to go, Chelsea are awarded a free-kick.*

The two teams' images, however, were diametrically opposed. Chelsea were Jean Shrimpton, Twiggy, David Bailey, David Frost, Terence Conran, Mary Quant and Michael Caine. Leeds were Jimmy Savile. Chelsea were the swinging sixties, the cavalier chancers; Leeds were the dour grafters, clunk, click every trip. The 1970 final was billed as a bitter clash between Sexton's long-haired dandies and Revie's austere short-back-and-sides. The beautiful south against the ugly, brutal, cynical face of the north.

Four minutes to go. The whole nation, the whole world, is watching. On a Wembley pitch turned into a quagmire by the Horse Of The Year Show, *Leeds are tearing Chelsea apart. Gray keeps waltzing past Webb, dumping him on his backside with his deceptive feints. Leeds are in their pomp, flaunting their talents. Big Jack opened the scoring with a farcical goal and then Sprake, typically, let Houseman's cross-shot underneath his body for the equaliser. Then Jones restored United's lead, thumping in the rebound from Clarke's diving header. As Wolstenholme announces that the Cup is finally bound for Leeds, I leave the room. When the four minutes are up I'll go back in and my headache will be gone and my team will have won the most famous club competition in the world.*

Raquel Welch, officially The World's Sexiest Woman, had once been spotted at Stamford Bridge sauntering down the touchline shouting 'Yoo-hoo, Ossie' at Peter Osgood. Ossie, Webbie and Hutch hung out with Twiggy, were photographed by Bailey and rubbed shoulders with Frostie. And Ossie, The King Of Stamford Bridge was once visited in his dressing room by The World's Coolest Man, Steve McQueen. If you wanted hedonism and glamour you'd go down Kings Road. If you wanted pub darts and bingo you'd go down Elland Road.

Four minutes to go and Revie has a premonition. He is overcome with a sense of disaster. He has to be physically restrained from running on to the pitch. I return from the kitchen to see a hunched and fidgety figure scowling on the bench. The old, robotic Leeds would have shut up shop, killed the game off. But the new attacking Leeds have let Chelsea equalise. The new Leeds have slowed down. Their muscles have stiffened. They have allowed Ian Hutchinson to steal in and head a free-kick past Sprake. 'Is there,' wonders Wolstenholme, 'no end to the misfortunes of Leeds United?'.

The received narrative of the 1970 final is that art and imagination overcame dull-eyed functionalism.

The reality is that, both on Wembley's gloopy porridge of a pitch and in the Old Trafford replay – the eighth-highest rated British TV programme, and the most notorious Cup Final, of all time – the mighty Whites outplayed the battling Blues. But they were beaten, ultimately, by a plucky, spirited side that refused to die. That kept coming back. The Wembley encounter had been astonishingly open, with Gray skinning Webb alive, but at Old Trafford, especially after Harris' karate kick took out the lanky winger, the game degenerated into a bloodbath.

Charlton floors Osgood. McCreadie almost beheads Bremner. The ball is an irrelevance. Astonishingly, no one is booked – or even sent off. In the last minute of extra-time Webb pops up from nowhere to head in the winner. Beauty has slain the Beast.

The Great Passover
Argument of 1971

Rita: 'You think you're somebody, don't you. I'll tell you something. You're not. You're nobody. You're just a piece of muck.'

1971. Leeds v West Brom. Suggett is clearly offside. The linesman has raised his flag but the referee, Ray Tinkler, is waving him on. Most of the Leeds, and West Brom, players have stopped but Brown passes to Astle and Astle scores. 'And Leeds,' Barry Davies says, 'will go mad . . . and they've every right to go mad . . . they have every justification for going mad . . . you can understand the feelings of those Leeds players.' Revie frowns and turns his eyes heavenward, as if looking for a sign. Then he wanders on to the pitch and shakes his head at the heavens. 'Don Revie,' sums up Davies, 'a sickened man.'

In 1970, their bodies drained by a brutal fixture pile-up, Leeds missed out on a never-before-achieved Treble. They lost yet another final, finished second in the League to Everton and were taken apart by Celtic in a thrilling, battle-of-Britain European Cup semi-final. Revie had reinvented the club through sheer force of personality. But it was, as I have pointed out, a conflicted personality. His most epic internal battle was between his technocratic rationalism and his neurotic fatalism. Given the abundance of talent at his disposal, he knew Leeds should have won far more than they did. When his scientific, fact-finding methods 'failed' he turned, more and more, to superstition. He believed in magic. He read the entrails. The spirits came at him at moments of great tension – like the moment Chelsea were awarded a free-kick at Wembley with four minutes to go.

Revie's superstitions tend to be dismissed, even laughed off, as crankish idiosyncrasies, but they were symptomatic of a profound insecurity, a gnawing anxiety, a deep fear of losing – and losing control. Off the pitch, Revie dictated his players' lives, controlling their diet, designing their kit, massaging their backs, sorting out their finances and even vetting their girl-friends. But he was forced to concede authority for the most important period of the week: the ninety minutes of a football match. In the early seventies, tele-vision pictures frequently caught him glowering from the dugout in his dark blue suit, sheepskin jacket and driving gloves. He wore this 'lucky' mohair suit to every game. Even when a great big hole appeared in his trousers, he continued to wear it. He always walked the same route to the dugout. He refused to return through the door of his home in the morning if he'd left something behind. He stopped wives and girlfriends wearing green or red dresses. He rubbed the orna-mental elephants that sat on his mantlepiece. He was influenced by his 'psychic' mother-in-law's predictions; he'd interpreted one of her dreams, about a barrel spilling out red apples, as a sign that Liverpool would beat Leeds − which, of course, they did. The night before the League Cup win, Cooper dreamed about scoring the winner against Arsenal; which, of course, he did. Every player had a good-luck charm, a pre-match ritual. Bremner would hand Revie his wedding ring for safe-keeping. Big Jack would be the last to run out of the tunnel and Reaney would always be third in line. Hunter always handed the ball to Bremner to carry out. Sprake always had a massage from Cocker before a match. Giles always put on his jockstrap, socks, boots, shirt and shorts − in that order.

'Look at him,' says Davies, 'looking at the heavens in disgust. So many fans on the field being taken off and more police on the field than players. And the Yorkshire spirit is

*really coming to the fore. There's a wrestling match going on
in the centre circle, but when all is said and done the goal
is going to stand. But what a cruel goal. Listen to the crowd
going mad.'*

Between winning the title in May 1969 and the Fairs
Cup, for the second time, in June 1971, Leeds played
some of the best football ever seen in this country. Few
English sides of any era could have lived with them.
In April 1970, Gray scored a goal that would be remembered by the 25,000 people who witnessed it for the
rest of their lives, ghosting past seven Burnley defenders
before slotting the ball home. The Lads knocked the
ball around with a swagger and a confidence rarely
seen, before or since, in the domestic game. They
smashed five past Chelsea, West Brom and Sarpsborg,
six past Nottingham Forest, Sparta Prague and Sutton
and ten past the amateurs of Lyn Oslo. But they won
nothing. Absolutely bugger all. And they were still
depicted as humourless, cloth-capped, whippet-fanciers.
They were still Dirty Leeds.

The frustration of this barren period was perfectly
captured in the title of Billy Bremner's 1970 autobiography: *You Get Nowt For Being Second*. In Revie's
thirteen-year reign Leeds were too often the brides-
maids. They might have won the League twice but
they were runners-up five times. They won the FA
Cup once but were losing finalists on three occasions.
The 1969-70 season was the closest they ever came to
realising their enormous potential. Many fans were
convinced they had been victims of a conspiracy. At
the end of the season, they were forced to play
seventeen matches in fifty-six days. The Football League

secretary, Alan Hardaker, refused to make any allowances for the fixture congestion. His view was that Revie and his team had twisted their way to the Top. He despised them so much that, when The Don became England manager, he refused a request to postpone First Division matches before vital internationals.

Revie had cultivated a public persona of a dour, controlling patriarch; an enigmatic man who always kept his cards close to his chest and never showed his true emotions. But his post-match interviews were becoming increasingly prickly affairs, revealing far deeper insecurities than this persona had suggested. After a radio presenter pointed out that a defender had received his seventh booking of the season, he snapped: 'There you go again, picking on Leeds United.' One or two of his normally-bland newspaper columns had turned into paranoic rants. It seemed that the more hoops his team jumped through, and the higher they climbed, the more the outside world conspired to block their progress. Perfectly good goals were being disallowed, legitimate penalty appeals were being turned down, doctored disciplinary records were being published, fixture pile-ups were being contrived. It was all part of The Plot Against Leeds.

Chewing fiercely, carrying a tartan travel rug under his arm, Revie gives out a sense of elected loneliness, of self-isolation. Normally, he refuses to allow his emotions to get the better of him, but now he appears to be overwhelmed by the immense stress of it all. He goes back to the touch-line to get the linesman. He pats him on the arm, appeals to his common sense, his sense of justice, his common decency. He manages, finally, to get the linesman to talk to Tinkler. But it's no good. The deed is done. His team's fate is sealed.

At the end of the 1970–71 season, a notorious offside decision in a home game against West Bromwich Albion 'cheated' Leeds out of the title. A small group of fans invaded the pitch, earning the club a four-match home ban at the start of the following campaign – which denied them another title. According to the conspiracy theorists, a sinister pattern was developing. Too many important decisions were going against them. For Revie, the West Brom game was a wake-up call, a kind of epiphany – the moment he realised that, whatever you did on or off it, the playing field would never be level. The gods of fate would never be beaten. The deck would always be stacked against Leeds United.

At the Passover service a few weeks after this game, I was in my last term at the Selig Brodetsky Jewish Day School and looking forward to going to the grammar school. I would soon be mixing with Gentiles for the first time in my life. I'd seen them on the terraces at Elland Road, of course, but I'd always been cocooned by my dad, uncles and cousins. As is customary on Passover nights, there were a number of heated arguments. The subjects at this particular seder ranged from the postal workers' strike to West Brom's offside goal. After the prayers and the exodus story and the meal, everyone, as always, did a turn. Jackie Lee told his usual jokes. His brother Benny, who was a semi-famous actor, did his 'You're robbing me' spiel about a factory boss searching the floor for bits of cloth that cost two shillings a yard. On this occasion,

Benny dedicated the routine to 'Ray expletive-deleted-because-children-are-present Tinkler'. My grandpa whistled "My Yiddishe Mama" and "Danny Boy". And I, as usual, rounded the sing-song off with a high-pitched version of "Glory, Glory, Leeds United". There were, as is the custom, four goblets of wine on the table: bring out, deliver, redeem, take. And a fifth cup for the prophet Elijah, the harbinger of the Messiah. And, as I saw one of my uncles shake a table leg to make Elijah's cup vibrate, The Great Passover Argument of 1971 broke out.

Revie decides to take decisive action. First he removes the owl, the civic symbol of Leeds, from the team shirt – birds, obviously, being harbingers of bad luck. And then he removes the 'curse' of Elland Road. During pre-season, he had received a letter from a fan claiming that gypsies used to live on the site before it became a football ground. When they were evicted they'd put a hex on the stadium. So he sends a car over to Blackpool to collect Gypsy Rose Lee.

Try as they might, Leeds just couldn't get back into the European Cup. Which, as one of the best teams in Europe, was clearly their rightful place. The problem was that they kept finishing second. In those days, you had to win the League to get into the world's biggest club competition, not just finish in the top four. And it was this failure which provoked the argument. If I remember correctly, it all started when the uncle who was vigorously shaking the table leg – trying to create the illusion that the Messiah had actually returned to earth and was happily drinking from his cup – said that Leeds would never win the European Cup. Not in a million years. Time was running out and they weren't getting any younger. Why wasn't a new generation of players coming through, like at Liverpool? And then another uncle pointed out that Leeds were cursed, as proved by the fact that Astle's strike was the most blatantly offside goal that had ever been scored in the history of football. The pitch invasion had been completely justified. My dad said that hooliganism could never be justified. And by the way, he added, neither could shabby suits. Having worked in Burtons, in the dispatch room at the giant Hudson Road factory, piecing all the bits – the trousers, the jackets, the waist-coats – together, he knew someone who'd measured Revie up for one of his lucky suits, which now – disgracefully – had a hole in the trousers. Auntie Millie said what did my dad know, he'd been in tailoring only five minutes. And, she added, Suggett had clearly been in an offside position when Tony Brown kicked the ball into open space on the West Brom right. Dad said he knew two things. Firstly, although the linesman had flagged for offside, the referee – like God – always had the final say on matters of opinion and fact. And secondly, he knew that Revie had come over as a schlump on national television, with his schmatty suit and his meshugah superstitions and his big behind hanging out of his frayed trousers.

Gypsy Rose Lee stands in the middle of the pitch, scratches the grass and throws some seeds down. Then she urinates over each corner flag. 'Now,' she tells Revie, 'you will start winning things again.'

Then Dad said that it was all over. Leeds were burned out, finished. And it was the players' own fault. They had, once again, blown it. All that talent gone to waste.

Why the heck, he asked, did they all freeze when the linesman flagged? Tinkler hadn't blown his whistle, had he? In fact, he'd waved Suggett on. So why did they stop? Why couldn't the silly sods have played to the whistle? Why had they – once again – come to a grinding halt on the threshold of the promised land?

White Heat

General Fisher: 'We will rebuild. Battalions of craftsmen will change the face of our cities. We will build towers. Towers. Towers, no less. Truly history has been made again.'

1972. Leeds United are just turning it on. Seven-nil up against Southampton and, as Davies tells the nation, it's almost cruel. 'And every man jack of this Leeds side is putting on a show. Hunter collects the ball deep in his own half and passes it to Gray. Gray pushes forward and passes to Bremner, who passes to Giles just inside the Southampton half. Giles passes forward to Jones who pushes the ball back to Hunter.' Leeds are on top of the world. Hunter hits a cross-field ball to Madeley. Madeley to Clarke. Clarke back to Bremner. Thirty thousand Leeds fans chant 'Ole!' 'And to say that Leeds are playing with Southampton is the understatement of the season. Bremner to Gray, Gray back to Bremner, Bremner backheels to Madeley. And poor Southampton just don't know what day it is.' And as Bremner hits a long cross-field ball to Reaney, who beats three players and finds Giles – who puts his left foot around his right and chips the ball to Clarke – I look out at the Leeds skyline, sturdy and prickly against the sky. And I can see – almost touch – the promised land.

Revie – and Gypsy Rose Lee – was right. My dad was wrong. Leeds weren't finished. They *did* start winning things again. Not only that, they started playing every other team off the park, week after week. They became entertainers, crowd-pleasers. They wore sock tags and Smiley badges and performed Busby Berkeley-style callisthenics during pre-match warm-up routines. Some days, I swear, they touched the football heavens. During one amazing month they thrashed Manchester United 5–1, Nottingham Forest 6–1 and – most famously of all – Southampton 7–0. They kicked branded foot-balls into the terraces after every home game. Peace, love and United. As their city became a super-region, they became Super Leeds. For the last two years of Revie's reign, the nearly men became the showmen. The dirty, cheating northern bastards had finally proved to everyone in Britain what an extraordinary side they were.

1972. Leeds v Spurs. The FA Cup quarter-final. The best game of football I've ever seen. Forty thousand people gasp in unison. It is a gasp of admiration, astonishment, awe. The team came out about an hour before kick-off, wearing track-suits with their names stitched on. Then they went into a beautifully choreographed workout routine. That's when the gasp came. A revelation. A sound unlike anything I'd ever heard, before or since. After the game, the players threw flowers into the crowd. It felt like they'd re-invented themselves – and their city. And football. Spurs had great players like Chivers, Gilzean and Jennings but they, too, seemed mesmerised by Leeds' wondrous patterns. After all the heart-breaks and false dawns and setbacks and near misses they'd come back with a better team, a new swagger, a media-friendly showmanship, a new beauty. And a desperate desire to be loved.

In 1972 Leeds returned to Wembley, and this time they didn't freeze. This time they won the Cup. Like the notorious Leeds–Chelsea battle, the 1972 Cup Final was hyped as an emblematic north–south clash. But now it was the Mighty Whites who were the emperors of cool. It was Super Leeds against Boring Boring Arsenal. Being the Centenary Final, it was watched by both the Queen and the Duke of Edinburgh. Before the game all the Cup's past winners, including the Gunners, had paraded their colours around Wembley. Leeds, being johnny-come-latelys, had not been among them. Not only had they never won the trophy, they hadn't even been formed when the first final was played. In 1872 the competition had been dominated by sides rooted in the public schools and Oxbridge. One final had even kicked off at eleven in the morning because the players didn't want to miss the Boat Race. Blackburn Olympic's defeat of the Old Etonians, in 1883, established football as the sport of the northern, if not the West Riding, working classes. But Arsenal were seen by old-school moralists as a beacon of Corinthianism. Sportsmanship, fair play and gentlemanly values still resided in Highbury's famous marble halls. The game itself wasn't an epic – far from it – but Super Leeds did enough to see off the old Corinthians. 'Clarke, one-nil!' screamed Coleman. And the Cup, finally, was bound for Leeds.

1972. Up until my bar mitzvah, up until I became a man, my parents wouldn't allow me to go to Elland Road without adult accompaniment. So I went with my dad or my uncles or my older cousins. Most of the songs started in the Kop but when they sang 'Lowfields, Lowfields give us a song' I joined in. Uni-ted, clap clap clap. And it's Leeds United, clap clap clap clap, Leeds United FC. I was so close. The wait was almost over. Soon I would experience the rawness, noise, intensity and camaraderie of the Kop; the sense of belonging I'd always dreamed about. Not long now. After I'd come of age. After I'd read my portion from the Torah and made a speech thanking all the guests for their suitcases and fountain pens. After I'd told the joke about the rebbe in the morning and the Revie in the afternoon. After that I'd be standing there, singing and clapping and chanting and roaring and swaying with the great mass of Leeds, Leeds, Leeds. The only Jew in the Kop.

By the time Leeds United won the FA Cup for the first time in their history, the local economy had been radically transformed. In 1972, only one-third of the working population was employed in manufacturing. The writing was on the wall for the city's two largest industries, tailoring and engineering. Tailoring outlets had failed to adapt to big changes in the market, such as the demand for more casual menswear. More people now worked in offices than in the clothing industry. Cohen's Labour had delivered Leeds from the past, blown things down, flattened the old and derelict. Between 1955 and 1967, his housing committee pulled down more slums than any other city apart from London. In the wake of the 1956 Clean Air Act, more than a hundred smoke-control areas were introduced. The Tories, led by Irwin Bellow and then Marshall, wanted Leeds to 'surge forward into the seventies' with its inner ring road, modernist high-rises and all-conquering football team. Bellow argued that the city should be brightened up. It should pioneer pedestrianisation. It should be rebuilt for shopping and offices and cleared of vagrants and travellers. Leeds town centre should become as lily-white as a United shirt. Marshall, who succeeded him, wooed developers like Ziff and architects like John Poulson. He launched Project Leeds, a long-term programme that placed the city at the heart of the service sector. 'New buildings born of new concepts are pushing their white rectangular columns into the sky,' oozed a council brochure. 'Exciting flyovers and splendid roads twist and spiral their course around the city centre.'

1973. To calm my nerves before my bar mitzvah, I think about that sublime passing movement against Southampton, a sequence that had been endlessly replayed on television for the past year, and would be endlessly replayed for years to come. A sequence that drew Oles! from the crowd and a bravura commentary performance from Davies and comparisons with Ajax's Total Football. Davies is a great commentator, but my favourite is David Coleman. Just hearing his voice pumps up my adrenaline. He creates a heightened spirit of excitement. Just before I climb up on to the bimah for my rite of passage, my initiation into manhood, I whisper a quick Colemanism to myself: 'This, then, the moment.'

Operation Eyesore was the new, go-ahead Conservative council's attempt to tell a different story about Leeds. It was time to clean its buildings, pave over its narrow, traffic-choked streets and create a shoppers' paradise. Leeds had always been a place of exchange, at the crossing, but now it was at the crossroads of the nation's motorway system, a distribution centre for much of northern England. Marshall promised that Leeds would, once again, become 'a city of importance and influence'. It was 'magnificently placed at the civilised centre of Britain'. All it needed was to believe in itself. Like Revie's team, it was bursting boundaries, swallowing up its surrounding landscape, sucking the life out of anyone who dared stand in its way. United were one of the most feared teams in Europe. But it still irked Revie – as he confessed to Shankly in one of their regular late-night phone calls – that they remained hated. Why couldn't people see that they had cut out the rough stuff and were playing beautiful football? Why wasn't he loved like Shanks or Sir Matt? The Liverpool manager told him he was being over-sensitive. Leeds *were* getting some long-overdue credit. There had been a slight wobble in self-confidence during the nearly-men years but they'd picked themselves up, dusted themselves down and started all over again. Just as the obituarists were sharpening their pencils, dismissing them as over the hill, they had come again. 'You're Super Leeds now,' Shanks reminded him.

1973. This, then, the moment. The moment that divides my

*life into two parts; the part before and the part after. The
moment when my life, or at least the way I view my life,
shifts. I am about to cross the threshold, to be initiated into
adulthood. The final stage of acceptance into the Tribe of Don.
I have sat on my father's shoulders, I have stood on the
Lowfields and now I have made it into the Spion Kop. Each
week I get to the ground earlier and earlier and climb higher
and higher, up the concrete steps, until finally I am at the Top,
at the place where all the shouts, chants and songs begin. I
can see the terraced housing on top of Beeston Hill. I can see
the frozen foods depot where my dad began his own ascent.
And the cemeteries where my great-grandparents are buried.*

Leeds began the 1973–4 season by winning their first
eight matches – and then cantered to a second League
Championship. For two years now they had been, quite
simply, mesmeric. After they had gone unbeaten in their
first twenty-nine games of the campaign even longstanding critics joined in the adulation. Dirty Leeds
were now Super Leeds. As the players displayed their
medals at a victory parade on the town hall balcony, it
was evident that the grime-coated shrine to Brodrick's
ambition had been scrubbed clean. Marshall called this
part of his renewal programme Operation Revelation.
A dilute acid solution had been brushed on the building's
stonework to loosen the soot and dirt. Low-pressure
pumps had then sent jets of water on to the masonry.
Revie told the crowd that they were now ready to
conquer Everest. Next season they would win the
European Cup, just as he'd predicted when he first took
over all those years ago. But the last few hundred feet,
he warned, were always the hardest to climb. This was
the crucial bit, the Hillary Step, the 'death zone', the

altitude above which oxygen was so depleted that no amount of acclimatisation would allow humans to function properly. This was where many of the world's greatest mountaineers had perished. One giant leap, though, one last push, and we'd be there. Next year in Jerusalem.

1974. A panoramic view of the new Leeds. The new, towering floodlights – the biggest in Europe. The old industrial land-scape is disappearing; the belching chimneys and massive brick edifices have gone. Giles to Bremner, who passes to Gray, who slides it to Hunter. And Leeds United are turning on a brilliant show. Skill, strength and athleticism. The other team are just not on the park. Hunter to Bremner, Bremner to Giles, Giles to Clarke, Clarke to Bremner, Bremner to Madeley. I can see the futuristic walkways in the sky. Madeley passes to Giles, who floats the ball into the goalmouth like a paper dart. The wild beauty of speed, the rushing motion, opening up new routes through vast hillsides, ripping up the landscape, wiping out the past. And I feel like William Terence Fisher or Joe Lampton or Frank Machin, standing on top of a hill carved out of millstone grit, lording it over the whole world. Reaney passes to Hunter and Hunter passes to Giles. Giles flicks up the ball and backheels it to Clarke near the halfway line. And we will build towers, towers no less. And we will rejoice in the beautiful. New buildings born of new concepts, pushing their white rectangular columns into the sky. And this, then, is the moment. The moment when history comes rushing towards us, making us feel lightheaded. I've been bar mitzvahed, I've read Torah in shul, I am a man. I'm at the top of the Kop. I have fully merged with the Elland Road noise. I belong.

*　　*　　*

The 1974 Local Government Act extended the boundaries, the very concept, of Leeds. It had become a market town in the seventeenth century, an industrial town in the last quarter of the eighteenth century and an industrial powerhouse in the Victorian era. And now, after two world wars and a depression, it was — as Harding, Wilson and Jenkinson had all prophesied — surging forward into the post-industrial future. Bigger, better, faster. Rising above the sordid, sweeping away its obsolete Victorian infrastructure, becoming a supersized, metropolitan district, with a population of 748,300. It was now the third largest provincial city in the UK. And it had created, in Marshall's words, an 'aesthetically pleasing' city centre, which boasted spacious, tree-lined pedestrian precincts. Every letter which left the post office was franked with the slogan 'Leeds Motorway City of the Seventies'. Which, in 1974 at least, seemed like a badge of honour.

In the beginning were the Chosen Ones. The adopted sons of Leeds. A one-off, golden generation. Sprake from Winch Wen, Reaney from Fulham, Cooper from Castleford, Bremner from Stirling, Charlton from Ashington, Hunter from Gateshead, Lorimer from Broughty Ferry, Clarke from Willenhall, Jones from Worksop, Giles from Dublin, Gray from Glasgow and Madeley from Beeston. The Don brought them — us — forth from the wilderness to a place at the crossing. And they produced a dizzying, electrifying surge of energy that changed the face of football and almost of fortune.

A few days before the 1974 victory parade, Revie told the celebrity-packed Queen's Hotel audience — and millions of *This Is Your Life* TV viewers — how the

Lads had been written off 'time and again'. But they were now League champions for a second time – and about to have another crack at the European Cup. His team's improved performances and results had not been the consequence, he said, of getting his chequebook out. As the team coach had made its way to Wembley for the 1972 Cup Final, he told Andrews, he'd spotted a bride on her way to church. This, he said, was a sign that The Curse had been exorcised. Gypsy Rose Lee had broken the hex. Super Leeds had gone on to win the Cup and then the League. Now for the Holy Grail.

3. Exile

'Though I've a train to catch my step is slow.
I walk on the grass and graves with weary tread
over these subsidences, these shifts below
the life of Leeds supported by the dead.

Further underneath's that cavernous hollow
that makes the gravestones lean towards the
    town.
A matter of mere time and it will swallow
this place of rest and all the resters down.'

Tony Harrison, V, 1987

1975. Leeds v Anderlecht. The European Cup quarter-final. Despite being at the top of the Kop, whenever Leeds go on the attack I can't see a bloody thing. The swirling fog has made it impossible to follow the game. During one Leeds attack I get into a conversation with three other lads. One of them asks if I'm Leeds. 'Of course,' I reply. 'Where you from then?' 'Leeds.' 'Where in Leeds?' 'Scott Hall Road.' 'Everyone's heard of Scott Hall Road. Biggest A road in't fuckin' country.' One of his mates unbuttons his flies and takes a piss. 'Where were you born?' 'St James' Hospital.' He says: 'Everyone knows Jimmy's. It's fucking famous.' I'm not sure what to do. Continue telling the truth? But every answer I give is so obviously 'Leeds' that it has, in their minds, to be a lie. They have decided, by my accent – which, admittedly, is beginning to lose its Leeds twang – that I am not a Loiner. That I must be an interloper. 'So where d'you go to school?' 'Roundhay.' I think it unwise to add: 'And before that, Selig Brodetsky Jewish Day School.' There is a long pause before they ask the final question. 'Name the Revie team then.' This one is easy. I look down at the dark concrete steps and smile. This is my party piece. The litany. The mantra. The Greatest Team In Football The World Has Ever Seen. I can recite it in four seconds flat. Sprake, Reaney, Cooper, Bremner, Charlton, Hunter, Lorimer, Clarke, Jones, Giles, Gray. But when I finish one of the lads, I can't remember who, punches me in the face. 'Madeley,' he says. 'You missed out fuckin' Madeley. From fuckin' Beeston.'

Decline and Fall

1974. My grandfather, David Saipe, who has lived in our house for the last five years of his life, is being buried. I will miss his lemon teas, his beautiful whistling and his card tricks. After his coffin has been lowered into the grave, and we say Kaddish – a prayer for the dead – uncle Louis, his brother, asks me to put the first spades of earth into the grave. He tells me that Moses saw into the promised land from the summit of Mount Pisgah and ascended Sinai to receive the Torah and then died in the wilderness. Just as we are about to reach the peak, we freeze. It's as if we can't quite believe it is happening to us. To our parochial, oval-ball town, our dirty old money box. We are out of our depth on the bigger stage. We lack the big-stage mental fortitude to support our talent. And everyone is against us. So we take refuge in the past. Which is the only thing to look forward to.

There is some pretty strong competition, but 1974 must surely rank as the most bizarre year in Leeds United's history. This was a year of political, economic and sporting upheaval. It began with Tory Prime Minister Edward Heath imposing a three-day week and ended with the IRA killing twenty-one civilians in a Birmingham pub.

The economy was in meltdown, there were two

general elections and the consensus politics of the last thirty years began to crumble. The leaders of the United States, West Germany, France and Israel all bowed out. From 1945 to 1973 the British economy had grown faster than at any other time in its history. Although punctuated by periodic crises, there had been full employment, a flourishing welfare state and the beginnings of a brave new society. But the global effects of the 1973–4 oil crisis, when the OPEC countries dramatically raised oil prices after the Yom Kippur War, had a seismic effect – especially on the industrial heartlands – and power cuts, soaring inflation and endless strikes were soon the order of the day. England sacked their World Cup-winning manager Sir Alf Ramsey and John Poulson, the Leeds-based architect who had designed such civic showpieces as the International Pool and City House, was convicted of fraud and jailed for five years. The country, it was generally accepted, was going to the dogs.

And yet, in the summer of 1974, like another smart northern boy who had climbed his way up the greasy pole, Revie was feeling on top of the world. After steering his team to a second League Championship he was appointed Ramsey's successor as England manager. The top job. As with the equally paranoid Harold Wilson – who narrowly won both general elections in February and October that year – it was to be all downhill from there. Some historians have drawn parallels between their tainted legacies, presenting both men's late-career eccentricities as symptoms of deep-rooted insecurities. Their technocratic revolutions had been based on science, rationality and a belief in progress. But, increasingly, they had succumbed to fatalism. Revie embodied the furious, maniacal energy of those upwardly mobile, inwardly anxious Northern Men who were living testimony to a meritocracy that underpinned the post-war settlement. He is regarded in a polarised way these days, worshipped by Leeds fans as a messiah but demonised by his myriad critics as a creepy, furtive – even sinister – figure who made his club's name mud and betrayed his country. His achievements, argue the latter, were built on his players' violent conduct. Attempted bribery, they allege, was not beyond him. But I see him as one of the towering figures of English football, a flawed genius.

In the beginning he believed in coaching, in learning from the rest of the world. He communicated, through his slow-burning presence, the idea that Leeds United were central to the city's concept of itself. In the end, as Brian Clough put it, he 'made them believe in luck, made them believe in ritual and suspicion, in documents and dossiers . . . in anything but themselves and their own ability'. Still, in the thirty-six years since his departure, not one of his sixteen successors has come anywhere near to emulating his achievements. For all the thousands of Loiners who came of age during the rise of the Revie empire, he made us believe in ourselves, our city, our team. He built a great side from scratch, in his own image; one that became an emblem of the city, embodying the fans' sense of belonging and desire for national acceptance. But Revie was both our glory and our problem; during the late seventies and eighties, when his empire collapsed in failure and humiliation, he left a Don-shaped hole that none of his successors have been able to fill.

It has become fashionable in recent years to see Revie's fall as symptomatic of the period's paranoia and entropy. As Wilson was telling aides about the supposed conspiracy to depose him – and how his holiday on the Isles of Scilly had being monitored by Soviet trawlers – Revie was briefing journalists about a media-backed FA plot to force him out of the England job. In his three years at Lancaster Gate he failed to forge an alliance with the England stars, missing the day-to-day involvement with his beloved Lads. His introduction of carpet bowls and bingo sessions had several long-haired, cowboy-booted members of the squad hooting with laughter. What was the point, they asked him, of a twelve-page dossier on a Scottish player they already knew inside out? As one of the England mavericks, Mick Channon, would later write: 'I don't think he could trust anyone.'

The Don's demise coincided with the fall of Northern Man. He left Leeds in 1974, the same year that Shankly quit Liverpool and Manchester United, four seasons after Busby's departure, were relegated. The angry idealists who had rebelled against the tired and leaden elite suddenly felt out of place in the New Britain. The Four Sons had morphed into *Monty Python*'s Four Yorkshiremen, lamenting the disappearance of the Old Britain, trying to outdo each other with tales of disillusionment. Whereas *Billy Liar*, like many other early sixties kitchen-sink movies, had expressed hope in a white-hot, technological future, dystopian films like *A Clockwork Orange* – some of whose outdoor locations were filmed in Leeds – took a brutal view of the 'progress' made in that decade, particularly the rebuilding of the north. In *Get Carter*, *Charlie Bubbles*, *O Lucky Man!* and *The Reckoning*, the north's prodigal sons returned home to a concrete wilderness of demolition sites, car parks and crumbling terraces. Their hometowns had not only been crippled by the decline of heavy industry but also corrupted by big business and concreted over by urban motorways, flyovers, shopping centres and tower blocks.

According to their detractors, Revie's Leeds were just another brutalist blot on this soulless, seventies landscape. They polluted football in the same way modernist architecture polluted their region's cityscapes. Like all those appalling arterial roads, they had ruthlessly sliced their way through cities and communities. Like the concrete tower blocks, they were an ugly monument to a deeply regretted decade. This goes some way to explaining the joyous reception that greeted the club's post-Paris collapse; in some quarters it was celebrated with a fervour normally reserved for the ceremonial dynamiting of a high-rise. It seemed apt that the showcase of modernist flat-building, Jenkinson's Quarry Hill complex, should be razed to the ground in 1977, the year Revie did a bunk to the United Arab Emirates. This 'defection', wrote Alwyn W. Turner, 'seemed somehow symbolic of a coarsening of public life in Britain. He had coached the Leeds United side that dominated the English League in the early seventies with what many considered deliberate brutality, turning gamesmanship into a martial art.'

'Bring me the head of Don Revie,' squawked Michael Palin in a late seventies *Monty Python* sketch that chimed perfectly with the national mood. Revie's influence was profound and yet, even in today's fickle world of sport, he was remarkable in how far and how fast he fell. After England failed to qualify for the 1976 European Championships, and looked set to miss out on the 1978 World Cup, the FA decided to sack him. Typically, he got his retaliation in first, accepting a lucrative offer from Dubai. An FA kangaroo court convicted Revie of 'treason' and banned him for ten years. All manner of people then queued up to form a verbal firing squad. He had 'disappeared', not by leaving his shoes on the shore or swimming out to sea – as various mid-life-crisis sufferers, fictional or otherwise (Lord Lucan, Reggie Perrin, John Stonehouse), were prone to so doing at the time – but by earning a fast buck off the very Johnny Foreigners who had put up the oil prices and caused the recession. According to some reports, he'd even sported a Reggie Perrin-type false beard on the plane out of England. The High Court judge who, two years later, overturned the FA's ruling called the saga 'a sensational and notorious example of disloyalty, breach of duty, discourtesy and selfishness'. Busby was knighted for his success at Manchester United and Shankly was – still is – worshipped as a secular saint. Revie, despite building one of English football's greatest ever teams, remains unforgiven.

For what, exactly? For creating the 'little West Riding hoods' in his own image, a dirty-tricks death squad composed of win-at-all-costs cheats? For resorting to bribery, although not one of the allegations levelled against him has ever been proved? For doing a runner to the Gulf for a £340,000, six-year contract? The FA had already sounded out Bobby Robson as his replacement. Revie asked them to pay up his contract and, when they refused, sold his story to the *Daily Mail* for £20,000 and boarded a plane to Dubai. The stigma of betrayal, however, was to dog him for the rest of his life. In 1983, when he returned from the Middle East, he was only in his mid-fifties, yet he was never to work in English football again. He died six years later, aged only sixty-one, from motor neurone disease. His weight had dropped to below eight stone. A few months before his death he came back to Leeds for a charity testimonial. Seated in a wheelchair, the frail, smiling messiah was given an emotional send-off by his devoted disciples. Although he'd managed the national team for three years, no representatives of the football authorities came to his funeral. His ashes were scattered at Elland Road. When the new season began there was no minute's silence, no black armbands and no recognition of the seminal role he'd played in the creation of the modern game.

The Damned United

Revie wasn't the only flawed genius to leave Leeds in 1974. Brian Clough's departure from Elland Road, a mere forty-four days after his arrival, has – thanks to Peace's seminal novel and its film spin-off – become an integral part of the Leeds United myth. The

appointment of Old Big 'Ead, although a little bewil-
dering given his persistent criticism of the team's
gamesmanship, didn't seem that mind-blowing at the
time. In retrospect, it could even be viewed as one
of those gambles entirely in keeping with the narrative arc of Leeds. The city had been 'brought out' of
its prickly isolation, the club had been 'delivered' from
the wilderness and, with Revie's ageing superstars
clearly reaching the end of their shelf lives, who better
than the brilliant, charismatic, flamboyant TV star to
'redeem' the club's reputation? Or, as he himself put
it, to bring more warmth, creativity and entertainment
to Elland Road.

This was neither the first nor the last time such a
gamble would be taken. The return of John Charles,
then considered one of the world's best players, had
almost bankrupted the club back in 1962. Signing Eric
Cantona, thirty years later, contributed to both the rise
and fall of Wilkinson's title-winning side. And, in the
first year of the new millennium, the biggest punt of
all triggered a spectacular meltdown. Like all of these
gambles, the Clough experiment seemed like a good
idea at the time. Its failure wasn't the reason United
ended up banished to the outer darkness for the next
fifteen years. The team, in fact, quickly recovered
from its Forty-four Days of Hell to reach the
European Cup Final. Since the publication of *The
Damned Utd*, however, the episode has become part
of the 'occult' narrative of Leeds. To the conspiracy
theorists it is yet further proof of a never-ending
plot, with Clough in the role of some Revie-obsessed
avenger out to destroy the club from within. The

critics have a surprisingly similar take on the saga, although clearly feeling that there was a poetic justice in Dirty Leeds' subsequent downfall.

I remember feeling very excited about Clough's arrival. He was box office; an opinionated, attention-seeking showman. What's not to like? He was also, by a country mile, the best young manager in Britain. He was a bit loopy, of course, and more than a bit anti-Leeds. The year before he had called for their relegation on the grounds of 'violent behaviour, both physical and verbal'. At his first training session, he told the Lads that, since they had won all their medals by cheating, they should throw them in the bin. He then attempted to remove all traces of his predecessor from the ground – although, contrary to urban myth, stopping short of setting fire to the Don's desk. And he banned all mention of the ex-manager's name and binned the wretched dossiers. But this was only a more extreme version of the 'redemption' that would be attempted in later years by less reckless figures like Howard Wilkinson and David O'Leary. Who knows, if he'd been given more time he might, indeed, have made Leeds more popular. They might, as he told Revie in an extraordinary TV face-off only hours after being sacked, have won the league with more style. He might have refashioned the side in his own flamboyant image – and even won them the European Cup. If Peter Taylor, his much wiser partner, had joined him at Elland Road, if he had been a bit more tactful, if the players had given him more of a chance . . .

In the real world, of course, Cussins' punt on redemption spectacularly, and expensively, backfired. Still, I can remember standing in the Kop, on a cold, rainy August night, reading our hated manager's programme notes before the QPR game and thinking he had a point. I can't have been the only one. Leeds, Clough wrote, had a record unsurpassed by any other in the history of the game. But people had begrudged them their success. 'I want to change that,' he declared. 'I think that Leeds have sold themselves short.'

His Yorkshire TV showdown with Revie has since passed into the game's mythology as a mouth-dropping, theatrical climax to a deeply personal vendetta; a managerial presidential-style debate in which Clough's sparkling, youthful JFK wipes the floor with Revie's saturnine, sweating Nixon. 'Why do I get the feeling this is all about you and Don?' Cussins asks in the film. 'Of course it's about me and Don,' came the reply. But it wasn't *all* about them – it was about what they represented. Their showdown was a clash between two brands of ambitious, insecure, iconoclastic Yorkshireman. Their differences have been wildly exaggerated by both the club's conspiracy theorists and their detractors. Yet they were both Northern Men climbing to the Top. They came from the same deprived area of Middlesbrough and both ended up playing centre forward for Sunderland and England. They moulded unfashionable, provincial teams into League Champions. They were inspiring leaders, great motivators and incisive man managers. They imposed rigid discipline on their players, refusing to allow any misbehaviour. And they were both patronised as small-town nobodies by the suits at the FA. The bullying, manipulative Sir Harold Thompson despised Clough and constantly addressed Revie by his surname. At an official dinner in 1976, the autocratic FA chairman – a former Oxford don – said: 'When I get to know you better, Revie, I shall call you Don.' The England manager replied: 'And when I get to know you better, Thompson, I shall call you Sir Harold.' Clough would have approved.

Watching the re-imagined version of their feud, some thirty-five years later, I couldn't help seeing them as different versions of Billy Liar. 'He'll have known my street, Valley Road; probably bought sweets from Garnett's factory where me dad worked,' says Michael Sheen's Cloughie. 'Best manager in the country, Don Revie . . . Peas in a pod, me and Don. Two peas in a bloody pod.' But by the end of *The Damned United*, as they trade high-speed verbal blows in the Calendar studio, Revie – squashed into an electric-blue blazer and dark tie – looks mentally drained, a man about to be undone by his fretful pursuit of success. The sprightly Clough, only a few hours after being humiliatingly sacked, looks all set to cross the threshold.

Revie's 'Family' had grown old together – many of them were now over thirty – and clearly needed over-hauling. After Busby retired, Leeds and Liverpool had emerged as the powers of the English game. Shankly had rebuilt Liverpool around outstanding youth team players and hungry unknowns like Kevin Keegan and Ray Clemence, laying the foundations for the success of the eighties. Bob Paisley went on to win four European Cups between 1977 and 1984 – and Joe Fagan and Kenny Dalglish continued the dynastic dominance. Revie decamped to England having failed to maintain the pedigree of his stock or groom a successor. He was both unable and unwilling to tear up the old blue-prints, to dismantle a great side, to ditch his neurotic and overcautious approach.

True, he had urged Cussins to appoint Giles – and the board had initially agreed. But Bremner, who also wanted the job, kicked up a fuss and the chairman, not wanting a split camp, caved in. As the Bremner–Giles rift had suggested, cracks were beginning to appear in the Family. Some players had privately criticised Revie for his increasing fascination with the runes, the tea leaf and the stink-eye. Despite the thesis-sized dossiers, the military-style planning – and Herbert's pre-match entertainment – his team did, indeed, keep selling them-selves short. As Clough pointed out, had they played with less inhibition and been weighed down by less superstitious nonsense, they might not have kept blowing up in the final furlong. And, as the Don himself privately accepted, the club's image needed a radical overhaul. The world was changing and Leeds needed to change with it. Shankly, Busby and Ramsey were gone, as was the euphoria of 1966. The national game, like society as a whole, was beset by 'declinism': a feeling that things were falling apart. If Cussins and the board hadn't bottled it, perhaps Leeds would have shed their reputation for insular dourness and been hailed as the new saviours of English football.

Mount Pisgah: The 1975 Choke

1975. Inflation runs amok, the trade unions are out of control and the country's economic foundations are being shaken by the pressures of global competition. Pundits, politicians and pop stars all declare Britain to be on the verge of the abyss. Anthony Crosland, the Foreign Secretary, tells the nation that 'the party's over'. Margaret Thatcher is elected leader of the Opposition. The body of the Yorkshire Ripper's first victim is discovered in Chapeltown. Some Euro-sceptic MPs, incensed by French referee Michel Kitabdjian's performance in the European Cup Final, attempt to exploit the Leeds defeat for anti-referendum purposes. A pro-European MP quips "There goes another half a million votes' when Lorimer's 'goal' is disallowed. David Coleman invites television viewers to look again at the incident, 'with the comments of Don Revie'.

Under Clough, Leeds made their worst start to a season in fifteen years, winning only one of their first six games. They were beaten by Liverpool in the first Charity Shield to be played at Wembley – Bremner and Kevin Keegan becoming the first British players to be sent off at the stadium – and finished ninth in the league. But they still came desperately close to capturing the Holy

Grail. Guided by the avuncular Jimmy Armfield, the pipe-puffing, organ-playing calm after the Cloughite storm, they went all the way to the European Cup Final in Paris.

'We are doing it for Don,' said Bremner, the day before leading the Lads out at the Parc des Princes. The great man himself was up in the heavens, sitting alongside David Coleman in the TV gantry. He might have left Leeds but they were still his chosen ones out there, playing their hearts out for him, running themselves into the ground in front of 50,000 spectators and a worldwide audience of millions. Nine of them were Revie's players. Six – Reaney, Bremner, Madeley, Hunter, Lorimer and Giles – had played in Leeds' first ever European tie a decade earlier. The European Cup, like its successor the Champions League, was the greatest club competition in the world. Provincial Western European cities like Milan, Turin, Munich and Manchester had always done well in the competition. Paris would be Leeds' turn. It had been a long, steep climb, but all those years of hard graft, enterprise and ambition were about to be rewarded. Leeds United were about to conquer Everest, to climb the Hillary Step. 'One day,' Revie had promised on becoming player-manager, 'this club will rule in Europe.' That day had surely come. Paris would eclipse everything that had ever happened to Leeds. It would redefine the way the city thought about itself – and the way the rest of the country thought about the city.

But the team that Revie had created in his own image – the team that had turned falling at the last hurdle into an art form – once again blew it. They had dominated the Long Sixties but, unlike the great empires that followed – Paisley's Liverpool and Ferguson's Manchester United – they failed to fulfil their awesome potential. Unlike his friend Shankly, who built a dynasty, Revie failed to create anything enduring or self-sustaining. After the Don, the deluge. Leeds went into serious decline for fifteen years, his six successors forced to carry the burden of a vanished imperial past. His era, as one of them argued, had been 'a noose around the necks of some managers'.

28 May 1975 should have been the day the great, ageing Revie team closed the deal. But, once again, they choked. Armfield refused to pick United's best striker, Duncan McKenzie, for the game. McKenzie, who scored thirty goals in eighty-one appearances during his two years at Elland Road, was a Clough signing; a self-styled 'cocky little bugger' who entertained his team-mates by jumping over Minis and throwing golf balls the length of the pitch. The Leeds fans loved him. Armfield argued that Paris was the Revie Family's last chance to win the European Cup. So he left McKenzie on the bench. Even when Terry Yorath hobbled off the pitch, he refused to bring on his mercurial striker. Leeds were a goal down – and Beckenbauer and his fellow defenders looked tired. Everything had started to go route one, via Jordan's head. 'We needed a goal and Jimmy should have put another striker on,' wrote McKenzie. 'Jimmy should have taken a risk because I may have changed the course of the match. Jimmy, in my view, bottled it.'

Bayern scored a second goal and the Revie empire, like the Long Sixties, was over. Giles left in the summer,

Bremner and Hunter a year later. In their memoirs all three players, while making the obligatory references to being robbed, cheated and betrayed, admitted that their beloved gaffer's neurotic caution and fear of failure were the reasons they kept stumbling at the final hurdle. Even when they had become Super Leeds, humiliating teams on a weekly basis, Revie accentuated the negative, worrying about what might go wrong rather than what was going right. His weird rituals and fatalistic routines stood in stark contrast to the upbeat, positive-thinking mind games of the Cloughies and the Shanklys. Some players took sleeping pills the night before a big match. Bremner would retire to his Queen's Hotel room and not be seen until the following morning. 'There was always a little bit of doubt in his mind about what his team could achieve,' wrote Gordon McQueen, who replaced Charlton at centre half. His fear of losing, said Lorimer, was his Achilles heel: 'In professional sport no one likes to lose. But you do appreciate that you win some games and lose some. The breaks go against you, there are poor refereeing decisions, lucky goals. As we progressed and things were not progressing so well he took it all personally.' Lorimer had come to loathe the dossiers. 'By and large you wouldn't be nervous when you sat down to listen to him, but by the time he'd finished you'd be on the verge of collapse with fear. He'd make the full-back marking me sound like the world's best defender, but five minutes into the game you'd discover he was the tosser you always thought he was before Don planted his seeds of doubt.' Shortly before he died, Revie told Giles: 'I know I should have let you lads off the leash years before I did.'

The more Leeds achieved, the more worried he became about losing everything and falling back into the abyss. His outstanding side, like those great tennis players who go wobbly-legged on match points, kept buckling under the pressure. They had started out as cocky, truculent outsiders, driven by a rough-and-ready, out-of-nowhere energy. They had quickly moved ahead of all their rivals. At the beginning of the seventies, they had started to play freewheeling, attacking football. And yet, when it came to those big occasions, they still kept choking. Three particularly big, one-off, all-or-nothing occasions stand out: 1965, 1970 and 1973. In 1965 Shankly drew his players' attention to the flat, eerie silence in the opposition dressing room. In the 1970 European Cup semi-final Celtic manager Jock Stein told his boys: 'Revie's shitting himself. I've never seen that man as nervous in all my life. He's as white as a sheet. If *he's* like that, what do you think his players are like? They are there for the taking, believe you me.' And, in the lead-up to the 1973 FA Cup Final, in contrast to the laid-back, casually attired Sunderland players – one of whom, during a live TV interview with Barry Davies, set off a laughter machine – the Leeds superstars, wearing ties, double-breasted suits and blank expressions, looked, in Davies' words, 'like a set of tailors' dummies'.

Nineteen seventy-three was the strangest choke of them all, stranger than the Liverpool and Celtic chokes that preceded it and all the chokes – Paris 1975, Charlton 1987, Aston Villa 1996, Valencia 2000, Watford 2006, Doncaster 2008, Millwall 2009 – that would follow. Super Leeds were at full strength and odds-on favourites to smash the Second Division side to smithereens. Naturally, according to Leeds fans, there was a bad referee. Ken Burns – already notorious for disallowing a perfectly good Lorimer goal in the 1967 Cup semi-final – refused to punish Dave Watson's foul on Bremner in the penalty area. And there was bad luck – the woodwork and two wonder saves from Jim Montgomery keeping Lorimer *et al* at bay. And the bad men who rule football jumped for joy (along with, it has to be said, the rest of the nation) when Ian Porterfield scored his famous winner. But, trudging on to the pitch for the second half, only a goal down, it was clear that something was wrong. The Lads were staring sullenly at the ground. A photograph of this emblematic moment appeared in most of the following day's papers. One of the captions read: 'United players appear to know their fate'.

The Fog

1979. A year after his death, I say a Kaddish for Harry Clavane, son of Phillip Clavanski, even though he was an atheist. And then I say a Kaddish for a generation who are dying in the wilderness, not quite sure, perhaps, if they have fully accomplished their task. A generation who got a glimpse of the promised land but will never enter it. And I say a Kaddish for Leeds, which has become a bleak, ugly termite mound on a washed-up landscape. Try as it might, the beastly city cannot shed its skin, erase its ugliness, scrub off the muck of ages. Before going to the Crystal Palace match I climb the steep hill to take in the cold, clean air and escape the fug below. We are all leaving Leeds now, fleeing the three Rs — the recession, the Ripper and the racism. At the game the Kop sing 'Nigger, nigger, nigger, pull that trigger' and make monkey noises and give Nazi salutes. The fog is everywhere. Up the river, down the river. Fog on the Aire and on the northern heights and on the bleak uplands that surround the theatre of hate. It seems to hang constantly over Elland Road, like some mysterious impenetrable miasma.

I left Leeds in 1979, the year Margaret Thatcher came to power and began to read the old, industrial north its last rites. In the eighties — as I lost my accent and found a new voice, and a new life, in the affluent, Loadsamoney south – I came back only for funerals. As my grandparents' generation were, one by one, laid to rest in the barren hills overlooking Elland Road, I couldn't wait to get the hell out and leave the increasingly poisonous atmosphere behind. I didn't want to end up drifting between two parallel existences: the old world of dark, depressing, broken dreams and the new one of sun, sea and sensual adventure. A year after my paternal grandfather, Harry Clavane, died, I went to the top of the hill and looked out at the vast panoramic sprawl of my benighted city. I had just witnessed Palace's teenage striker Vince Hilaire being taunted with monkey noises and Nazi salutes. I vowed never to return to Elland Road.

After we had said a Kaddish for Harry, uncle Louis congratulated me on the short story I'd just had published in a newspaper. It was a Billy Liar-type fantasy about scoring the winning goal in a European Cup Final and writing a best-selling novel – and then waking up to find it had all been a dream and that I was still living in a city of concrete flyovers, psychopathic skinheads and serial killers. The Motorway City of the Seventies, the brave new world of shopping centres and high-rise flats, had turned out to be crass and materialistic. Post-war northern regeneration had been a mirage, as had the fanciful notion that a tired, post-imperial society could reinvent itself as a white-hot technological powerhouse. As the corpses of its dead parent industries slowly rotted, Leeds became a tough and unforgiving place. And Elland Road became the home of a nasty, embittered and racist element. There was a growing aura of menace, a climate of fear and paranoia. A sense of victimisation. The city, like its football club, battened down the hatches and adopted a bunker mentality. It became, once again, identified in the public mind with the darker, more primitive side of life. Property experts advised businesses to move out. The town centre became a night-time haunt of disorderly youths, tramps and alcoholics.

As the centrifugal force of seventies Britain quick-ened the spiral of talent, power and influence down to London, the capital reasserted its authority and Leeds turned in on itself. Halfway through the decade it began a slow and steady decline. Manufacturing, the basis of its wealth, collapsed and unemployment soared; in 1976 it reached 5.5 per cent – fifteen years later, it had almost doubled. Between 1979 and 1990, as jobs in the new hi-tech industries were generated in the south, manu-facturing in the north fell from 31 to 22 per cent. Leeds seemed to be slipping into poverty and isolation and out of the mainstream of British society. There was a tangible sinking feeling, a perception that, like the country as a whole, it was going to hell in a handcart. There was a retreat into an imaginary, nineteenth-century golden age. The leading architectural critic Kenneth Powell, a member of the Victorian Society, highlighted his hometown in his 1985 pamphlet *The Fall of Zion*. Slum-clearance programmes were all very well, he argued, but look what had replaced the back-to-backs: ugly, brutalist, high-rise flats.

The Gipton, my dad's 'utopian' estate, was a no-go area. Seacroft shopping centre, like most civic show-pieces, had become a concrete monstrosity. In their haste to get rid of the old and embrace all that was new, shiny and modern, the developers had mutilated the town centre and unleashed an aggressive, self-aggrandising Titan which had greedily swallowed up the rolling surrounds of a once proud and independent people. My parents' generation had swept away, concreted over, their grimy past. They had climbed out of poverty, escaped their economic incarceration and reaped the benefits of the consumer boom. My generation had been born into this brave new world but we were entering adulthood in an era of dystopian gloom, lost illusions and reduced expectations – and in a Leeds which had stopped making things: clothes, writers, football teams.

The old Leeds was dying and the new Thatcherite service economy had yet to be born. During the inter-regnum, a stalking beast cast its morbid shadow over the city. On 30 October 1975, a milkman discovered the body of Wilma McCann, the Yorkshire Ripper's first victim, in Chapeltown. Twelve weeks later Emily Jackson, another prostitute, was battered to death in Sheepscar. Peter Sutcliffe committed at least another dozen murders over the next five years. His third killing took place in a field outside my school and the fourth was at Chapeltown Community Centre. I can still remember the 'voice of the Ripper' – which turned out to be a hoax message – being played at Elland Road. As the monster prowled the streets, killing with hammers, screwdrivers and Stanley knives, some fans wore badges boasting that United were 'more feared than the Yorkshire Ripper'.

Dead Leaves in a Gale

1978. Leeds v Manchester City. The FA Cup third round. Always the station, always the train. On match days, Leeds Central becomes a blood-soaked battleground. Three years earlier I had seen some battered City fans lying unconscious – and, for some reason, shoeless – on the floor of the station. City had got their revenge plenty of times since then and, when Leeds drew them at home in the Cup, retribution was in the air. The visitors go 2-0 up and Leeds fans invade the pitch, trying to get the match abandoned. City keeper Joe Corrigan sticks two fingers up at the Kop and is knocked to the ground. The game is held up and police horses ride on to the pitch. Both teams are taken off and the rioting continues for about a quarter of an hour. The FA ban Leeds from playing home cup ties for three years.

The late seventies were not just loon pants, lava lamps and Abba. They were also – in my neck of the woods at least – the National Front, the Service Crew and the Ripper. By 1983 the so-called misery index, calculated by combining the unemployment and inflation rates, had reached an all-time high. Nor indeed were the Thatcherite eighties, as revisionist historians are now so fond of claiming, all about material girls, shoulder pads and council house sales. They were about Greed Is Good, Big Bang and City traders breaking open champagne while miners queued outside job centres. For the first time since the war, Britain imported more manufactured goods than it exported. Many northern districts became traumatised. The two great legacies of the Industrial Revolution, association football and big cities, became demonised. As the fulcrum of the British economy moved from north to south, and Thatcher's counter-revolution ravaged communities in the old manufacturing heartlands, Leeds failed to attract the new, faster-growing industries in light engineering, chemicals, electrical goods and cars. During my infrequent, prodigal son returns, I encountered a world of strikes, layoffs and tribalistic bigotry. The local newspapers were all cataclysm and collapse.

There is a strong, and understandable, tendency to romanticise a jumpers-for-goalposts golden age when football pitches looked like the battlefields of Flanders, assorted firms and crews spent their Saturday evenings trashing railway carriages and multi-millionaire players, bloodsucking investors and a globalised Manchester United had yet to ruin our lives. But there is no getting away from it: the beautiful game had, by the mid-1980s, become rotten to the core. The decay in football's infrastructure had become chronic. Decrepit stadiums groaned and leaked. Concrete terraces crumbled. Hooliganism, high unemployment and the disasters at Heysel and Bradford in 1985 turned 'the people's game' into a drab, hostile, often vicious affair, watched by ever-dwindling crowds, 'a slum sport played in slum stadiums increasingly watched by slum people', as a *Sunday*

Times leading article famously concluded. It was no
longer able to support ninety-two professional clubs
and, until the 1987 stock market crash caused a slump
in property values, plans were being drawn up for
mergers. Charlton Athletic and Bristol Rovers had to
move grounds because they could not pay the rent.
Ugly play, foul language and violence all contributed
to a dramatic fall in attendances as TV companies began
to look to other sports. League crowds fell by nearly
a quarter between the 1979–80 and 1982–3 seasons.

For some, the tipping point was that 1971 Leeds–West
Brom game when a group of Leeds players surrounded
the referee after Astle's 'offside' goal. About twenty spectators ran on to the pitch, beer cans, toilet rolls and
sandwiches were thrown from the Kop and a linesman
sank to his knees after being hit by a can. Four years
later, the world woke up to 'the English disease' when
Leeds fans ripped out seats and rioted after the European
Cup Final. In 1976, weeks of pitch invasions led to the
erection of steel fences at grounds; spectators were caged
like animals in wooden stands. In 1977, drunken Scottish
fans ripped up sections of the Wembley pitch and
dismantled one of the goals after their bravehearts had
slain Revie's England. In the eighties, there were three
terrible tragedies – at Bradford, Heysel and Hillsborough
– in which a total of 191 people died. The first two
crowd disasters took place in a nightmarish three-week
period in May 1985. Fifty-six people were killed at
Bradford's ground after a dropped cigarette set light to
a wooden stand. Then thirty-nine Juventus supporters
lost their lives in Brussels when a wall collapsed following
a charge by Liverpool fans. English teams were banned

from Europe, some of the country's best players – like Glenn Hoddle, Mark Hughes and Mark Hateley – moved abroad and Thatcher tried to bring in ID cards. To the Iron Lady, football supporters were as much of a menace as striking trade unionists; according to her minister Kenneth Clarke, she regarded them as another 'enemy within'. Hooliganism was not to blame for Hillsborough, but the tragedy was the result of crude methods of crowd control born of years of violence on the terraces.

In the fifteen-year exile that followed Paris – during which time six managers (the first three outsiders, the second three Revie-ites) all failed to stop the rot – the only time Leeds United came close to topping a table was when their racist yobs finished second in a National Front-sponsored League of Louts. Typical Leeds: always runners-up. The Service Crew's clashes with other 'military units' provoked more headlines than any on-pitch battles.

The most notorious incident occurred on the same afternoon as the Bradford tragedy: one young man died after a wall collapsed on him and eighteen police offi- cers and fifty fans were hospitalised after United supporters went on the rampage in Birmingham.

During this exile it is hard to recall more than a handful of noteworthy footballing moments – or even noteworthy football players. John Sheridan and Ian Snodin were good in midfield, Ian Baird was a combative presence up front and, towards the end of the eighties, David Batty came through the ranks. But that's about it. Nineteen seventy- eight, for me, was the watershed year. Jordan and McQueen were both sold to Manchester United – 'ninety-nine

per cent of footballers want to play for them and the rest
are liars', McQueen explained – and Armfield was sacked
to make way for Jock Stein. The Celtic legend lasted 44
days, as long as Clough, before resigning to manage
Scotland. Jimmy Adamson was then appointed, but seemed
completely out of his depth. In 1980 the six-year experiment with outsiders was ditched as the board looked to
'our own' to get Leeds back into the big time. Clarke
was the first of Revie's men to take over but, during the
1981–2 season, his team won only ten games before dropping into Division Two. Eddie Gray's young, skilful and
inexperienced side made a valiant attempt to shed the
Dirty Leeds tag, but kept losing to older, more experienced and dirtier sides. Enter Little Billy, the captain of
the crew, who – as I used to remind everyone at the
Passover meal – 'for the sake of Leeds United would break
himself in two'. In 1987 he guided his dour, utilitarian
team to an FA Cup semi-final and the first ever top-flight
play-offs. They lost both and a year later Bremner, too,
went the way of all Revieites. Trying to manage Leeds
United, he explained, had been 'like trying to sweep up
dead leaves in a gale'.

The Four Yorkshiremen

*1983. Britain is the sick man of Europe. There is gang warfare
on the terraces. The north is a place of dearth. The abraded*

cities and failed industries are creating new ghettoes of the dispossessed and the abandoned. Politicians can't be trusted. The England team is shit. The country is torn, once again, between north and south and rich and poor. Football has long ago lost the glamour that came from winning the World Cup and is sleepwalking to pariah status, possibly extinction. Thatcher wins a second election and my dad loses his job. When he first started at Lyons, twenty years ago, it was a growing ice cream and frozen food company. It had eighty-five depots throughout the country, serving shops and cinemas. Then it shrank to sixty depots. The supermarkets arrived, supplying the shops and the cinemas, and sixty became twelve. Then his depot closed down and he became an auditor, travelling around Britain, visiting the few remaining depots. Then twelve became six. And then they didn't need any more depots – they just stored the ice cream in a huge, central complex. Now they no longer need auditors. And, along with two million others, he is on the dole.

In 1983, having completed my history degree and spent a year fighting the education cuts as a member of a revolutionary cadre, or Vice-President Education as my student union post was officially known, I decided to stay on in Brighton. Following the recession of the early eighties, unemployment had risen to three million. Everyone I knew in Leeds seemed to be out of work – my dad, my brother and most of my friends. The Iron Lady was still in power, the economy was shrinking and Leeds United had just spent the first of eight miserable seasons in the Second Division. Revie was six years into his Middle Eastern exile, leaving only an imprint of his brilliant, flawed personality. The

New Wave canon stared at me accusingly from a dusty bookshelf, reminding me who I was and where I came from, but the novelists themselves seemed to have disappeared off the face of the earth. Or gone out of print, which is pretty much the same thing.

Towards the end of the eighties, just before leaving Brighton to take up a teaching post in the Thatcherite heartland of Essex, I bumped into Kate Storey. After the obligatory small talk, and the obligatory Essex jokes, I asked after her father. Like many of his contemporaries, she said, he was suffering from writer's block. He now whiled away the hours scanning the 'S' shelves in bookshops, looking for copies of his novels. These searches were, on the whole, unsuccessful. Like his fellow West Riding escapees, Storey had been part of a crack battalion of cultural pathfinders who had benefited from the new inclusiveness – which, it turned out, had only been applicable to a small minority – and, in the process, severed the bonds of their upbringing. They had gone beyond their old lives, escaped their provincial back-waters – and found that they didn't quite belong.

Storey hadn't been completely forgotten, though. His home town had installed plaques in honour of three Wakefield writers and artists. The first marked the home of the Victorian novelist George Gissing, author of *New Grub Street*. The second celebrated the sculptor Barbara Hepworth. And the third, which was dedicated to him, was attached to the wall of the council house he had grown up in before the war. Only it was the wrong house. The tenant who now lived there, and who was very hostile to the idea of a plaque being fastened to his wall, complained to a local newspaper that he'd 'never heard of fucking David Storey anyway, so what's it all about?'. Kate's dad had considered this to be a very good question.

In an influential early eighties essay, the cultural commentator Ken Worpole had said – albeit from a more politically attuned perspective – more or less the same thing. What had been the point of the kitchen-sink generation? Worpole compared the flow of talent to London in the so-called golden age to Herod's massacre of the innocents. 'In post-war Britain,' he wrote, 'state education succeeded where Herod most conspicuously failed by selecting out a significant proportion of the academically most able working-class children. [But] for many working-class children, success was actually the beginning of their problems.' The grammar schools, he argued, had cut a huge cultural swathe through proletarian life, disinheriting academically able children from their families and traditions. 'Whatever happened to that generation of novelists who made their names in the late fifties and early sixties?' wondered Blake Morrison, himself part of a new generation of northern writers. 'Interest in them seems to have closed down as inexorably as the pits which dominated their landscapes. In their time these men were success stories . . . Not any more.'

I once spotted the white-haired Keith Waterhouse wandering into a Brighton watering hole. A friend told me that he lived in a flat around the corner. The last thing I'd read of his had been *Billy Liar on the Moon*, back in the late seventies. Fisher, now a middle-aged fantasist, still hadn't caught the train to London. Instead, he'd married a local girl and settled down in an affectless northern estate. Like Billy, the Four Sons – all

upwardly mobile beneficiaries of the post-war settlement who had barged through the privileged ranks of
the Oxbridge elite and stormed the citadels of literature – were having a midlife crisis. They felt cut off
from their past, alienated from the present and uncer-
tain about their future. They had spoken for a rising
generation of provincial braggarts who had made their
mark in the years between Suez and Wilson's first
government. To me, they remained – along with Sillitoe,
Braine, Barstow and all the other forgotten men of
English literature – heroic, almost mythic, figures. They
had put themselves, and the West Riding of Yorkshire,
on the map. They had written about the region's biting
winds and football's communal baths and the heady
possibility of escape. Their novels had fleetingly occupied, as Tony Harrison put it, the 'lousy leasehold' of
literature. But, as William Terence Fisher himself had
warned, 'a man can lose himself in London'. The capital
had drained the regions of its talent. A hundred years
after sucking in unemployed farmhands from the hamlets
and towns of the Home Counties, it had devoured the
children of the new industrial poor, consigning them
to the dustbin of social history – or at least to the
grumpy-middle-aged-men-out-of-time files.

Alan Bennett's TV series *Talking Heads* and Harrison's
epic poem *V* sustained me through these years of exile.
They were like comfort blankets; howls in the wilderness, powerful elegies for lost worlds. Many of the references and allusions in the former were not only
pre-Thatcher but pre-sixties. Bennett's monologues,
dotted with Loinerisms – 'ginnels' (alleyways), 'roaring'
(crying), 'spother' (fuss) – depicted a Leeds that really

only existed inside his own head, an Atkinson Grimshaw world of corner shops, grubby back-to-back terraced houses and cobbled streets. The Leeds-born Grimshaw's paintings, which had found poetry in the smoke, fog and gaslight of late nineteenth-century Yorkshire, had briefly come back into fashion, appearing on the covers of ghost stories and on cake tins. In his 1980 play *Enjoy*, which flopped in the West End, Bennett cruelly exposed the fantasies of town hall planners who believed they could socially engineer the future.

Life might have been a continual struggle, sighed the Four Yorkshiremen, but at least the old Leeds had given them a sense of community. 'Northern writers,' Bennett wryly observed in a 1984 interview, 'set their achievements against the squalor or the imagined squalor of their origins, and gain points for transcendence . . . "Look we have come through" is the message.' The black, steaming, polluted city continued to live on in their memories. They returned to the gaslight, tram and cobble era again and again, writing with bitter-sweet nostalgia about picture palaces, dance halls, grimy factories, grand Victorian offices and elegant shops. In his memoir *City Lights*, Waterhouse recalled a Leeds of rock-solid, Yorkshire confidence. All that had gone. In one of his *Daily Mirror* columns he wondered what had become of *A Poet Goes North*, a BBC film in which John Betjeman gently railed against the destruction of Leeds' Victorian past. The Betjeman programme was made in 1968 but never broadcast. Forty-one years later a copy was found on top of a cupboard in the offices of Leeds Civic Trust. The poet had warned that new development and slum clearance were destroying vital pieces of the country's history. 'It's all done with the best intention,' he said, standing in front of a Leeds tower block, 'but if you lived in one of those flats I wonder if you wouldn't look back with regret at the old days when you had a back-to-back house.'

When *V* was broadcast in 1987, right-wing columnists and MPs declared themselves to be shocked by its 'torrents of obscene language' and 'streams of four-letter filth'. Harrison declared himself to be shocked by both the graffiti Leeds United skinheads had daubed on his father's headstone and his beloved city's descent into the abyss. Written in the aftermath of the miners' strike, and set on a hill-top cemetery in Beeston overlooking Elland Road, the poem used the darkening national mood as a backdrop to Harrison's own internal torment. His face-off with a United hooligan, who had taken the traditional short-cut from the football ground back into town, symbolised his own estrangement from his family, class, community and city. In the poem, he tries to erase the drunken fan's graffiti, to scrub away the obscenities. But he couldn't make them, or indeed his own alienation, go away.

White Riot

1984. I return to Leeds for my uncle Louis' funeral and look out at the post-industrial wasteland and say another Kaddish for a last, lost tribe. Louis had once told me that, when his generation were all long gone, the Jewish cemeteries would collapse. It was, he had said, all down to subsidence. If we dig out the treasures from the rocks beneath, the rocks will react. We have mined the treasures beneath us and we have ripped up our landscape and we have created cracks in the ground. I look down at Elland Road, which has become a brutal, dangerous, misanthropic place. Then I see Leon Apfel and ask him how Albert's doing.

The Service Crew, the notorious 'firm' of Leeds hooligans, took their name from the service trains fans used on match days instead of the heavily policed specials. They were formed in the mid-seventies, not long after the Paris riots, uniting all the independent crews of Shipley, Harehills, Seacroft, Gipton, Armley, Beeston and Bramley under one banner. They replaced the Kippax, a more informal grouping of tough, working-class men who had served their time following Revie's Leeds. The Kippax had a strict code: enjoy your drink but avoid trouble unless it came looking for you. They recruited among ex-miners who had a strong, Scargillite collective tradition. The Crew, eventually bolstered by the Very Young Team – a band of thieves who brawled at rock concerts – were a far more sinister breed. They were fashion-conscious – favouring designer labels like Burberry, Ellesse and Stone Island – xenophobic and sadistic.

Many of their ex-military generals, having exchanged Stanley knives for publishing contracts, now claim that they were simply high-spirited Jack the Lads, proud inheritors of an English warrior tradition. 'The Leeds firm occupies almost legendary status in the annals of hooligan history and I felt flattered to be asked to write their story,' wrote their biographer, BBC journalist Caroline Gall, in 2007. The real story, however, is very different from the titillating hoolie-porn served up by these apologists. The Crew were a violent bunch of *Clockwork Orange*-style, racist Droogs who ran riot across the country, punching and kicking their way into notoriety. They were behind the infamous riots at West Brom in 1982, Chelsea in 1984 and Birmingham in 1985. Worst of all, during a match at Bradford in 1986, which took place only a year after the fatal fire at the Odsal, several members of this 'legendary firm' set a chip van alight.

And yet the Crew's former members, aided by their hagiographers, continue to glory in the gore of a 'golden' era. The further United sank on the pitch, the more they tested their superiority off it. We are Leeds and we fought them on the beaches of Bournemouth, on the half-demolished housing estates of Hunslet and on top of the cold, windswept hills that overlooked Elland Road. In the eighties, the Kop – my old spiritual home – became a violent and fenced-in ghetto, the object of national scorn and derision. Like English football as a whole, the club was in a rut. As a teenager, I had naively considered the ground to be a microcosm of the new meritocracy. We had Our Albert – the first black footballer to play in an FA Cup Final – a Celtic spine and several Jewish directors. The Kop's ballads had been the soundtrack to my integration. On leaving the cocoon, however, I soon realised the extent to which Dirty Leeds were reviled in the outside world.

Occasionally, on Sussex University campus, I would overhear references to 'the Leeds scum'. It was clear that both leftie, middle-class students and Thatcherite, working-class Brightonians associated the club's players and fans with brutal thuggery. Although I was trying to reinvent myself as a rootless cosmopolitan, I came close to blowing my cover during one late-night, drink-fuelled debate in the student union bar. Football hooliganism, I pointed out, was part of the game's rich proletarian tradition, a form of resistance through rituals to the pressures of a capitalist society in crisis. This was complete bollocks, of course, but so was the perception that Elland Road had always been a corner-stone of white, working-class racism. What about Johanneson? Many of the black and Asian immigrants who came to Leeds in the fifties and sixties saw him as a role model. And what about Speedy Reaney, the defender George Best described as his toughest ever opponent? Wasn't he of mixed race?

From the fifties to the seventies, thousands of Afro-Caribbeans – principally from Jamaica, St Kitts and Nevis and Barbados – moved into Chapeltown. They were part of a massive national recruitment programme; the factories needed nightworkers and the National Health Service needed nurses. Just before this migration, a few thousand Africans had settled in the inner-city suburb. Built for the prosperous, Christian middle classes in the early 1900s, it was immortalised as a quintessential Edwardian district by Gordon Stowell in his novel *The History of Button Hill*. Stowell resented the Jewish 'invasion' of the suburb; 12,000 of the city's 20,000 Jews lived there between the wars. In the early fifties, it was a multicultural melting pot. By the seventies and eighties it had become a byword for crime, drugs and prostitution; according to a *Sunday Times* investigation, it was Britain's primary no-go area. When I left the Hilltop cemetery, after uncle Louis' funeral in 1984, I took a bus back to our old house in Moortown. Just for old time's sake. The bus threaded its way northwards, through Chapeltown and Moortown, on an arterial road that told the story of Jewish social mobility – indeed, of immigration – far more eloquently than any local history book could. The story of immigration in Leeds – Irish and Jewish in the nineteenth and twentieth centuries, Afro-Caribbean and Asian after the Second World War – is one of constant movement; of newcomers moving to the city, settling close to the centre and then gradually moving outwards towards the suburbs.

As the bus passed the familiar landmarks – the large dome of the neo-Egyptian New Synagogue, Cantor's fish and chip shop, the rugby league headquarters, the Jewish National Fund offices where my mum used to work – I noticed that many of the kosher shops and shuls had been supplanted by West Indian barber shops and mosques. The Jewish Institute and the Judean Club had been replaced by the United Caribbean Association and the West Indian Centre. In the ten years between my grandfather's and uncle's funerals, the last Jews had moved out of the area and a new shtetl – a black ghetto – had been created. Like my grandparents' generation, these immigrant communities also seemed trapped in their narrow, insular world. Unlike my parents' generation, though, integration appeared to be a pipe dream. Unemployment in Leeds had risen from 2.4 per cent in January 1974 to 5.5 per cent in January 1976. A quarter of the jobless lived in the Chapeltown ghetto, where youth unemployment was as high as 60 per cent. On one notorious November night in 1975, gangs roamed through the area hurling bricks at windows and overturning cars. The following evening, Bonfire Night, police cars were attacked by a large mob. The local paper accused the force of violence and intimidation – and of fabricating evidence. In 1981, three months after a race riot in Brixton, South London, the area erupted again. The police claimed the riots had been stage-managed by political extremists but, as one councillor put it, 'everyone knew a time-bomb was ticking'.

In 1974, at my grandfather's funeral, I had asked my old school friend Leon Apfel about Albert. The Apfels had been good friends of the Johannesons back in the sixties. Leon said that Albert's wife Norma had left him to make a new start in Jamaica with their two young daughters, Alicia and Yvonne. Johanneson had been Revie's first signing in 1961. Two seasons later, his fifteen goals had kick-started the revolution. In 1965, he had frozen, like the rest of the team, in the FA Cup Final – but had still been given a hero's ovation at the civic reception. In 1969, one of the greatest years in the club's history, United won their first ever League Championship without his help. He played his last game the following season and was sold to York City. In 1984, at uncle Louis' funeral, Leon told me that Albert had been an alcoholic for several years. The last time he called round to the Apfels' house, he had handed Leon's dad all his trophies and medals because he was afraid he would end up pawning them for beer money.

In the early seventies, while Albert was struggling at York, I can remember a new song being added to the Kop's ever-expanding anti-police repertoire. To the tune of 'Michael, Row the Boat Ashore', they sang: 'The River Aire is chilly and deep, Oluwale; never trust the Leeds police, Oluwale.' On the night Johanneson's team-mates were winning the title at Anfield, and he was out getting bladdered in the town centre, David Oluwale's body was drifting down the River Aire. Oluwale was a Nigerian-born vagrant who had come to Leeds during the first wave of black immigration. He was a scholarship boy, had been educated at a grammar school and was one of many immigrants seeking a better life in post-war, post-colonial Britain. He died, at the age of thirty-eight, after being chased along the waterfront by two police officers. His body was discovered face-down in the Aire. Oluwale was buried at Killingbeck Cemetery, in a pauper's grave, at the top of a windswept hill overlooking the town centre. A 1971 inquiry revealed he had been the victim of horrific, systematic, police brutality.

Things were never quite the same after Albert's demise, although Terry Connor, a Chapeltown lad, lit up Elland Road for a brief spell. The black teenager scored on his debut against West Brom in November 1979, and then grabbed another six goals in the next ten matches. But after he left in 1983, two years after Chapeltown exploded into riots, there was a seven-year 'colour bar' until Vince Hilaire and Noel Blake were signed from Portsmouth. In the eighties, as the floodgates opened and a new generation of England-born black players broke through, Elland Road became a recruiting venue for the National Front and the British Movement. The NF's newspaper, the *Flag*, was openly sold outside the ground. The swastika replaced the Smiley badge, neo-Nazis started up racist chants in the Kop and black players were regularly pelted with bananas. 'Leeds United supporters are proud to be called racists,' thundered one editorial in *Bulldog*, the NF's youth magazine. 'If you're not British don't come to Elland Road.'

Many of the black and Asian fans I spoke to for this book told me they had boycotted the stadium during the exile years. 'The racism was appalling,' wrote Caryl Phillips. 'One minute you're on the terraces and they're high-five'ing you and you're hugging them, and the next minute they're doing the jungle sounds and the banana noises and monkey noises.' Shakeel Meer, who came to Leeds from Pakistan, became a fan because of Johanneson. 'When I heard they had a black player, I thought Leeds United must have a progressive team. That it didn't matter to them what colour you were, or what background you had.' But, after being pelted with coins at one match, he refused to return to the ground.

Phillips, who went to my dad's old school in Gipton, remains proud that a contemporary of his – Cyril 'Ces' Podd – became one of the first black players to break the mould. Although born in Leeds, and a United fan, Podd played for Bradford City – a record 504 times. During the sixties, like Phillips, he had been a regular at Elland Road. Albert, he told me, had been his hero. He used to sneak into the stadium as a tiny kid, under the old Lowfields turnstiles. It was only when he got a bit older and hung around with the other black lads that he was called names and made to feel unwelcome. 'I got on really well with the Bradford fans though,' said Podd. 'They were my security.' He went back to Leeds only once, to play in a reserve match. After the game he saw Johanneson, who begged him for money. Podd felt he had got out of Chapeltown just in time, 'before the rot set in'. Albert died alone in a council estate tower block at the age of fifty-three. He had been dead for several days before his body was discovered. He was so broke a single seashell was listed among his few possessions.

Cracks in the Ground

1987. I watch Manny Cussins' funeral cortège pass Elland Road, where players and backroom staff have formed a guard of honour, on its way to the cemetery. On top of the hill I spot Bremner and Gray and the rabbi who had made that 'rebbe in the morning, Revie in the afternoon' gag all those years ago. Today it doesn't matter that NF leaflets are being sneaked into Leeds United programmes. Or that when United play Spurs, Leeds fans sing: 'The yids are on their way to Auschwitz, Hitler is going to gas them again, no one can stop them.' Or that when United play Chelsea, the Chelsea fans sing: 'Put a Jew, Jew, Jew, in the oven gas mark two.'

Or that there are swastikas daubed on synagogue walls. Or that 'Hitler was a Leeds fan' decorates a subway wall near the ground. Or that a mist is coming down from the moors and is uncurling above the rooftops and entering through turn-stiles which keep the mutually murderous fans away from one another with their bread knives and steel toecaps. Today I feel proud. Especially when the rabbi calls Manny Mr Leeds United. And then says: 'There is hardly an institution, hardly an organisation, hardly a charity in Leeds which has not benefited from his vision.'

In a series of articles written for the *Jewish Telegraph* in 1987, a few months before he died, uncle Louis reflected on the Jewish community's successful integration into Leeds life.

In his last ever newspaper column he wrote: 'I am proud and happy that I am a Jew, and even prouder and happier that I am an English Jew from Leeds.' The only time he had ever come across any public anti-Semitism, he added, was when Burnley chairman Bob Lord had urged a Variety Club audience to 'stand up against a move to get soccer on the cheap by the Jews who run television'. Lord, upset by Cussins' criticism, had then compounded the offence by boycotting Elland Road. In those politically incorrect times a Ron Atkinson-style ostracism was hardly to be expected, but very few people in the game took Cussins' side. The saga was presented as a silly spat between two jumped-up northern businessmen. Some columnists even argued that there *were* some powerful Jews in television, like the Grades and Sidney Bernstein. The Tory MP Alan Clark recorded in a diary entry how, while watching Bernstein being ennobled in the Lords, he had loudly 'muttered and mumbled about "Jews" in order to discomfit his relations who were also clustered in the gallery . . . The House took it quite well, a few guffaws.' I can recall reading several pieces arguing that the indigenous Football League chairmen would, indeed, be unwise to sell out the working man's game to a race who were disproportionately represented in the entertainment business.

My uncle, I'm afraid, was in denial. There had been a resurgence of anti-Semitism in the seventies. Conspiracy theorists directed their readers' attention to the Jewish names on Harold Wilson's resignation honours list. And they pointed out that Lord Kagan, Harold Lever, Sam Silkin and Gerald Kaufman had all been members of the former Prime Minister's kitchen cabinet. And that Siegmund Warburg was Harold's man in the City. And that the legal fixer Arnold Goodman and the publisher George Weidenfeld were also friends of his. And weren't Jack Lyons (a Leeds philanthropist), Ernest Saunders, Gerald Ronson and Anthony Parnes – all arrested during the late eighties in the Guinness share-trading scandal – of the Mosaic persuasion? In the eighties several Westminster old boys complained about Thatcher's over promotion of Jewish parvenus like Leon Brittan, Nigel Lawson and Michael Howard. The Iron Lady's cabinet, as Harold Macmillan sneered, was 'more old Estonian than Old Etonian'. During the 1985–6 Westland affair, a Conservative MP expressed the hope that Brittan's replacement at the Department of Trade and Industry would be a 'red-blooded, red-faced Englishman'.

To my uncle, however, the journey was almost complete. The second- and third-generation Jews were almost there. In his lifetime Leeds Jewry had moved out of two ghettoes – the Leylands and Chapeltown. The Leylands had been demolished and new immigrant groups now occupied Chapeltown. Throughout the century there had been a steady rise in the community's economic status, with people leaving working-class tailoring to enter the middle-class professions. The children and grandchildren of black and Asian immigrants would, he felt sure, make similar progress. He admitted, however, that there was a price to be paid for integration: demographic decline. There had been an increase in the numbers marrying out and a decrease in the numbers going to shul. The Jews were shrinking. In his father's time the population had numbered 8,000. In the fifties, when tailoring was still a major industry, it had peaked at around 30,000. In the seventies it had dropped to 20,000. 'Judaism,' he noted, 'appears to be on the way out . . . the wheels are wearing thin.' In digging out the treasures from the rocks beneath the landscape, he concluded, we had created cracks in the ground.

4. Redeem

'The symbolic role which Cantona played of putting Leeds United on the map operated for the city of Leeds more widely, which the club symbolically represented. Like the football club, the city of Leeds has faced difficult problems in recent times as it has had to reorganise itself to compete in the new global economy created by multinational corporations, which has decimated much of the traditional manufacturing areas of Britain's economy on which the prosperity of most northern cities, like Leeds, was based.'

Anthony C. King,
The Problem of Identity and the Cult of Cantona, 1995

1987. Brighton v Leeds. Second Division, last game of the season. I am sitting on my hands, surrounded by Brighton fans, trying to stifle my twitching. I have lived in the town for most of the decade, but I don't really belong here. I am an interloper. They all hate Leeds and Leeds. It's a bit like that scene in The Great Escape *when Gordon Jackson and Richard Attenborough are pretending to be Germans. I have to keep my mouth shut and my emotions in check or they will twig that I am Leeds. I got in by showing several stewards and policemen an envelope displaying my name and address. They decided, by my accent, that I couldn't possibly be a scummy northerner. A few minutes before the end Edwards scores the winner and I stand up and sing: 'We are Leeds, we are Leeds, we are Leeds.' Which is a bit of a giveaway really. A bit like Gordon Jackson saying 'thank you' after the SS man has cunningly wished him 'good luck'. But so what? The exile is over. We're back. I can't wait to leave Brighton and return home. And, as the train pulls into Leeds station, the fog has cleared and, for the first time in years, I can actually see the river. The dirty river that provided the power for the wool and textile mills of old, industrial Leeds. That flows through the city giving it new life and energy. And isn't dirty any more.*

The New Leeds

I came back to Leeds at the end of the eighties. Not to stay. I just wanted to spend some time with my mum, dad and brother. And not just at funerals. I felt I had drifted away, lost touch with my roots, severed the bonds of my upbringing. I hadn't been near Elland Road – nor a synagogue – in years. I was 'in between jobs' and had a bit of spare time after leaving teaching. Going to the Brighton game had reignited my sense of belonging. Besides, I had heard that Leeds was changing.

I met my dad for a beer down by the waterfront. Like everyone else, he'd had a bad eighties. He'd lost his old job at Lyons frozen foods, and spent a few years on the dole. But things were looking up; he'd recently been appointed secretary of the Leeds Jewish Workers Co-operative Society. And Leeds was getting back up on its feet, scrubbing itself clean and starting all over again. As in the sixties, it was rebuilding its town centre for shopping and offices – in an architectural fusion of glass and metal, this time, rather than concrete. It was attracting a new generation of young, upwardly mobile professionals, who were settling in the middle of town next to the new shops and offices. Its old manufacturing base was disappearing but a thriving service sector was expanding to fill the gap. An estimated £2.5 billion had been invested in large-scale commercial, retail and residential property. Twenty-thousand new jobs were created. Between 1988 and 1995, the Leeds Development Corporation transformed the waterfront. The government showered money – £15 million a year – and power on the quango, which was run by a supermarket entrepreneur. City Square was pedestrianised. The Dark Arches, once a cardboard city for homeless vagrants like David Oluwale, became a trendy market boasting myriad gift shops and craft stalls. The Calls, once a notorious centre of low life, became a fashionable eating area, symbolised by a state-of-the-art water sculpture called Regeneration. Brodrick's Corn Exchange was converted into a specialist shopping centre. First Direct opened the UK's first call centre. The DHSS transferred a thousand London employees to Quarry House, the largest building ever constructed in Leeds. And Asda redeployed 1,500 of its staff to a new head office just around the corner from Leeds station.

During the late seventies and early to mid-eighties, the city had closed ranks and folded back into the worst of itself. Now everything was changing and up for grabs. Leeds was about to metamorphose into a shiny, corporate entity, a boom-time, celebrity-city-living metropolis. New markets were opening up and new money was fuelling a post-industrial, postmodern convulsion; another great leap forward. Nobody, said my dad, used to talk about the river in his day, nor even remember it was there, let alone go for a drink on its banks. But now it was dotted with pavement cafés, minimalist restaurants, designer-boutique hotels, cappuccino bars and chic clubs. Derelict mills, warehouses and scrapyards had been converted into loft apartments, offices and hotels. Like the city itself, it was being cleansed.

The Last Champions

1992. The Sergeant is about to take the salute at the victory parade. An estimated 150,000 people, more than one-fifth of the city's entire population, have lined the streets. After eighteen trophy-less seasons, Leeds United are, once again, the champions of England. The Sergeant has buried the ghost of old Don. He has liberated the club from Revie's legacy and set up a youth system that will produce a new generation of Leeds, Leeds, Leeds. And he has promised to rebuild the team around the enigmatic Frenchman who stands next to him on the makeshift art gallery balcony. Holding aloft the Championship trophy, the Frenchman tells the crowd: 'Why I love you? I don't know why, but I love you.' The crowd serenades him with 'La Marseillaise' and repeated choruses of 'Ooh, aah, Cantona. Oohaah Cantona.' Then the Sergeant and Eric and the rest of the new, regenerated Leeds United are transported through the shiny city centre in an open-top bus. They cross the river, speed past the railway station, wiping out the past, hurrying – once again – to embrace the future.

★   ★   ★

The 1987 play-offs had turned out to be another false dawn. After winning at Brighton, and celebrating with an overexuberant conga around the Goldstone Ground – which had to be broken up by mounted police – Little Billy's youngsters stumbled, in time-honoured fashion, at the final hurdle. They lost the first ever play-off final to Charlton, despite going ahead in extra-time, and an FA Cup semi-final to Coventry – after leading with twenty minutes left on the clock. The following season they finished seventh, eight points adrift of a promotion place. After another shaky start – only one win in six games – Bremner was sacked by Leslie Silver. Silver, whose grandparents had emigrated from Poland in 1899, had been chairman for five years. After the Second World War – as a bomber pilot he'd flown sixty-five missions in Europe and the Far East – he'd set up the Leyland Paints company. Like my uncle Louis, and the city's 'demolition man' Karl Cohen, he joined the Jewish socialist organisation Poale Zion. He built up a huge business empire in Yorkshire, London and Newcastle and was approached, in April 1982, to join the United board, just weeks before Clarke's team were relegated. 'You interested in football?' Cussins had asked him at a Jewish charity do. 'Want to come on the board?' Silver asked what it would cost. 'Nothing,' lied Cussins. The interest payments on the cash borrowed to pay for new signings Peter Barnes and Kenny Burns had left United on the verge of bankruptcy and the new director had to cough up £200,000 to keep away the bailiffs.

Silver was a passionate fan, a local businessman who, in the tradition of Reynolds and Cussins, ran the club out of a sense of civic duty. He idolised the Don – their families occasionally holidayed together – but after Bremner's side began to slump he felt it was time to go outside the Family. Revie's adopted sons – Clarke, Gray and now Bremner – had taken them close to the brink. United had languished in the Second Division for the first five years of Silver's chairmanship and fans had repeatedly called for his head. His last throw of the dice was Howard Wilkinson. The former Sheffield Wednesday manager had led the Owls back into the First Division in 1984. He was nicknamed 'Sergeant Wilko', a moniker that alluded, somewhat ironically, to the American comedy sitcom character Sergeant Bilko while at the same time acknowledging his tough, no-nonsense, strict-disciplinarian persona. The Sergeant was determined to dismantle the Revie legacy. His first act was to remove all the pictures of the Lads from the walls – 'crutches,' he said, 'for people who still basked in the reflected glory of those bygone days'. Then he sacked Norman Hunter as coach and kicked Herbert Warner, the unofficial in-house comedian, off the team bus. There were no gypsies involved, no chopping up of desks or burning of dossiers, but it was still an exorcism.

In some ways, however, he was a continuation of the Legacy. Wilkinson was a deep-thinking technocrat, a single-minded Yorkshireman who paid great attention to detail and left nothing to chance. His teams were mercilessly well prepared and rigorously drilled. His ethos had a familiar ring: grit, graft and solidarity. 'Training was intense,' recalled Gordon Strachan. 'We pushed ourselves – players going down, throwing up and coming back again.' There was no place for vanity, selfishness or greed. With Graham Taylor and David Pleat, Wilkinson had been part of a new generation of forward-thinking coaches who had graduated from the FA's Lilleshall headquarters. He was renowned for his organisational skills, rigorous fitness programmes and tactical know-how. He even commissioned dossiers on opponents. When he arrived – their eighth manager in fourteen years – Leeds were in real danger of slipping into the Third Division for the first time in their history. They were a second-rate side with a dilapidated training ground and run-down changing rooms. In his first full season, they were promoted as champions. In their first year back in the top flight, they finished fourth. The following season they won the League, becoming the last ever First Division champions. The Sergeant had not only worked another Revie-type miracle, he had speeded up the process, dragging them out of the wilderness and into the elite in only half the time it had taken the Don.

Wilkinson galvanised Leeds at the dawn of a new football boom. The euphoria generated by Bobby Robson's England team, which had reached the 1990 World Cup semi-finals, spilled over into rising attendances – and the fans' good behaviour in Italy allowed English clubs back into Europe. Despite being knocked out by Germany on penalties, England returned home as heroes. But it was another, less trumpeted, event in 1990 that proved to be the real turning point. The publication of the Taylor Report, commissioned in the wake of Hillsborough, paved the way for the 'second era' of English football. Lord Justice Taylor concluded that the danger of Hillsborough-type incidents occurring would be significantly reduced by the introduction of all-seater stadiums and CCTV cameras. His proposals amounted to football's version of a slum clearance scheme, producing a gradual change in the social composition of crowds; a shift from unskilled and manual workers to the skilled and professional classes. The FA document *Blueprint for the Future of Football* argued that the sport should now follow 'the affluent middle-class consumer'. In this way, hooligans would be priced out of the market and families would return. In the bad old eighties, football had been the love that dared not speak its name. Thatcher's proposed identity cards were an attempt to criminalise fans. The good Lord Justice, however, rejected her Football Supporters' Bill and argued that if you stopped treating people like animals they would stop behaving like animals.

Football was once again socially acceptable. The soundtrack to this media-led, lad-infused, aggressively marketed revival was Puccini's soaring aria 'Nessun Dorma', which the BBC used as its Italia 90 theme tune. Its descant was New Order's 'World in Motion', the first World Cup song to be halfway hummable. Leeds' own musical contribution was 'Why I Love You, I Don't Know Why, But I Do', the pop group Ooh La La's homage to Eric Cantona. The defining moment was Paul Gascoigne's big blub after England's semi-final defeat, an uncontrollable sob which would be endlessly replayed and dissected by philosophers, cultural historians and TV pundits. And its bible was Nick Hornby's *Fever Pitch*. The Arsenal fan's best-selling, touchy-feely, confessional memoir touched a nerve. It sold over a million copies in the UK and launched a thousand lad lit tomes. Traditionalists denounced the genre as yet another example of the Great Sell-Out: the commercialisation and gentrification of the working-man's game. But suddenly, thanks to Taylor, Pavarotti, Gazza, Hornby, Cantona and *Loaded* – a ground-breaking New Lad magazine dreamed up by two Leeds United obsessives – it was okay, cool even, to be a football fan. *Loaded* made a phenomenal impact on the men's market, although some of its readers were a little perplexed by its references to the Don, Little Billy and Bites Yer Legs Hunter. Sandwiched in between signature pieces on Page Three Babes, the *Bullitt* car chase and *Sweeney* rhyming slang were homages to Smiley badges, sock tags and the bacon sarnies you could buy outside Elland Road back in the good-old-bad-old-seventies.

The clownish, but extraordinarily talented, Gascoigne was an obvious icon for the emerging generation of New Lads who adored birds, booze and footie. Lads who, in the words of *Loaded* editor James Brown, had 'the best fucking time of their lives'. Dirty Leeds, on the other hand, seemed unlikely poster boys. But, as the magazine's editorial board pointed out, the dour Wilko had signed flair players like Strachan, Gary McAllister, Tony Dorigo and Rod Wallace. The Sergeant's most famous signing of all was the *enfant terrible* of French football. A few months after quitting the game, following a three-month ban in his native country, Cantona was persuaded out of retirement by Wilkinson. King Eric became an instant cult figure at Elland Road, giving interviews on art, philosophy and poetry. 'A natural room-mate for David Batty,' quipped

Wilko. Four months after Cantona's arrival – with home-grown youngsters like Batty and Gary Speed coming through the ranks and Strachan and McAllister pulling the strings in midfield – Leeds stunned Manchester United, the rest of the footballing world – and Wilkinson himself – by winning the title.

I was in Leeds, having a cappuccino with my dad and brother in a waterfront bar, on the day United beat Oldham to go top of the league for the first time in seventeen years. We all had tears in our eyes. The Lads, as we still called them, didn't lose another league match for four months. Three particular games stand out that season: the 4-1 spanking of Aston Villa, the 6-1 demolition of Sheffield Wednesday, both shown live on national television, and the 3-0 thrashing of Chelsea. In the last of these flawless exhibitions of passing and finishing, King Eric scored one of the best goals I have ever seen. Receiving Strachan's throw, he nonchalantly flicked the ball over Paul Elliott's head and played some keepy-uppy before lashing it triumphantly into the top corner of the net. Super Leeds United.

Big Bang

The Premiership was launched in 1992, 104 years after the foundation of the Football League. The top twenty-two clubs ditched the League's traditional TV deal, taking up an offer from new satellite force BSkyB – and English football entered the space age. Nothing would ever be the same again. As the football economy began to swell – bigger TV contracts, new stadiums, rocketing ticket prices, freer movement of players – the domestic game was transformed beyond recognition. The big clubs began to look for the bigger bucks and the bigger strategies. The Premier League, aiming at the global TV markets of the new satellite world, became a closed shop, shutting out the smaller clubs from the lower divisions. For all ambitious, upwardly mobile teams, it was sink-or-swim time.

Before 1992, English football was a parochial business, its clubs mostly run by self-made industrialists like Reynolds, Cussins and Silver – local worthies who put their hands in their pockets and made interest-free loans. After 1992, as a new business ideology invaded the game, these custodians became a dying breed. In the space age, English football would be reincarnated as a mind-blowingly lucrative, globally dominant commercial free-for-all. As the Premier League conquered the world, top-flight clubs gobbled up the TV millions and became vigorous exploiters of their own 'brands'. Attendances soared and the new, state-of-the-art stadiums became safe environments in which to enjoy the sublime skills of the world's best players. The Sky deals spectacularly reversed the game's long economic decline. Back in 1965 the BBC had paid a mere £5,000 for the right to screen *Match of the Day*. In 2007, the total figure for Premier League rights was estimated at £2.7 billion. The exposure and hype that came with this high-octane, round-the-clock coverage brought millions of pounds into football through sponsorship deals, replica kit sales, eat-drink-and-sleep merchandising and perimeter advertising. The rich got richer and the poor got poorer. Those joining the goldrush saw their assets soar, while those unable to get in on the boom were marooned in the financial wilderness. Between 1992 and 2008, forty of England's ninety-two professional clubs were involved in insolvency proceedings. In the 2009–10 season, HMRC issued winding-up petitions against eight teams.

Before 1992, provincial nobodies like Leeds, Derby and Nottingham Forest could become European giants. The English champions could be pursued by the likes of Ipswich, Watford and Southampton – as Liverpool were when they completed a hat-trick of titles in the early eighties. After the revolution, only Chelsea – bankrolled by Roman Abramovich's squillions – would spring from the proletariat to become established in the top four for any length of time. In the Premier League's early days, Aston Villa, Blackburn and Newcastle, all run by rich local worthies, gave global brands Manchester United and Arsenal a run for their money. But to get into and stay in the promised land – soon to be renamed the Champions League – this time around would require more than just a driven, single-minded, visionary leader – a Revie, a Clough or even a Wilkinson. It would also require the megabucks of a Russian oligarch or an Arab sheikh. Inequality in football is nothing new; the English League has always had strong and weak teams. But, after 1992, money conquered all.

The North Will Rise Again
(It's Grim Up North)

1992. Sheffield United v Leeds. The penultimate game of the last ever First Division season. When it's over, and Leeds have won the League, I drive across the river to Elland Road, the techno anthem 'It's Grim Up North' blaring on the radio. In a distorted monotone voice, as if he's reading the Saturday afternoon football results, the lead singer deadpans: 'Bolton, Barnsley, Nelson, Colne, Burnley, Bradford, Buxton, Crewe, Warrington, Widnes, Wigan, Leeds . . .' Everywhere I look windows are festooned with blue white and yellow flags. Some fans have climbed on to the Black Prince statue and are singing 'Ooh, aah, Cantona. Oohaah Cantona'. I buy a T-shirt from the megastore bearing a retro Smiley badge and the legend: 'Peace, Love and United'.

In 1992, on the cusp of football's second era, Leeds United were English champions and a new multimillion-pound East Stand – the biggest cantilevered structure in Europe – announced their re-emergence as a leading footballing power. At the end of the year, having just witnessed Wilko's Wonders defeat Stuttgart in a European Cup tie in Barcelona, James Brown and Tim

Southwell dreamed up the idea of a new magazine. Launched two years later, *Loaded* was unashamedly northernist in its celebration of great indie bands like Joy Division, New Order and the Smiths and the nihilistic clubs of Manchester, Leeds and Liverpool. At the end of the eighties, the rave scene had spilled out of Manchester's Hacienda nightclub into other provincial cities. As acid house exploded, and illegal warehouse parties spread across the Pennines, superclubs like Back To Basics, Up Yer Ronson and Vague opened in Leeds. A new generation of cocky, iconoclastic northerners – cultish novelists, jumped-up journalists, swaggering artists, achingly hip DJs and hedonistic pop stars – invaded staid and stuffy London, throwing themselves about town, flaunting their talent.

At the end of the nineties, Brown launched a new Leeds United magazine – entitled, with a degree of inevitability – *Leeds Leeds Leeds*. It featured hip comedian Vic Reeves talking of his love for 'Reaney, Revie, Clarke . . . all geniuses'. There was a tribute to the awesome size of Tony Yeboah's backside and an interview with the notorious gangster Mad Frankie Fraser, who had once been jailed in Armley prison; a tenuous connection, perhaps, but Mad Frankie claimed he'd 'always got a soft spot for Leeds'. In future issues supermodel Rachel Hunter, wife of Rod Stewart, would reveal that her son's middle name was McAllister, a homage to her favourite player Gary, *Trainspotting*'s Irvine Welsh would write a piece on the Hibs–Leeds connection and a long list of other zeitgeisty celebrities would be outed as fans: Jeremy Paxman, the Kaiser Chiefs' Ricky Wilson, Mel B from the Spice Girls, Radio 1 DJ Chris Moyles, *Newsnight Review*'s Mark Lawson and the award-winning novelist Caryl Phillips.

LLL was unashamedly 'Leeds-ist' in its celebration of local bands like The Wedding Present and the Kaiser Chiefs. Brown wrote a poignant piece about arriving back home and choosing which of the two paths to follow. There was now, he argued, a clear choice to be made. His generation could either be optimistic or pessimistic about the new Leeds. They could eagerly anticipate its gentrified future or revel in its tawdry past. It all depended, he half joked, on which direction you chose to walk after you left the station. If you turned left, and walked through the new concourse, you would emerge into a glitzy, happening wonderland changing at a furious, unfettered pace. If you turned right, and walked down the steep slippery steps, you would soon find 'that there's still much left of the old place: the yelling paper sellers . . . the Scarborough Taps where in the late seventies the NF and the Service Crew chose to drink'.

To the horror of the city's boosterists and marketing consultants, many of Brown's fellow escapees turned right. They wrote about, and drew inspiration from, the squalid areas that most people chose to avoid. Peace, Brown, Phillips and Damien Hirst were part of a nineties explosion of young, provincial talent. They embodied the furious energy of a new generation of ambitious Northern Men who, like the previous generation, were determined to use their talents to enlarge their social horizons. At the beginning of *Nineteen Seventy Four*, Peace's first novel, a cocky young crime journalist returns home to his insular, tribal community. At the beginning of his last British-based novel, which also takes place in 1974, a cocky young football manager returns to God's Own Country to confront another insular, tribal force: Leeds United. Both Ed Dunford and Brian Clough experience Leeds as the cold, grimy, unforgiving place its tourist board insisted had long since disappeared.

While growing up in the city, Hirst made an unsettling discovery in his next-door neighbour's house. One day, Mr Barnes just disappeared. The young Damien climbed over the fence and came across an amazing store of objects. There was sixty years of existence in the house: parcels of money, alarm clocks, hundreds of tubes of toothpaste – all completely empty and neatly organised – and magazine pictures of women, round figures, with nipples and pubic hair drawn in. The entire house was an installation, and it inspired a series of collages that caught the attention of the London art world. It proved that there was an innate glamour to, and money to be made from, northern grimness. Bleak was cool, and insouciance in the face of such bleakness even more so. The Young British Artists, wrote the critic Gordon Burn, were interested 'in the dirt that accrues beneath the laminate surface of shiny things'. After meeting Jay Jopling – a pinstriped, Leeds United-obsessed art dealer – Hirst became the YBA's unofficial leader. There was a strong Leeds core to the notorious grouping: Hirst, Jopling, Carl Freedman and Marcus Harvey. 'In the early days,' wrote curator Gregor Muir, 'there was a noticeable northern contingent descending on private views and causing mayhem. With their thick Leeds accents, Hirst and Freedman were among the most prominent . . . for a brief moment it was entirely desirable to be an artist with a northern working-class background.'

Ooh Aah: The 1992 Choke

1992. Alex Ferguson, whose team haven't won the title for twenty-five years, gets a call from Wilkinson, whose team have just won their third title in twenty-three years. Wilkinson wants to re-sign Denis Irwin. Ferguson says the defender is not for sale but how about Cantona? According to the Sergeant, the Frenchman has become a disruptive influence on team spirit. So he sells him to Manchester United, his biggest rivals, for only £1.2 million. No stars, no egos, no big-time Charlies. No one is bigger than the club. The new Leeds, like the old Leeds, don't do mavericks. Even if they score hat-tricks, win them trophies and enhance their global appeal. Wilko's Leeds are honest grafters not flamboyant Fancy Dans. Three years later Cantona returns to Elland Road and rubs their noses in it, scoring in a 4-0 hammering. After the match Leeds sack Wilkinson. At the end of that season Cantona retires after leading Manchester United to four Premiership titles and two doubles.

Eric Cantona is fond of fish metaphors. 'When the seagulls are following a trawler,' he once told a press conference after kung-fu kicking a Crystal Palace fan, 'it is because they think the sardines are going to be thrown into the sea.' Three years earlier, less famously, he had concluded a fax to Wilkinson with another gnomic utterance: 'The salmon that idles its way downstream will never leap the waterfall.' Eric had refused to accept Howard's Way and was offloaded to Manchester United.

The 1992 title should have been the springboard for the rebirth of Super Leeds. A new all-singing-all-dancing Premier League, lashings of TV money, a lucrative and high-profile European Cup campaign, a huge and passionate fan base, a long list of celebrity supporters, a state-of-the-art youth academy, the best midfield in the country – Strachan, McAllister, Speed and Batty – and an imperious, collar-turned-up sexiness. 'The title should have been a massive catalyst for the club,' McAllister argued. 'We could have moved on, especially after we'd beaten our biggest rivals to the championship . . . it might have been the start of something big.' At the start of the following season, Cantona's hat-tricks against Liverpool and Spurs sealed his cult status. When, on a balmy autumn evening in the Nou Camp, Leeds beat Stuttgart – the tie had to be played at a neutral ground because the Germans had fielded an ineligible player in the second leg – to set up a second-round European Cup clash with Rangers, 'we are the champions, the champions of Europe' suddenly seemed a slightly less ludicrous rallying cry than normal.

And then? An implosion, of course. After selling their adored talisman to their biggest rivals – possibly the worst transfer decision in the history of football – Wilko's Leeds went into freefall, incredibly going the whole of the inaugural Premiership without an away win. It was the worst title defence since Ipswich's in 1963. No team has ever been relegated immediately after winning the league, but Leeds came pretty close.

The problem, argued Wilkinson, was that no one had expected them to win the title in the first place; least of all their manager. Not only two years after promotion. His team, he claimed, had peaked too early. According to the received narrative of the 1991–2 campaign, they had stolen the championship from under the other, mightier, United's noses. The bar had been raised to an impossible height, expectations were out of all proportion to reality and, Wilkinson conceded to a journalist, the only way was down. There had been bad luck – the inspirational Strachan, for example, being injured for most of the season. There was, once again, bad refereeing: another crucial European Cup 'goal' – Strachan's at Rangers – being wrongly ruled offside. And the bad men who ruled football had only gone and abolished the back pass, a typical anti-Leeds measure. Passing back to the keeper was a great Leeds tradition, an art perfected by Reaney, Madeley and Hunter and passed on to a new generation of Sterland, Whyte and Fairclough. This new establishment stitch-up, the latest instalment in the Plot Against Leeds, had made an admittedly suspect defence even more jittery.

But the Cantona sale was the tipping point. Leeds fans were devastated. Eric's irresistible cameos had restored their belief that Leeds could really beat Manchester United to the First Division championship. He was the swaggering anti-hero *par excellence*, their most exotic recruit since Johanneson. His misunderstood-maverick persona mirrored their own anti-establishment identity. He loved them – he didn't know why but he did – and they loved him back. They wore onions and berets to matches. When he scored he put his hands on his hips and stuck his chest out, like a Roman emperor acknowledging the adulation of his subjects. The old Leeds anthem 'Marching On Together' was rewritten as 'Marchons Ensemble'. 'Leeds fans did not merely admire Cantona's manliness or his style,' wrote sociologist Anthony C. King, 'but loved him in the way that someone might love their partner.'

The acrimonious divorce, in November 1992, was a clear signal – to the fans, the players and the rest of football – that Leeds were, once again, selling themselves short. Everyone remembered how McQueen and Jordan's cross-Pennines defection had precipitated the eighties collapse. Cantona's departure resurrected that grimy-old-parochial image; as if they couldn't quite accept that they were, or deserved to be, the champions of England. A mere 20,457 turned up at Elland Road to see the crucial European Cup first-round tie against Stuttgart. They had arrived at the threshold only to discover that, once again, they were out of their depth. According to their personal mythology, they hadn't won the title – Fergie's men had thrown it away. During the final six games of the season, the Reds had lost at home to Forest, drawn at Luton and then been defeated at West Ham and Liverpool. Leeds were the plucky underdogs who'd come from nowhere to over-come impossible odds and take advantage of the other, more famous, United's implosion. There were distinct echoes of Revie's early 'professionalism' in the way Wilkinson had used a residual, and in some cases visceral, anti-Leeds feeling to nurture a siege mentality. When, for example, the former Liverpool captain Emlyn Hughes wrote in the *Daily Mirror* about his absolute loathing for the club, the offending column was pinned up on the dressing room wall. Once again, it was us against the world.

Cantona's arrival had not only provided the momentum that won them the league. It had been a sign that the club had finally shed its dour and insular image. That it was willing to embrace elegance, flair and entertainment. That, like its fizzy and flashy city, it had been redeemed. The influential national fanzine *When Saturday Comes* had praised the new, improved, attractive Whites. The influential local fanzine *The Square Ball* had expressed pride in Eric's foreignness and criticised sides who destroyed the beautiful game by 'substituting aggression and brute force for skill'. Cantona's departure was the cue for a return to the atavistic tribalism of the seventies; as the team got sucked into the quagmire of a relegation struggle, the French 'Judas' received hate mail, had fireworks pushed through his letterbox and was subject to vile abuse during home clashes with 'the scum'.

Them against us can be a useful thing in football. But once Leeds had shed their plucky-underdog status and become the team to beat – the country's brave new European hopes – a more ambitious, positive outlook was surely required. There was a ghost in Wilko's well-drilled, highly efficient machine. Eighteen years after hounding Clough out of Elland Road it had still not been laid to rest. On ITV's popular *Saint and Greavesie* football show, the two pundits twittered on about the bruises and batterings they'd received at the ground back in the good-old-bad-old-days. Wilko might have sacked Bites Yer Legs from the coaching staff but his critics still dismissed his side as a bunch of bruisers intent on destruction. Leeds, they claimed, had clawed their way out of the Second Division by becoming kick-and-rush merchants, long-ball specialists; even bringing in a glorified bovver boy, Vinnie 'The Axe' Jones – famous for squeezing Gazza in a sensitive area – to roughen up the opposition. Most of their goals had come from headers, long-distant strikes and set pieces. They were English champions by default and now, in time-honoured fashion, they had lost their nerve and were about to disappear from the elite. Same old nearly men, always choking. Their dull, unimaginative Yorkshire boss had been found out.

By banishing their biggest star – the biggest star in the Premiership – to Old Trafford, where he would inspire his new team to their first title win in twenty-six years, help them establish a domestic hegemony that endures to this day and emerge as football's first corporate marketing tool, the message had been made clear: Dirty Leeds couldn't handle supremely talented players. According to King, the fans had seen in Cantona's Frenchness a means to assert their own aspirations to cosmopolitanism; they were 'able to distin-

guish Leeds as a team, symbolically represented by
Cantona, that was different and superior to the rest of
the English league'. Eric's departure meant they would
never be able to hack it with the big boys. Cantona,
like Johanneson and Clough – and even Duncan
McKenzie – epitomised the flamboyance and sense of
adventure Leeds had always failed to accommodate.
'He just wasn't Howard's type of player,' explained
director Bill Fotherby. Howard's type of player now
seemed to be ageing workhorses like Ian Rush and
Mark Hateley or overweight has-beens like Tomas
Brolin, who cost £4.5 million and ended up playing
only nineteen games. Stripped of their awesome four-
some in midfield, they were laid bare as a hard-working
bunch of journeymen destined, at best, for mid-table
mediocrity. Batty was sold to Newcastle, McAllister was
sent to Coventry – to join Strachan, who had become
player-manager there – and Speed was dispatched to
Everton.

King Eric's elevation to the rank of demi-god had
jarred with Wilkinson's team ethos. The gaffer argued
that the title had not been been won by crowd-pleasing
back heels or sublime flicks, but by harnessing traditional British virtues such as grit, commitment and
aggression. He explained that Eric had put self before
side every time, demanding to be picked for the team
every week or not play at all. Wilko had been unable
to give him such a guarantee. Cantona had become
'unmanageable . . . he likes to do what he likes when
he likes and then he fucks off'. After fucking off down
the M62, for a ludicrously-cheap fee, Eric went on to
become Ferguson's man of destiny, the player who

defined a decade of English football, the high-octane fuel that propelled the Reds' extraordinary bid for world domination. Typical Leeds.

5. Take

'[Leeds United are] a symbol of the city and the entire region . . . Yorkshire's great white hope . . . a source of mass inspiration and dogged, defiant pride, in a football elite that seems increasingly devoid of both'

The Rough Guide to English Football – A Fans' Handbook, 1999–2000

1996. France v Spain, European Championship, Elland Road.
I walk out of the station and turn left, through the shiny
new concourse and out into a reinvented city centre which is
replacing its old brick buildings with tall structures of steel
and glass. Its fizz and chutzpah are attracting the big brands
and the designer names and the affluent employees of regional,
national and international businesses. It has taken a long
time for the bleak old Leeds to die and for the shiny new
one to be born. This new Leeds yearns for national recogni-
tion – 'live it, love it' – aspires to be a European city-state
– 'Barcelona-on-Aire' – and dreams of becoming a twenty-four-
hour, global metropolis of movers and shakers – 'the city that
never sleeps'. It has a flourishing financial services sector and
shops till its plastic weeps. I enter the grand arcade of the
Victoria Quarter, look up at a flag bearing the motto 'Admire,
Aspire, Acquire' and walk past the Brooker Flynn's frontage
at the ritzy, five-floor Harvey Nicks and several upmarket,
exotic watering holes. And then past the Goths posing outside
the circular Corn Exchange, through the Dark Arches – now
called Granary Wharf – and across the river to Tetley's Brewery
Wharf and Clarence Dock. There is new money everywhere.
Up the river, down the river. Superstar DJs are racing up the
M1 to play at Leeds' new superclubs. Yuppies are moving
into city-centre apartments. Thousands of football fans of all
nationalities are flocking to the gentrified jewel of the new
north for Euro 96. There is a sense of opportunity, growth,
fun. Leeds is riding high, fuelled by the speculative boom and
a mood of giddy optimism.

The New Money

In June 1996 Elland Road hosted three UEFA European
Football Championship games. Euro 96 – official slogan:
'Football Comes Home' – was the first time the tour-
nament had taken place in England and northern civic
leaders used it to show the world just how far their
cities had come since the dismal eighties. Leeds United
directors used it to show off their 17,000-seater, two-
tier, £5.5-million East Stand. A year later, when U2
played a gig at the ground and Bono told a packed
house how kids in Dublin used to talk 'with stars in
their eyes' about Leeds United, the urban renaissance
appeared to be complete.

Euro 96 was the perfect opportunity for Leeds to
showcase its new, European-style urbanity. The emergence of a powerful, visionary leader in the tradition
of Colonel Harding, Charles Wilson, Charles Jenkinson
and Frank Marshall was another sign of this regeneration. In his seven years in office, Jon Trickett had
brought a 'continental feel' to Leeds and shed, once
and for all, the anachronistic image of flat caps, slag
heaps and Tetley Bitter men. There were no more
whippet jokes or Hovis adverts. No more *Good Old
Days*, live from the Leeds City Varieties. No more 'of

course I'm sophisticated I've been to Leeds' Harry Enfield piss-takes. The Labour leader had been to Graham Stringer's Manchester and he had seen the future. Leeds, like its big rival, would become a living metropolis not an archaeological site. A city for twenty-four-hour party people, a magnet for hedonists looking for a great night out; a boom town not a ghost town.

In 1996, Harvey Nichols, an icon of retailing, opened its first regional store outside London and the £40-million Royal Armouries, a national museum, was relocated on the redeveloped waterfront. Trickett introduced a 'Funday, Sunday' scheme which launched seven-day shopping. Licensing hours were increased for trendy clubs, bars and discos – like Dave Beer's Back II Basics, the Orbit and the Majestyk – sparking a night-time economy boom. Café proprietors were encouraged to place tables and chairs on pavements. A French boules court and chess tables appeared in one of the centre's squares. Property owners were urged to cut rents to encourage late-night shop opening. Using government urban-aid money, a Trickett task-force lured film festivals, heritage events and global music celebrities – among them Madonna, Michael Jackson and the Rolling Stones – to the city. The burgeoning bars and music culture provided an ideal springboard for new talent, like Kaiser Chiefs and Corinne Bailey Rae. Grants were given to illuminate buildings and fund the hosting of big sporting events like Kellogg's Tour of Britain and the Classic Cycle Race. 'Swinging granny' Lorna Cohen donned her Lady Mayoral chain and went out clubbing with the London media. Football fans from around the world, who had come to watch games involving France, Spain, Bulgaria and Romania, sampled the heaving nightlife of the self-styled Barcelona-of-the-north – the council even published rainfall charts to prove that Leeds was drier than the Catalan city – bopping at happening nightclubs like Nato, Uropa, the Underground, Planet Earth and the Cockpit, eating at trendy eateries like Anthony's, Kendells Bistro, Chaophraya and Brasserie Blanc, drinking at cool bars like Cuban Heels, the Observatory, Café Mex and Jumping Jacks and, after recovering from their hangovers, shopping at the refurbished Corn Exchange and the glass-enclosed Kirkgate Market.

Leeds' rebirth as the biggest legal and financial centre outside London was part of a northern-based economic revival generated by the growth of knowledge-based services. Chic city revellers thronged its pedestrianised streets, renovated mills and swanky arcades. Gated, high-tech developments provided homes for the high-earning professionals who worked in the neighbouring glass-and-steel towers. Leeds was on its way to becoming the archetypal postmodern city; a 24-7, late capitalist wonderland encapsulating the shift away from indus-trial production and towards the service sectors, finan-cial services, retailing and tourism. It was cool, cosmopolitan and cutting edge, its rejuvenated centre a glittering celebration of big European money.

Which was more than could be said for the foot-ball team. While the city was attempting to transform itself into a global, corporate entity – and that French Judas Bastard was weaving his magic at Old Trafford – Wilko's Wonders continued to idle downstream. Cantona's departure had triggered a four-year spell of austere and sterile football, probably best characterised by Carlton Palmer's ponderous performances in midfield. It had signalled the end of Wilkinson as a manager and the beginning of Ferguson's pomp. And it had left a hole in Leeds fans' hearts that all the vilification of the Frenchman for his defection could never fill. Wilko never recovered from overseeing a wretched display in the 1996 Coca-Cola Cup Final, a 3-0 mauling by an average Aston Villa side. In their first major final for twenty-one years, and entirely in keeping with their nearly-man inheritance, they had choked. After only seven games of the 1996-7 season – following a home-turf hammering at the hands of Cantona's team – the Sergeant was given his marching orders.

He was sacked by Bill Fotherby, who had taken over the chairmanship from Silver. Fotherby was a fedora-wearing, cigar-smoking motormouth, the link between old-school directors like Reynolds, Cussins and Silver – established businessmen who invested their self-made millions in their boyhood club – and the new generation of director-entrepreneurs. He might not have been Jewish – 'I would never deny it if someone said I was' he once joked – but was fond of using the Yiddish patter associated with the community. I remember him at my dad's fiftieth birthday party, telling stories about the golden age of tailoring. His impersonation of the Yiddish-speaking tailor who took him under his wing as a small boy made me cry with laughter. With my dad's brother Leon by his side, he had run Cussins' clothing factory – and the two of them went to Elland Road together to watch the Revie boys. Not long after he became a director, he negotiated a twelve-month, £50,000-sponsorship deal with Burton. As part of that deal, one of its thrusting young executives, Peter Ridsdale, was invited on to the board.

In 1996, Fotherby persuaded Silver to float the club on the stock market. After the Taylor Report, the ownership structures of clubs were beginning to change. Spurs were the first to become a public limited company. 'Everyone is doing it,' Fotherby told Silver. 'Spurs, Manchester United, Newcastle . . . we can't afford to miss the boat.' Alan Sugar made £22 million when he sold part of his Tottenham stake to the investment group Enic. Martin Edwards, whose father, Louis, accumulated his majority Manchester United stake in the fifties and sixties, made £93 million from selling shares. And Sir John Hall eventually made £100 million out of floating Newcastle. Fotherby wanted a piece of the action. In August, Leeds United became a plc and Chris Akers' London media company, Caspian, took control, with backing from leading City financial institutions. Akers, a former Swiss Bank corporate financier, unveiled his sunny vision in the club's prospectus: 'We intend that Leeds should form the cornerstone of our strategy to create one of Europe's leading sports, leisure and media groups, underpinned by a multi-sport and leisure facility available for the community.' Caspian's strategy was to expand beyond football and build a 14,000-seater indoor sports, conference and concert arena adjacent to Elland Road, which would generate revenue for the club and provide long-term security for the group.

The thirty-one-year-old plc chairman, who had made his name brokering cable television and sporting rights deals, was attracted to the prosperity and 'zing' of the regenerated city. The arrival of Harvey Nichols, the personification of London style, was a symbolic moment but Trickett's disposal of the family silver – council-owned city-centre buildings – had already brought in £4 billion worth of property investment. In a drive to attract new entrepreneurs, the council leader had coined the phrase 'Intelligent City'. Between 1991 and 1997 employment grew by 12 per cent, double the national figure. Millionaires like David Hood, co-founder of Pace Micro Technology, the internet entrepreneur Peter Wilkinson, and Paul Sykes, the property tycoon, were part of a network of young movers and shakers who had cut their teeth in the Thatcherite services boom. The Caspian board reflected the city's shift from a manufacturing, and particularly textile, based economy to a modern hub of commerce and opportunity. Big brands like Asda, BT and First Direct had all flocked to the north's Knightsbridge. 'An affluent local population,' argued Trickett, 'will bring life to the formerly-deserted core of a nine-to-five city centre and provide a local market for a growing service sector.' According to the 1991 census, only 900 people inhabited the centre; sixteen years later, 14,000 residents were living in 372 apartment blocks. A strong business group started following United around on foreign trips. After Leeds won the title in 1992, one supporter told the *Yorkshire Post* that he had travelled 50,000 miles to follow the club, timing his business trips so that they would coincide with their fixtures. 'We want to forge a real brand value in the Leeds United name,' explained Jeremy Fenn, Akers' right-hand man.

Just as the flamboyant, showboating Cantona had not been Howard's type of player, so the taciturn, grim-faced Howard was not Caspian's type of manager. George Graham, his replacement, was more up their street (quite literally, in fact, as he lived near Akers in north London); as a double-title-winning manager with Arsenal, he was a brand name. And the old-school, old-Labour Silver was clearly not their type of chairman. The seventy-one-year-old millionaire socialist argued publicly that it was time for both new blood and new money. A plc, he stressed, should be run by the new breed of brand-obsessed, corporate thrusters who were far more in tune with football's space age. 'Now you are talking of millions not making a difference,' he said. 'The chairmanship needs professionalism and high-quality management.'

Speaking to me twelve years later, however, he hinted at another, darker reason for quitting. He had wanted out for some time. 'I remember Manny getting some anti-Semitic remarks when he wasn't making things happen. I thought that if Leeds weren't successful the Jewish community would get hammered. When we won the championship I was very popular as a Yorkshireman. But when things went wrong, I was criticised by some fans as a Jew.' Some Leeds fans denounced him as a 'shyster' who had sold the club's heritage to a London-based investment firm and walked away with a cool £2 million. Under Silver, Leeds had won their first – and to this day only – trophies since the Revie era. Just before he stepped down his house was burgled by a group of men wearing balaclavas. They handcuffed him to a door, escaping with cash, jewellery and £200,000 worth of antiques. 'It was the final straw,' he said. 'I wanted to get out of the public limelight. I'd never been comfortable in it.'

Publicity Pete

1998. The world is changing and Leeds must change with it. It must reinvent itself for the coming decade; for a new century, a new millennium. In the new globalised economy, anything will be for sale to anyone. There will be no return to boom and bust. Leeds United will – must – become a global brand, a modern entertainment corporation. Or they will get left behind, sink back into oblivion. They must buy into the aspiration of an optimistic, freewheeling, property-booming, credit-card addicted era. They must chase the dream.

Peter Ridsdale was more than comfortable in the public limelight. In 1997, Caspian appointed him chairman – at an Elland Road banqueting suite in front of three hundred corporate sponsors – with strict instructions to 'grow the brand'. He ticked all their boxes. He was youthful – twenty-two years younger than Silver – energetic and a good communicator; the ideal chairman to help the brand chase the rising financial rewards of the TV rights boom. Moreover, he was steeped in the mythology of Leeds. Ridsdale was brought up in a terraced back-to-back in *Billy Liar* land. He was desperate to escape a life of provincial confinement; his mother warned him that if he did badly at school he would end up working at the nearby Burton factory. As a young boy, he experienced a personal epiphany in 1965 while camping overnight at Elland Road to get an FA Cup Final ticket. That piece of paper, he said, was the equivalent of Charlie Bucket's golden ticket to Willy Wonka's chocolate factory. Although he left school with only one O-level he worked his way up to the post of ICL regional personnel manager. After being headhunted, ironically by Burton chairman Sir Ralph Halpern, he became the managing director of Top Man. Then came his second Willy Wonka moment when Bill Fotherby offered him a place on the Leeds United board. Ten years later – an even more mind-blowing experience – he was offered the chairmanship. Now he felt as if he'd won the pools. 'I was no Leslie Silver,' he wrote in his autobiography, '. . . football was becoming more business-like, and so its revolution presented me with an opportunity.'

By the time I interviewed him for a *Sunday Mirror* profile in 1998 the board had renamed itself Leeds Sporting plc and Ridsdale had reinvented himself as Publicity Pete, the very model of a modern football chairman. His inner circle reflected the new corporate forces that were thrusting the city skywards: high-flying Asda chief Allan Leighton, forty-eight; Stephen Harrison, forty, an executive at a spectacles firm; David Spencer, fifty, who had run a catering company, and Richard North, fifty-one, the finance boss of a brewing firm. North and Leighton, he proudly told me, were 'among the top non-executive directors in the country'.

Being steeped in Leeds folklore meant Ridsdale was painfully aware of the Revie legacy. He hated the way TV presenters and phone-in show callers still blathered on about Dirty Leeds. Although he worshipped that great Leeds side he referred to them as 'nearly men' – which upset the golden age alumni. Revie had been a product of his time, he told me. He had started out as a forward-thinking technocrat but had ultimately succumbed to a paranoiac fatalism; a belief that the media, indeed the rest of the world, were out to get him and his team. The club had a massive and passionate customer base but were trapped by tradition. Ridsdale's mission was to erase this bunker mentality, shed their reputation for thuggery and reinvent Leeds as something more than just gritty, try-hard underdogs forever busting a gut against the odds. In order to keep up, go toe to toe, with the giants of football – the Manchester Uniteds and the Arsenals, the Milans and Madrids, the oligarchs and sheikhs – they would have to buy into aspiration. Wilko had lost the plot, he said, but George had stopped the rot. Graham and Leeds were meant for each other. Both were desperate for rehabilitation; the ex-Arsenal manager had been banned from football after receiving £425,000 in connection with two transfer deals and United were still trying to ditch their dirty-cheating-northern-bastards image.

As football moved from a small to a global business, Leeds, although not able to match their spending power, still had two big advantages over their rivals. Firstly, a fan base that would gobble up all the merchandise and keep coming through the turnstiles, week after week. And, secondly, a state-of-the-art youth academy at Thorp

Arch that would – 'mark my words' – deliver the most talented crop of youngsters this country had ever seen. This was the dawn of a new era of football, Ridsdale said, and the Brand Leeds juggernaut was unstoppable.

My Babies

1999. When I arrive at York station, which is actually closer to United's new state-of-the-art training ground than Leeds station, I have a sudden flashback. The last time I was there, in 1963, I was wearing a suede coat with a fur collar and my hair was slicked back. It was my dad's first big job, his big break, his new beginning. On my way from Leeds to York he had pointed out a big spaceship which appeared to have crash-landed on the edge of the city. The taxi driver takes me through the picture-book village of Boston Spa, across the River Wharfe until eventually we come to a long, winding driveway. At the end of the driveway is a little wooden hut. I am greeted by a man called Jack who asks if I am an "ostile'. Jack explains he isn't allowed to let 'ostiles through. Not even fans. I tell Jack that it is harder to get into the Thorp Arch complex than to get out of the prison across the road. Jack doesn't smile. The wrought-iron gates glide open and, after I enter the inner sanctum, immediately click shut.

In his first season, Graham rebuilt from the back and steered the team away from the relegation zone. In his

second season they finished fifth and qualified for the
UEFA Cup. Another revival, it seemed, was on the
cards. At the start of the 1998–9 campaign, there was
even title talk. United flew out of the traps and were
unbeaten in their first six games. But, after the seventh
game, the new messiah packed his bags and returned
to North London. Leeds, he said, had gone as far as
they could; his new charges, Tottenham, had a much
better chance of restoring their former glory and
breaking into the European elite. Leeds Sporting immediately went for another 'brand name' – Martin O'Neill
– but the deal fell through and, besides, their caretaker manager's hunger and ambition had made a big
impression on Ridsdale.

David O'Leary, like Graham, was an Arsenal legend.
He had spent nineteen years at Highbury, winning
several trophies, before Wilkinson signed him on a free
transfer in 1993. After playing only fourteen games he
suffered an Achilles injury and retired at the age of thirty-
seven. Graham made him his number two at Elland
Road but when he begged his mentor to blood gifted
youngsters such as Jonathan Woodgate, Alan Smith,
Stephen McPhail and Paul Robinson, George told him
they weren't ready; his refusal to watch the kids had
provoked academy director Paul Hart into resigning
his post. O'Leary was also frustrated by Graham's
penchant for dreary, goalless draws. At the end of the
Scot's first campaign, having watched their team score
only twenty-eight times – the lowest total in all four
divisions – the Kop adapted an old Vera Lynn classic
– 'We'll score again, don't know where, don't know
when' – as its new anthem. The fans had even taken

Tony Yeboah's side against Graham when the Ghanaian striker hurled his white shirt at the manager after being substituted; Yeboah's stunning strikes – including a dipping volley against Liverpool which was voted *Match of the Day's* goal of the season – had, for a brief period, filled a Cantona-shaped hole.

Once installed as Graham's permanent successor, O'Leary wasted no time in blooding 'my babies' – as he, somewhat nauseatingly, kept calling them – turning them into an exhilarating, swashbuckling side. He immediately elevated Woodgate, Smith, McPhail and Robinson – whom he likened to four new signings – to the first team. He sold Jimmy Floyd Hasselbaink to Atletico Madrid, bringing in more young players with the £12 million fee. Smith scored with his first touch against Liverpool at Anfield. Robinson's display at Old Trafford had Alex Ferguson in raptures. And, only nine months after his first full start, the nineteen-year-old Woodgate won an England cap. In O'Leary's first season in charge, United finished fourth and again qualified for the UEFA Cup. Turnover was rising and profits were on the up. The initial Caspian plan had been to grow the brand slowly but with rival brands, like Manchester United and Chelsea, now borrowing so heavily, Ridsdale decided to up the ante. This time around, Leeds United would get more than just a glimpse of the promised land. Like Revie, he dreamed of conquering Everest. But football had changed so much since the Don's day. There was a new world order of footballing city-states. The Premier League had been founded on money, a get-rich-quick market had been ratcheted into place and a new, debt-loading breed of Premiership speculators was curling towards our shores. It was a whole new commercial game; everything was moving faster and becoming more mobile and efficient. To get a slice of the action this time around, Leeds needed to be in, and stay in, the world's biggest club competition: the Champions League. It was time to spend their way into the elite.

Encouraged by O'Leary, the chairman started pushing for more player investment. 'In the summer of 1999,' said Jeremy Fenn, United's Managing Director since the Caspian takeover, 'Peter was getting more involved in the transfer deals. It was quite clear there was a desire on the part of Ridsdale and the manager at the time to spend more money on players. Things came to a head when there were some stories in the paper about myself constraining progress at the club through a lack of desire to open up the chequebook, and I used that as an opportunity to say this is not for me.' By this time Akers had also gone – as had Richard Thompson, the third member of the three-man Caspian board – and Ridsdale's clique was running the show. Publicity Pete wasted no time in reinventing Dirty Leeds as a vibrantly populist, family-friendly, European-style club. He installed bright signs at the stadium directing families to the Leeds United Crèche, the Leeds United Playgroup and the Leeds United Mums and Tots Enclosure. Fans were encouraged to buy cappuccinos rather than Bovril and, if they had the dosh, enjoy corporate entertainment with black-tie service in the Leeds United Pavilion – built on the spot where a greasy spoon café had once stood. The general feeling, both inside and outside Leeds, was that 'the brand', as vice-chairman

Leighton put it, 'was about to deliver'.

Leighton's two favourite buzzwords, as I discovered when we met for a two-hour, off-the-record briefing, were 'brand' and 'zap'. Several pundits had claimed that it was he, not Ridsdale, who was pulling the strings. After a six-year stint as a teacher I had become a journalist and, after moving to the *Sunday Mirror*, I suddenly had access to all United's movers and shakers. I had even met the mysterious sheikh, a member of Bahrain's ruling dynasty, who was rumoured to be planning a Saudi-based takeover. Sheikh Abdulrahman bin Mubarak Al-Khalifa – 'but, Anthony, you can call me Abdul' – was a year older than me and had 'fallen in love with the Mighty Whites' after watching the 1970 FA Cup Final. He wanted to talk to a Leeds-supporting hack so Leighton had brought us together. Leighton, like Ridsdale, was one of the new breed of ambitious, football-loving businessmen, a grammar-school arriviste who had turned Asda around and was now hoping to do the same thing for the Leeds brand. Shortly after Asda's HQ had relocated to Leeds, he was approached to be a United director. It presented, he said, 'an interesting opportunity to look at football from a business perspective'. Leighton, like Publicity Pete, certainly talked the talk. He told me he hated the old-boy network and relished taking on the establishment. After grammar school he'd been to technical college and then spent eighteen years at Mars before making his name at Asda. 'We created this culture that we were underdogs and we were going to fight back,' he said. 'For Asda, read Leeds United.'

Everything, declared Leighton, was in place for an

assault on the big boys, the global brands. O'Leary had turned Graham's obdurate, defensive unit into a free-flowing, gung-ho, attacking team. Ridsdale ran a cosmopolitan, outward looking, positive thinking club. The new chairman was a hugely popular figure within the game. His compassionate and dignified handling of the murders of two Leeds fans, Chris Loftus and Kevin Speight, before a 2000 UEFA Cup semi-final against Galatasaray had won him universal respect. He had seen the stab wounds and sent his driver to pick up blood from a neighbouring hospital in Istanbul. He was with Philip Loftus when he identified his brother's body. Nobody doubted that he cared. He had opened a crèche, dispatched United's stars into schools, supported local anti-racist initiatives and rooted out the hooligans. He was the chairman of Education Leeds, a New Labour-inspired 'public-private partnership' which had taken over the city's schools in the wake of a damning Ofsted report. With Ridsdale and O'Leary in charge, the club would deliver not only results, and eventually trophies, but also the kind of beautiful football that would win over the public.

Leighton praised the *Loaded* lads for popularising the brand through *Leeds Leeds Leeds,* the club's irreverent new magazine. He admired the chutzpah of these cheeky young men who were kicking against the pricks, getting up the noses of the stuffed shirts. David Mellor, a former Conservative minister and a big Chelsea fan, had even denounced the mag on his phone-in radio show. Great accolade, great publicity. All this youthful energy, this 'zap', as he put it, was coming out of the brand. The board had grandiose plans to develop the stadium, had invested heavily in a nursery which was growing the next generation of stars and were implementing ground-breaking community programmes. The nation, he laughed, was shocked to discover that it actually liked Dirty Leeds. We had become media darlings. Now we were entering new and lucrative territory. Our cool and sexy appeal would cross class, regional, even national boundaries. The most important thing, concluded Leighton, was to instil confidence. To 'zap not sap'. That was his thing – in football, in business and in life. 'Sap is taking energy out of organisations, zap is keeping people up; attack, charge, be confident, be positive. It's so simple. Zap is "I'm good", sap is "I'm average". That's the choice.'

Billy Liar on the Moon

1999. Thorp Arch again. At the end of the year, I interview O'Leary. When I enter his office he is moving his 'babies' around on a large wooden desk, using gold coins to work out his best formation for the Port Vale game. 'King David is in his counting house,' I write, 'counting out his money.' The coins all have tags with names like Kewell, Woodgate, Smith, Bridges and Bowyer written on them. He tells me that Leeds United are back on the map. They have been reinvented, 'given a good name'. It's been a long time since people have actually liked Leeds. Everybody used to hate them, including O'Leary himself, but now that's changing. With all his babies coming through, the board don't actually know their luck. And neither does he. 'I still have to pinch myself that I'm manager of Leeds United.' It's now or never. At the end of the year – the century, the millennium – this is surely our last chance to rise above the sordid and rejoice in the beautiful. To cross the threshold into the promised land. To become champions of England and then Europe. With the right backing, O'Leary says, Leeds can be like Manchester United in a few years' time. 'I don't sit back on things. I'm ambitious, I'd love to win the Premiership.' I ask him which players he has targeted. He says only young players with potential. Players who will develop under his tutelage. Players who bristle with technique and raw ability.

Take

Players who Leeds can polish into gems. Players who will stay the course and win the club lots of trophies.

In the 1999–2000 season, O'Leary's babies zapped their way to the dizzy heights of the Premiership's top three. Suddenly, they were box office. They had qualified for the Champions League and would now be able to tap into a deep reservoir of television money. Getting through to the group stages guaranteed millions of pounds of income in gate receipts and sales of broadcasting rights. Ridsdale had set the template for a new type of football chairman. He had a public image, wrote the *Guardian's* Jim White, 'that most club chairmen would sell their shareholders for'. When I interviewed O'Leary in the last month of the old millennium, his team were on fire. They had won fourteen out of their first nineteen games and their fast and furious football had been praised by media pundits. Ridsdale had struck a deal with Sky to release £8 million for new players and the chairman, board and manager had all agreed on a Viv Nicholson-spend-spend-spend pursuit of the all-conquering Reds. Like Trickett, they were out to dethrone the Mancs. Sky was so impressed it took a stake in Leeds Sporting after turnover had jumped from £37 million to £57 million – which included a 56 per cent rise in TV revenue and a 33 per cent increase in gate receipts. O'Leary told me he wanted the club to be mentioned in the same breath as Ferguson's men. Revie's scrappers had a reputation for brutality and cynicism. But his Leeds, the new Leeds, would be popular, admired, loved even. He was determined, he said, to make them everyone's second team.

At the beginning of the 2000-1 campaign, his babies barnstormed their way through to the second stage of the Champions League. Turnover soared to £86 million and operating profit leapt to £10 million. Gate receipts rose by a third, merchandising revenue by 40 per cent and television income doubled. It was at this point that Leeds Sporting, intoxicated by success, began to borrow against future success. It's easy to be wise after the event. Leeds was a booming city, the fourth largest in England. According to the 2001 census it had a population of 715, 404. The club's fan base was expanding and the brand was growing stronger by the month. Football had become a game defined by rapacity and greed – a winner-takes-all ethos – and the top teams were building their success on a high level of debt. Pretty soon a quartet of elite clubs, bolstered by Champions League money, would morph into an unofficial mini-league. Leeds needed to get into that mini-league or they would be left behind in the stampede for wealth.

'We devised a winning strategy and knew what was required,' wrote Ridsdale. 'We had to spend. We either aimed for the moon because that's where we'd find the television income and future European revenue. Or we settled for a mid-table survival strategy with all the restrictive prudence attached.' So in came Dominic Matteo for £4.25 million, Olivier Dacourt for £7.2 million and Mark Viduka for £6 million. To fund this £17.45 million investment the club turned to insurance adviser Ray Ranson, who had previously acquired finance packages to cover the signings of Eirik Bakke, Michael Bridges, Danny Mills and Michael Duberry. Ranson arranged short-term loans which were insured with a German-based company whose interest rates were higher than bank charges. The quarterly payments were substantial – and the extra insurance was expensive and had to be paid upfront.

A growing band of sceptics now pointed out that borrowing had never been a feature of the Revie era – and that Manny Cussins had been famously reluctant to get the chequebook out. Ridsdale pointed out that when the Don delivered Leeds from the wilderness, and even when the Sergeant had brought them out of their eighties exile, it was still possible to be dragged into the elite by the boot straps; to succeed through a combination of talent, application and luck. Nineteen ninety-two had changed everything. After the gold rush, football clubs had to buy success. Look at Blackburn. Owned by steel magnate Jack Walker, they had won promotion to the new Premier League, spent millions of pounds and, three years later, become champions. The higher Leeds went, the tougher the competition would become and the more money it would take to sustain their momentum. Lacking a wealthy investor, Leeds needed silverware and regular Champions League football to finance their ambition. The billionaire-infused, hyper-inflated Premier League was all about 'aiming big'. It had become big business on an unimaginable scale. Biggest income, biggest audience, biggest earners, biggest egos. It was attracting the biggest footballers on the planet, billions of viewers worldwide and billions of pounds from global TV rights, merchandising and the highest ticket prices in Europe. A big-bucks strategy was required to assemble a team that could compete in a big-bucks culture. Confronted with this new Darwinian reality, Leeds could either become ambitious high-fliers or mid-table might-have-beens. Eric Cantona was right: they could either leap the waterfall or continue to idle their way downstream.

With the original Caspian management team of Akers, Fenn and Thompson no longer there to rein him in, Ridsdale went for the great leap forward. The board borrowed another £60 million against future success. At the same time, they changed the Caspian ground development plan from refurbishing Elland Road to building a new, state-of-the-art, 50,000-capacity stadium on the outskirts of the city. To finance this, they would have to sell their old ground for £20 million. They would then find a naming rights sponsor for the new venue, who would secure a long-term deal for £40 million. Ridsdale turned to former Wall Street operator Stephen Schechter, a showman and financial wizard who had raised £50 million for Newcastle United the previous year. Schechter pointed out to London and New York lenders that Leeds was the biggest city in England with only one professional club – and that their supporters were unusually dedicated. Ridsdale informed his shareholders that the rates of borrowing for this securitisation loan were low, and that the new funds would push Leeds towards annual Champions League qualification. The board spent half of the loan – the biggest ever raised by an English football club – on clearing existing bank debt and developing Thorp Arch. The other £30 million was spent on bringing in new players, including Rio Ferdinand from West Ham for a record fee of £18 million.

The Kaizer Chief

2000. Leeds makes Nelson Mandela an Honorary Freeman of the City in front of a crowd of 25,000 at the opening of the £12 million Millennium Square. He is introduced by Lucas Radebe, the club captain of Leeds United. The Leeds band Kaiser Chiefs, who have come from nowhere to sell records by the bucket load, took their name from Radebe's old team. His story reads like a classic, rags-to-riches fairytale: a young man from an impoverished background gets a chance to shine on the highest level, takes that chance, succeeds and becomes a national hero. Mandela tells the Chief: 'You are my hero.' The gardens at the Civic Hall are renamed the Nelson Mandela Gardens. A few months later, the Chief shows me around Diepklouf, the Soweto zone he grew up in. He takes me to the small house he lived in with his brothers and sisters at the height of the anti-apartheid struggle. Lucas carried a knife and was active in the student movement which, he says, hijacked government vehicles and dispensed vigilante justice. When he was fifteen, his parents sent him away to school in a so-called independent homeland to train as a teacher. He was bored by his studies and to pass the time he played football. His skills brought him to the attention of Kaizer Chiefs. In 1991, while in a car with one of his brothers, he heard gunfire. He and his brother looked around to see who had been shot. Then he felt a pain in his back and noticed that he was covered in blood. The bullet had entered his back and passed out through his thigh. Although nobody was ever arrested and charged with the shooting, the Chief thought that somebody must have been hired to shoot him. Somebody who resented him joining Kaizer Chiefs, perhaps. But when I interview Radebe's mother about her role as coach of the local football team – called, I glowingly note, Diepklouf Leeds United – she tells a different story. Lucas was shot, she believes, because he stood out, was different from, the crowd. He was resented because he went away to train as a teacher. They tried to kill him because they were 'jealous of his ambition'. But the thing about her son, she says, is that he doesn't think there is a limit on ambition. 'Lucas,' she says, 'has always chased the dream.'

At the end of the eighties, when a more socially liberal and multicultural Britain was beginning to emerge, Leeds United were still perceived as a racist club. Many teams had a similar history of far-right involvement on their terraces, but the antics of the Service Crew were particularly notorious and, between the Chapeltown riots and Hilaire's arrival seven years later, 'the Whites' had become more than just the club's nickname. The emergence of Leeds United Fans Against Racism and Fascism, a supporter-led initiative involving the local Trades Council, the police and Leeds players, went some way towards curbing offensive chanting. Left-leaning groups of fans, whose opinions were echoed in the fanzine *Marching Altogether*, launched a number of anti-racist initiatives in an attempt to achieve supremacy over the hooligan element that had tarnished the club's image for almost two decades. *Marching Altogether* featured funny cartoon strips like 'Eric The Hooligan', a pre-Judas homage to the great French maverick, and '101 Things To Do With A Nazi Skin'. According to Cantona's biographer, 'it was an extraordinary reversal of the xenophobic values which were and still are attached to the Leeds support'. On the cover of its first issue of November 1988, Hilaire was pictured standing next to a white Leeds star. The editorial pulled no punches: 'Leeds United and Leeds fans have had a terrible reputation over the last few years thanks to the morons who have shouted abuse at black players. Such behaviour is illegal and unacceptable and it has come close to permanently ruining our great club.'

The civic boosterists were keen to rebrand Leeds as, in Trickett's words, 'a place where people from all different ways of life are thrown together, where horizons are broadened'. It was becoming, he insisted, one of the most cosmopolitan cities in the country, with 'people of different creeds, races and origins living in harmony'. The council's promotional material cited Albert Johanneson's historic appearance in the 1965 Cup Final, the Chief's friendship with Mandela and Harpal Singh's breakthrough into the squad as key stages in the 'journey towards multiculturalism'. Singh, the son of a Bradford bus driver who came to England from India, was on the verge of becoming the Premiership's first ever Asian footballer. He joined Leeds when he was twelve and played in youth teams alongside Smith, Woodgate and Robinson. According to the club magazine, he would blaze a trail for young Asians and be a role model for a generation of youngsters seeking to follow him into the game. A TV programme on the 'Asian breakthrough', featuring Leeds and West Ham as model clubs, opened with a shot of the talented midfielder. 'One player who knows the importance of integration,' it informed viewers, 'is Leeds United's rising star Harpal Singh.' It concluded that 'the future for football in the community and Asians within the professional game is looking bright.'

This 'rebranding' as anti-racist helped improve the club's image. *Leeds Leeds Leeds* proudly pointed out that United had a long history of employing black players. Gerry Francis had joined as an amateur from Johannesburg in 1957 and Johanneson became Revie's first signing four years later. By the time Chris Whyte, Chris Fairclough and Rod Wallace were starring in the 1991–2 title-winning side, a small number of black and Asian supporters had started coming to home matches. The integration of black players into the game was the single biggest factor in the decline of terrace racism. Football had become one of the few places where black British people were allowed to excel publicly. Crowds had become more mixed. Wilkinson signed Brian Deane, another proud son of Chapeltown, from Sheffield United. Yeboah's dead-eyed finishing lit up Elland Road for a year. The inspirational Jimmy Floyd Hasselbaink came, conquered and then followed the money to Spain, before ending up at Chelsea. And then came the Chief, one of the most popular Leeds players of all time.

When I spent a week shadowing Radebe in Soweto, he told me that he was initially wary of the club's racist reputation. But the supporters had taken him to their hearts and there was a part of him now that was forever

Leeds. He would never forget the time Wilkinson had called him into his office with Yeboah and another South African, Phil Masinga. The Sergeant said he would be starting all three of them in the same match for the first time. 'Nelson Mandela is my hero,' he told them. 'I would like you to succeed for this reason.' Caryl Phillips, who flew in from New York to present Jack Charlton with an award, had boycotted Elland Road for the past ten years. Radebe's captaincy, he wrote, marked a turning point. The Chief had brought him, and many other black fans, back into the fold. 'If [Ridsdale] can touch the different communities of the city, and bring them under the banner of Leeds United,' he concluded, 'then this might well prove to be the most valuable, and profitable, legacy of his charismatic chairmanship.'

The Last Hurrah: The 2001 Choke

2001. Valencia v Leeds. Estadio Mestalla. The Champions League semi-final. The last four of the European Cup. O'Leary's babies have shaved their heads. Fists clenched, eyeballs bulging, testosterone oozing from every pore, this is their – our – last hurrah. The last chance to become one of the most powerful clubs in Europe, to be part of a new world order of titanic footballing city-states. To close the deal on

Paris. Leeds are at the base of the final summit slopes, at the Hillary Step, about to become a great European city. And this time they've done it the right way, with the right image, the right marketing tools; reinventing the brand, shedding the Dirty Leeds legacy. Unlike Old Big 'Ead, they've cleansed the temple. Unlike the Sergeant, they've locked up the ghost of old Don. Bring out, deliver, redeem — and now, finally, 'take'. They have gone further in this season's competition than any other British team, even Manchester United. And, after a 0-0 draw with Valencia in the first leg, they are only ninety minutes away from the Champions League Final.

On their way to the Champions League semi-final, Leeds had played some dazzling attacking football and collected some notable scalps including AC Milan, Lazio, Deportivo La Coruña and Anderlecht. But, after a goalless first leg at Elland Road, they were humiliated in Valencia. I can still remember the shock of seeing the shaven-headed, semi-feral warriors running on to the pitch at the soaring, ecstatic Mestalla Stadium. This misguided act of team bonding — a bit more full-on than the bingo sessions and carpet bowls of the Revie era — was a last, all-or-nothing bid to release Leeds from its tainted past. And it smacked of desperation. The babies looked beaten before the game had even started; like sullen convicts being led to the gallows. Their up-and-at-'em, us-against-the-world, menacing aggression — Travis Bickle meets the Service Crew — was no match for the technically superior Spaniards. Smith was sent off for a two-footed lunge which O'Leary called 'a disgrace'. Bowyer had not even made it on to the pitch, banned after stamping on a Valencia player in the first leg. Same old Dirty Leeds. Same old nearly men, always choking.

Being knocked out in Spain knocked the stuffing out of their Premiership campaign. United finished fourth, failing by one place to get back into the Champions League. At the end of the season it was revealed that the debt had risen from £9 to £60 million and that the wage bill was £38 million and rising. This was not just the result of expensive buys; the wonderkids were now coming out of their youth contracts and were due hefty pay rises. Another season of failure – defined, quite simply, as not qualifying for the Champions League – would be a financial catastrophe.

Still, on New Year's Day 2002, the big-bucks-chasing-big-bucks strategy appeared to be back on track. Reinforced by the Toxteth Terror, the legendary Robbie Fowler, Leeds stuffed West Ham 3-0 to go three points clear at the top of the table. And they looked a fair bet to stay top until the end of the season. At the very worst they might finish third, which would still get them back into the Champions League. As thousands of fans poured out of Elland Road, singing 'We are top of the league, I say we are top of the league', there was a tangible feeling that the babies were, finally, maturing into a side of world-beaters. And there were lots more rookies coming through on the Thorp Arch academy conveyor belt. And O'Leary, it appeared, had money to burn. And it was not just the scoreline, it was the manner of the victory: two predatory strikes from Viduka and a sublime chip from Fowler. No wonder Liverpool fans called him god. No wonder O'Leary, on signing him two months earlier, had argued that four strikers – Smith, Viduka, Keane and Kewell – were not enough. As I chatted excitedly to my brother about the upcoming FA Cup tie at Cardiff, neither of us had any idea about the board's £60-million gamble. No one had. If we'd had any idea, would we have cared? They seemed to know what they were doing. Football was booming, Leeds were flying and O'Leary exuded self-belief. He had even asked for the Cardiff game to be switched to the Welsh city's showcase Millennium Stadium, which at the time was hosting the Cup Final while the new Wembley was being built. It would, he said, be 'excellent preparation for us if we go back there in May. We're well capable of beginning and finishing our Cup campaign there.' The entire edifice of the brand was based on confidence. And, on 1 January 2002, confidence was sky high.

Admittedly, there had been a slight hitch when the board had been forced to drop their plans for a glitzy, state-of-the-art, out-of-town football stadium – another potentially lucrative revenue stream. But at least this meant we were now staying at Fortress Elland Road, the giant spaceship on the edge of town, our spiritual home. The chairman had blamed his failure to sell the all-important naming rights for the new ground on the post-9/11 economy. But a more likely cause had been the bad publicity surrounding 'Bowyergate'. In January 2000, an Asian student had been beaten to within an inch of his life in Leeds City Square. Two of O'Leary's babies, Bowyer and Woodgate, had been arrested for taking part in the assault.

6. Wilderness

'Leeds were going to be this new model club, the Barcelona of England, a sporting hub for the community. They were going to reinvent the football club and reinvent Leeds as a non-racist city. Financially it would have collapsed anyway. But Bowyergate brought back the racist, lumpen, violent image that they'd been trying to shed. That precipitated the decline. Now what are you left with? A horrible stadium that hasn't been touched, a horrible area and third division football'

David Conn, 2008

*2000. City Square. Jonathan Woodgate totters out of the hip-
and-happening Majestyk nightclub. He and his mates have
been on a pub crawl. They've visited a lap-dancing club and
knocked back pints of rum and vodka cocktails in a succes-
sion of trendy bars. The Majestyk, which in the last century
was variously a temperance hotel, a cinema and then a bingo
hall, has mutated, at the beginning of the noughties, into an
emblem of Leeds' twenty-four-hour, hedonistic night-life
economy. Woodgate staggers past the Queen's Hotel and sees
a punch being thrown. Gripped by the pack instinct, he starts
to run, following the shouts through City Square. He falls
over, twisting his ankle. He gets up and runs past the station
and aims a flying kick at a fleeing man. Then he sees Lee
Bowyer running by. He makes it to Boar Lane and limps
past the Square On The Lane pub, where he and his friends
had started out on their binge earlier that evening. He turns
right and sees a fight taking place.*

Leeds United on Trial

There were teeth marks on Sarfraz Najeib's face. It had been fractured in six places and his leg was broken. During the trial, Hull Crown Court was told that Bowyer, Woodgate and their friends had chased him and his brother Shahzad through the city centre. In his original statement to the police, Najeib said that one of his attackers had shouted out, 'Do you want some, Paki?' But, with no independent witnesses, the judge insisted that racism had played no part in the events. The first trial collapsed when my own paper, the *Sunday Mirror*, published an interview with Najeib's father claiming the attack was racially motivated; the judge ruled the article the 'most serious form of contempt'. But the assault had not taken place in a vacuum; incidences of racial harassment in the city had increased almost thirteenfold between 1995 and 2001. And only a few months earlier, the deputy chief constable of West Yorkshire had admitted that his force did 'not have the full confidence of the minority ethnic communities'.

Woodgate was found guilty of affray but his friend Paul Clifford, who had bitten Najeib's face, was convicted of causing grievous bodily harm and sentenced to six years in prison. Bowyer was acquitted of causing GBH.

He had played out of his skin during the trial and Leeds fans, incensed by an FA ban on him playing for his country, had adopted 'Bowyer for England' as their battle cry and voted him player of the year. Once again, the accusatory finger of racism had been pointed in their direction. A *Daily Mirror* front-page headline depicted their box-to-box midfielder as 'boozing, pot-smoking, violent, racist, cowardly, unapologetic, odious' and invited the 'little scumbag' to sue. During the court case he'd been taunted by opposition fans with 'Bowyer's going down' chants. He was now the most demonised figure in British sport. At Elland Road, however, he was elevated to the status of a folk hero. Although the crowd's love affair with the player – as with Cantona before him and Smith soon afterwards – ended in vilification, Leeds were tainted not only by the attack but also by their fans' response. The 'racist' club had spent the past decade trying to cleanse itself. As the BBC's Fergal Keane observed in a *Panorama* programme on the trial, they 'were confronted with the most damaging crisis in their history, a crisis that couldn't but summon up memories of the bad old days at Elland Road'.

In the last ten years, Woodgate has talked about becoming a new man and Bowyer has pointed out to several interviewers that, despite being cleared of all charges, he is 'still thought of as guilty'. Lucas Radebe insisted that neither player was a racist and in *Leeds United On Trial*, O'Leary wrote that a member of the reserve team, 'a Leeds-born Asian', was often seen 'chatting and laughing with Bow and Woody'.

This was the first public mention of Harpal Singh since the coach had told a television crew, four years earlier, that the youngster would 'eventually become a first team squad member'. Like Johanneson in the sixties, there had been a huge burden of expectation on Singh's shoulders. George Graham had compared him to Michael Owen but, although his successor's much-vaunted policy was to give youth its head, Singh never made the grade. After O'Leary splashed out £3 million on Jason Wilcox, the New Owen disappeared. Following loan spells with three clubs, he was eventually sold to League Two strugglers Stockport. In the 1990s, a report by Jas Bains and Raj Patel claimed that the vast majority of professional club officials felt Asians were physically inferior. It spoke of 'good intentions' but also of under-representation, lack of access, denial of opportunity and the 'inability of too many officials, scouts, coaches and managers to look beyond the negative stereotypical images still held of British Asians'. Zesh Rehman became the first Asian to play in the top flight in 2004 before moving from Fulham to QPR. But a Commission For Racial Equality survey of the same year identified only ten Asians at Premier League academies, 0.8 per cent of the total figure. In the sixties and seventies, blacks had been stereotyped as skilled footballers but poor tacklers. It was claimed that they couldn't cope with Britain's cold winters and lacked dedication. The likes of Ces Podd and West Ham's Clyde Best had blown away those myths. According to Bains, Asians were being held up by different stereotypes – like not eating the right food and having no interest in football.

The latter myth would have been easily dispelled by any weekend stroll through the ribbon of green bordering the red-brick houses of Beeston. In Cross Flatts Park, which overlooks Elland Road, hundreds of young Asians played football from dawn until dusk. But tensions had been simmering in the traditionally white working-class area – which in the past thirty years had become home to a number of first- and second-generation citizens from Pakistan – since the murders of two Leeds fans in Istanbul in 2000. Bowyergate brought these tensions to the boil. Ridsdale's refusal to follow England's example and ban the players until the case had ended, even going so far as to fly Bowyer to and from court for some games, enraged the Asian community – and completely undermined his campaign to reinvent the club as a cosmopolitan, community friendly business that took anti-racism seriously.

During the period of the trial, parts of Leeds and Bradford were scarred by some of the worst racial unrest for twenty years. There was a revival of the old Kop chant 'Town full of Pakis, you're just a town full of Pakis' and, at one notorious game at Leicester, United thugs hurled abuse at the British-born Turkey international Muzzy Izzet. When Leeds fan Shakeel Meer confronted a group of supporters who had been chanting offensive songs about the trial, he was told it was 'the Paki's' fault for getting the stars arrested. A chat-room contributor recalled Kopites shouting, 'Oy get back to your fucking shop, you should be selling beers and fags not coming here and watching football' at two Asians. Najeib's father said the club had showed 'no shame or responsibility' in their handling of the affair. In his book, O'Leary recalled being taunted in the school playground for being a 'Paddy'. But, while condemning racism, violence and binge-drinking, he also implied that Leeds United, not Najeib, were the principal victims of the whole episode, revealing that they had received hate mail from 'misguided Asians [who] apparently wanted to declare a jihad, a holy war, on the players . . .'

Three-and-a-half years after the trial ended, on 7 July 2005, Mohammad Sidique Khan, Shehzad Tanweer and Hasib Hussain took part in the largest and deadliest terrorist attack on London's transit system, killing fifty-two commuters. Sidique Khan, the leader of the gang, was one of a group of second-generation Pakistanis called the 'Mullah boys', formed in the mid-1990s as a response to the drugs issue. The Beeston-based group kidnapped young addicts and, with the consent of their families, forcibly cleansed them of their habits. Tanweer, who was born in Bradford and grew up in Beeston, had trials for Yorkshire County Cricket Club and starred in midfield for Holbeck FC. He also boxed and excelled in athletics. His uncle, Bashir Ahmed, told a reporter: 'He was just a good British boy growing up, a sports fan from a good family. It is hard to accept what must have happened to him.' Hussain, like Sidique Khan, went to Matthew Murray High School in Holbeck. Months before the terrorist attack, the school won an award for promoting racial harmony. According to his friends, he was quiet and lacked confidence. Overshadowed by his older brother Imran, his main outlet for expression was his first love – football. He was part of a close-knit group, which also included Sidique Khan and Tanweer, who played football every week in Cross Flatts Park. A few days after the terrorist outrage, one of the group was quoted by the *Wall Street Journal* as saying: 'It was them. Why aren't they here if it wasn't them? They never missed a game.'

Some British race relations experts have argued that thirty years after the establishment of any sizeable ethnic minority community there will be riots. Thirty years after East European Jewish immigration into Leeds there was a mini-pogrom in the Leylands. Thirty years after Afro-Caribbean immigration into Chapeltown there were violent clashes with police. And, thirty years after Pakistani immigration into northern England, there was urban unrest in Leeds, Oldham, Burnley and Bradford. An investigation into the civil disorders concluded that 'parallel lives' and ethnic segregation had generated deep-rooted divisions. According to Shiv Malik, who spent several months in Beeston researching the 7/7 bombers, 'it takes about thirty years for a sizeable second generation to establish itself and then become frustrated with its status, both within its own community and the wider society. This frustration arises in part from a question of identity. Whose culture and values do you affiliate with? Those of your parents or of your friends? Those of your community or of your country? Religion – in this case a purified and politicised version of Islam, far from the traditional "folk" religion of the first generation – is a natural way of transcending this cultural dislocation. It gives you a sense of belonging.'

On receiving an honorary degree from Leeds Metropolitan University in 1997, Caryl Phillips praised Leeds' openness to strangers. He recalled growing up in a district where the black, brown and white working classes lived, worked and played side by side. While

Elland Road in the 1960s was hardly a model of cross-cultural integration, it undoubtedly gave my previously marginalised tribe a sense of belonging. Through passionately supporting – and generously financing – the club, the Jews made a place for themselves in the city. It is hard not to contrast their integration into Revie's Leeds United with the Asian community's alienation from the modern-day incarnation. Many second- and third-generation Jews – Ziff, Cohen, Cussins, Simon, Morris, Bellow – played a pivotal role in the rise of both the team and the city in the sixties. Today, many second- and third-generation Asians struggle with their dual identities, feeling themselves to be neither Pakistani nor British. They are 'British' outside the home, wearing Western clothes, smoking and following football. But inside it they wear the salwar kameez, defer respectfully to their elders, dutifully take care of chores and observe daily prayers. Most juggle their parallel lives with skill. Some even marry white women. But when it comes to issues such as Iraq and radical Islam, the tensions are at their highest; they led Sidique Khan, one of the London bombers, and his wife Hasina to split up. Parallel lives become secret lives. Parents, friends and imams lose control and influence.

Since the London bombings there has been a deepening distrust between mainstream society and a growing number of isolated Muslim communities. Many areas of Leeds are off-limits to young British Muslims. Conversely, certain Muslim enclaves are seen as no-go areas for whites; surveys have revealed that these communities have the highest rates of unemployment, the poorest health and the fewest educational qualifications of any faith group in the country. Approximately 60 per cent of British Muslims live in the poorest areas of Leeds – Beeston, Harehills and Hyde Park. Some of the film crews swarming into Beeston after 7/7 were surprised to find Muslim lads, whose families had arrived after the Second World War from Pakistan, Bangladesh and India, speaking with broad Yorkshire vowels, working in chippies and playing football. But it was clear that very few of them, if any, followed their local team. In an *Observer* feature on the estate, which appeared on the Sunday after the bombings, a young man called Imran declared: 'I would rather die than support Leeds United. I would never support Leeds; they're a bunch of racist scumbags.'

The Fall

2001. The trial is over and Leeds put Bowyer on the transfer list and drop him from the team for refusing to pay a club fine. Bowyer complains of 'victimisation'. Leeds beat Everton 3-2 and after each goal the players come over to salute Bowyer, who is sitting in the stands. It is their way of showing solidarity with their beleaguered team-mate. It is a huge V-sign to the board, the media, the world. A banner in the crowd warns the board: 'Lose Bowyer – lose the title'.

And then came the Fall. Football's most notorious financial collapse. Having borrowed heavily to live the dream, the brand imploded. Panic set in and confidence nose-dived. The club were devoured from within by a toxic combination of excessive debt, self-doubt and bitter in-fighting. They plummeted, like a stone in the well, until they hit rock bottom. For the next five years, separated from the golden umbilical cord of the TV largesse, they were locked into a dive; a fast-moving, downward vortex in which losses and high wages fed debts, which in turn produced yet more losses and yet more debts. O'Leary had been right about beginning and finishing the 2001-2 Cup campaign in Cardiff. The Welsh underdogs cut the Premiership leaders down to size, winning a nasty, brutish encounter 2-1. Violence erupted in the stands. Police with dogs were called in to restore order and the rattled Irishman had to be restrained from taking a swipe at the Cardiff chairman. Something had snapped.

The 'Bowyergate' verdicts had just come through. Bowyer was acquitted but Woodgate was sentenced to one hundred hours community service for affray. O'Leary warned his players against speaking publicly on the trial but then wrote a book – *Leeds United On Trial* – which gave the distinct impression that he himself was trying to cash in on it. He vigorously denied this charge, of course, but his observation that 'as many, if not more, detectives from the West Yorkshire police force were employed in the detection of this crime as were used in the hunt for . . . the Yorkshire Ripper' did not play well with the local Asian community. And his suggestion that it might have been better had Bowyer and Woodgate been jailed did not play well with the Leeds United community.

The shameful saga sapped, in Leighton-speak – and then rapidly began to unravel – a club whose solidarity and sprightly enthusiasm had been a feature of their seemingly unstoppable ascent. In football's new global age, stories about binge-drinking and violent disorder – never mind accusations of racism – were bound to undermine Leeds Sporting's attempt to rebrand itself as a modern entertainment corporation. 'It seemed that wherever I went in the world,' wrote O'Leary, 'from Madrid to Dubai to Rome, television networks such as CNN were providing daily bulletins on the fortunes of the Leeds United players at Hull Crown Court.' As his team were dumped out of the UEFA Cup by an average Dutch club, and then slid down the table, the self-styled naive young manager buckled under the strain. He publicly criticised his team for underper-forming. He had rows with Danny Mills, Robbie Keane and Olivier Dacourt. He fell out with Kewell; 'Harry thought he was a Zidane,' he said. 'He wasn't.' His rela-tionship with Ridsdale broke down. Woodgate faded to a cadaver. Net debt had reached £82 million and the annual wage bill had jumped to £53 million. United finished fifth in the Premiership, once again outside the Champions League places, which was a poor finish for a team that had cost £66 million. Attendances had fallen following a terrible run – they went half a season with just two wins – and gate receipts were badly down. With the operating profit of previous years trans-formed into an operating loss of £8 million, Leighton expressed his alarm at the way the club was being run. The big-bucks-chasing-big-bucks strategy had been blown out of the water. Spend, spend, spend was over;

it was time to sell, sell, sell. Ridsdale advised O'Leary
to toe the party line, but the coach went off-message
and publicly opposed Ferdinand's sale to Manchester
United. This gave the board the perfect excuse to sack
him. He left at the end of the 2001–2 season, the first
of nine men to manage the club during the decade.

In order to reduce the level of debt, and protect
shareholder value, Leeds were forced to sell all their
top players. The timing for a fire sale could not have
been worse. The transfer market was collapsing so
most players, apart from Ferdinand – offloaded for an
astonishing £29 million – had to be sold at a loss.
Rival clubs, knowing Leeds were desperate, exploited
their obvious distress to pick up discount buys. The
slump in form also contributed to a drop in the players' value. And the introduction of the transfer window
– a fixed period during the year in which clubs can
buy or sell players – exposed Leeds to end-of-window
brinkmanship. Keane went to Spurs for £7 million,
Bowyer to West Ham for £100,000 (six months after
Leeds had agreed a £9 million fee with Liverpool), Woodgate to Newcastle for £9 million, Fowler to Manchester
City for £6 million. The downward spiral – loss of
confidence, panic, more loss of confidence – was now
unstoppable. Becoming a selling club undermined
morale, which led to a further loss of form, which
then produced another fall in attendances and a slump
in television income. Leeds Sporting was now in the
grip of a £103 million debt. Sell, sell, sell had been
a complete disaster.

Initially praised to the skies for his ambition, Ridsdale
was now perceived by a vocal section of fans to be a

liability. According to several media commentators, he had become giddy with his own celebrity. His retort was that every single decision had been backed by the whole board – and he blamed O'Leary for spending a fortune and failing, on two successive occasions, to deliver Champions League football. O'Leary, in turn, blamed Ridsdale for signing the cheques. And the supporters, myself included – who had been high on the opiate of success and fully convinced that Leeds would, at long last, return to the elite – felt completely bewildered by it all. One minute we were in Champions League heaven, the next we were in Hades. The gamble on going global, on becoming a permanent fixture in the world's biggest club competition, had spectacularly backfired. Just as Leeds were about to close in on the promised land, they had spontaneously combusted. A nation rejoiced. 'You'd have to be from another planet, one where football doesn't exist,' wrote Danny Kelly in *The Times*, 'not to understand exactly why the fall of one of the game's most prominent clubs has been the biggest excuse for a national knee-trembler since VE-Day.'

The Goldfish Years

In May 2004, a hundred years after the formation of Leeds City, Leeds United dropped out of the top flight. On being expelled from the Football League, City had been obliged to sell off all their players at knockdown prices at the Metropole Hotel, just across the road from the railway station. This ceremonial auctioning of footballing flesh raised £10,000. Leeds United's auction lasted a full two years, at the end of which – unsurprisingly – they were relegated. Three years after that they dropped down into the old third division, were placed in administration, sold off their stadium and training ground and came within a whisker of being expelled from the League.

The first fire sale came during Terry Venables' reign. O'Leary's successor lasted only nine months, during which time he was forced to offload Ferdinand, Keane, Fowler, Woodgate, Bowyer and Dacourt. Ridsdale's final, desperate throw of the dice was the appointment of Peter Reid as caretaker manager. The former Sunderland boss kept Leeds up following an end-of-season win at Arsenal, but the squad had been stripped bare. As debts of £103 million were announced, Ridsdale resigned. A number of stories were then leaked about his financial recklessness, some of them no doubt apocryphal.

He was succeeded by 'Professor' John McKenzie. The Prof immediately set about rubbishing the previous regime, even though, towards the end, he'd been an integral part of it. He denounced the private jets and helicopters, the fleet of company cars and the £100 million the board had allowed O'Leary to spend. And he outed Ridsdale as a tropical goldfish enthusiast, at the club's expense. The ex-chairman admitted spending £240 on their upkeep but protested that 'nobody ever raised it as an issue. If they had, I'd have fed them myself.' Still, the damaging revelation of his £20-a-month habit served its purpose. McKenzie happily publicised the bill as an emblem of excess. The removal of the tank from his office, like Cloughie's bonfire of the dossiers and Wilko's purge of the Revie-ites, symbolised the end of an era.

The first three players out of the Prof's revolving door were Harry Kewell, Danny Mills and Nigel Martyn. Immediately after relegation from the Premiership, Paul Robinson was sold to Spurs, followed by Mark Viduka to Middlesbrough and Dominic Matteo to Blackburn. The departure which hurt fans the most, though, was Alan Smith's. Born and bred in Leeds, Smith was canonised and then pilloried within the space of a week. After kissing the badge in time-honoured fashion, the People's Smudger was mobbed at Elland Road in his last game for the club. But as soon as he announced he was high-tailing it across Saddleworth Moor, going back on a pledge 'never to sign for Manchester United', he instantly replaced Ridsdale as the People's Enemy.

The mysterious McKenzie, after sacking Reid in November 2003 with relegation beckoning and bringing in Eddie Gray for a second stint as manager, then packed his bags; after only nine months in the post he had bolted, never to be seen again. Trevor Birch became chief executive and negotiated a series of standstill agreements to stop the club going under. But, when Kevin Blackwell was appointed manager, only two established first-team players remained on the books. One of them, Gary Kelly, was on £46,000 a week.

In March 2004, as Blackwell stabilised the team by signing players on free transfers and low wages, another new board, headed by insolvency expert Gerald Krasner, rode to the rescue. Leeds were two and a half years into meltdown and seemingly destined for administration. At first the £22 million takeover was welcomed by fans. The consortium put £5 million into the club and cut the wage bill from £38 to £18 million. Then they borrowed £15 million from property developer Jack Petchey, which was spent paying off creditors. The club, however, still had significant debts and an unpayable wage bill that produced a loss of £29.7 million. Time for another fire sale. 'They hadn't lived the dream,' said Krasner, referring to the Ridsdale regime. 'They'd lived the nightmare. The squad was too big, wages were too high and some butchery was needed.' All the remaining star players, the Thorp Arch training ground and a new crop of 'babies' – including Aaron Lennon, Scott Carson and James Milner – were flogged in order to bring in some firefighting money. Inevitably, United were relegated after fourteen years among the elite. This was hard enough for supporters to stomach, but when Elland Road was sold to the council on a sale-and-lease-back arrangement there was uproar. Managing director David Richmond returned to his house one day to find his front gates padlocked. A sign saying 'Richmond Must Go' had been placed against them. And so he went. As, eventually, did the rest of the board, selling up to Ken Bates in January 2005 for £10 million.

The cantankerous, seventy-three-year-old Monaco tax exile, acting on behalf of an off-shore firm based in the Cayman Islands, appeared an unlikely saviour. For twenty years, before a certain Russian billionaire made him an offer he couldn't refuse – an estimated £17 million – Bates had been Mr Chelsea. Flash Cockneys, as Venables had discovered, are traditionally given short shrift at Leeds. A song about shooting the 'Chelsea scum' has been part of the Kop's repertoire ever since the notoriously brutal 1970 Cup Final replay. Undeterred by such tribal opposition, and using the wealth he had gained from the Roman Abramovich sale, Bates managed, for the time being at least, to side-step the bailiffs. In 2006, against all the odds, Blackwell steered Leeds into a top-six finish and the Championship play-offs. But we know our one-off-all-or-nothing-big-occasion history. On a wet and demoralising afternoon in Cardiff the team, once again, froze. When the Leeds players walked out at the Millennium Stadium, they appeared to be spooked by the indoor fireworks. Watford duly thrashed them 3-0. After a poor start to the following season Blackwell was axed and Bates brought in his good friend Dennis Wise. Wise was not a popular figure

in Leeds. This was partly due to his Chelsea connec-
tions, but also to the fact that he lost twenty-five games
in his first season in charge – condemning the team to
a second relegation in three years.

Leeds United had never experienced life in the third
tier of English football before. Not even in the
prehistoric, pre-Revie age. The schadenfreude was
uncontainable. In some parts of the country the Ipswich
goal that sent them down into what was now called
League One sparked minor celebrations. And the pitch
invasion that followed the goal revived memories of the
bad old days of football hooliganism; every transgression,
from the 1971 anti-Tinkler protest to the 1982
Hawthorns riot was recounted in vivid detail. The Fall
of Leeds was presented as some kind of early noughties
morality tale, a parable of greed, excess and hubris. How
deluded of the club to think they could build a team
to match the citadels of Manchester and London, let
alone Milan and Madrid. They had pulled out the credit
card, gone on a wild spending binge and the bill had
fallen due. Now it was payback time. 'It is tempting,'
wrote the *Daily Telegraph*'s Sue Mott, 'to believe in some
kind of supernatural retribution.' The ghost of old Don
had returned, once again, to haunt United. Giles Smith,
in *The Times*, pointed out that 'in any argument about
right and wrong in football, a reference to Revie's Leeds
United is the nuclear option. There is, quite simply,
nowhere to go after that. There has never been a more
horrible team . . .'

The lower the club sank the more, it seemed, his
team's 'horribleness' was invoked – inside as well as outside
Elland Road. In his first press conference as manager,

Wise had pointed to the pictures of Bremner, Charlton and Hunter hanging on the wall – restored after the early nineties Wilko purge – and said that his boys would emulate their 'nastiness and togetherness . . . I have spoken to the players here and I have told them that I want them to be like the Leeds United of before, and they were horrible.' Two years later, after replacing Wise's successor Gary McAllister to become the club's ninth manager in ten years, Simon Grayson revealed that similar pictures of Bremner, Charlton and Hunter had adorned his bedroom wall as a kid. On the tenth anniversary of Bremner's death, the letters HYC – Huddersfield Young Casuals – were sprayed on his statue outside Elland Road. Wise said he had a special message for the HYC: 'I'd just like to say up yours.' This went down a storm with the fans but incensed several scribes, one of whom depicted his relationship with Bates as a reincarnation of the 'rancorously defiant' Revie–Bremner partnership. In one review of Peace's *The Damned Utd*, a literary critic not previously known for his interest in football felt moved to condemn the Bates–Wise regime as 'an institution corrupted by Revie's paranoia'.

No one does paranoia better than Leeds United. In May 2007, with relegation virtually assured, the club was declared insolvent and went into administration, its debts calculated by administrators KPMG at £38 million. HM Revenue & Customs challenged the fact that they had entered a Company Voluntary Arrangement, leaving most creditors with a much lower return on the money they owed. So KPMG terminated the CVA and held an auction to sell the club. Bates

In the 36 years since Revie's departure, only one Leeds manager has delivered a major trophy. Howard Wilkinson, whose side lifted the 1992 title, removed all reminders of the Revie years from around Elland Road.

Eric Cantona holds the 1992 championship trophy aloft. 'Eric likes to do what he likes when he likes and then he fucks off,' said Wilko. After fucking off to Manchester United for only £1 million, Eric led Alex Ferguson's side to four Premiership titles and two doubles.

David O'Leary, on the touchline during a 1-1 draw with Liverpool in October 2001,
guided Leeds to three consecutive top-four finishes between 1998 and 2001.

Peter Ridsdale 'enjoys the dream', parading United's new £18 million signing
Rio Ferdinand – a world record fee for a defender – at Elland Road in November 2000.

O'Leary and Ridsdale tell a press conference why they have signed Robbie Fowler –
seated between them – from Liverpool for £11 million. And why four strikers – Alan Smith,
Mark Viduka, Robbie Keane and Harry Kewell – are not enough. 14 months later debt-ridden
Leeds are forced to sell Fowler to Manchester City for £6 million.

A shaven-headed Alan Smith in action in the Champions League semi-final second leg against Valencia in May 2001. Leeds lost 3-0, Smith was sent off for a two-footed lunge and 'the dream' was over.

When the trial was over, Leeds put Bowyer on the transfer list and dropped him for refusing to pay a club fine. Woodgate paid the fine but buckled under the strain. 'Bowyergate' undermined the club's attempt to rebrand themselves. Once again, the accusatory finger of racism had been pointed in their direction.

Fans give a message
to Ridsdale during the
Everton-Leeds match
at Goodison Park in
February 2003.

Harvey Nichols,
an icon of retailing, opened
its first regional store
outside London in 1996 –
and became an instant
symbol of the New Leeds.

The Billy Bremner statue outside the Elland Road stadium. It was erected in 1999 and is as close as modern Leeds gets to a signature piece of public art.

Presenter Jeff Stelling reminisces about the Golden Age with (*left to right*) Jack Charlton, Paul Reaney and Norman Hunter on the 2009 Sky Sports show *The Revie Years*.

Simon Grayson congratulates Jermaine Beckford after the striker's goal knocks
Manchester United out of the FA Cup in January 2010.

Current Leeds chairman Ken Bates. In May 2007, with relegation virtually assured,
the club was declared insolvent and went into administration. Bates then, controversially, bought
it back from the receivers as the front man for an offshore group of resolutely-anonymous
investors. For failing to meet the terms of the Football League's insolvency rules, United were
forced to start their first ever season in the old third division with a fifteen-point deduction.

Jermaine Beckford celebrates after scoring the winner against Bristol Rovers on the last day of the 2009-10 season. This was the goal that earned Leeds their first promotion in 20 years.

Beckford's strike partner Luciano Becchio is carried off the Elland Road pitch by fans after the Bristol Rovers game. Despite pleas on the Tannoy to keep off, the green turf quickly disappeared beneath a sea of delirious white.

then, controversially, bought it back from the receivers as the front man for an offshore group of resolutely anonymous investors. For failing to meet the terms of the Football League's insolvency rules, however, United were forced to start their first ever season in the old third division with a fifteen-point deduction, a handicap voted for by almost all the other League clubs. This was presented by Chairman Ken as a 'stitch-up' and produced another gallery-pleasing quote from Wise: 'They've not only taken my arms and legs off, they've cut me balls off as well.' The soundbite immediately appeared on street vendors' T-shirts. At the start of the following season, despite – or more likely because of – the points deduction, Leeds won their first eight games and by Boxing Day led the division. One month later, completely out of the blue, Wise resigned to become executive director of Newcastle United.

As in the 1980s, Leeds decided to look to their own to get them back into the big time. The Revieites were getting on a bit, so Bates turned to two Wilkoites for salvation. McAllister, a star of the 1992 title-winning side, took them to the 2008 play-off final with a pleasingly aesthetic brand of football. But, in their first ever appearance at the new Wembley, they lost to Doncaster – another lamentable performance – and after a poor start to the following campaign, including a humiliating Cup defeat at the hands of non-league Histon, he was sacked. Bates then appointed another old boy, Grayson, who had regularly warmed the bench – occasionally alongside Cantona – during the 1992 title-winning season. On arrival at Elland Road, the former Blackpool coach was blunt and to the point.

'The club have reached rock bottom,' he said. 'We can't go any lower.'

The Team That Never Was

2009. By Leeds City station I sit down and weep . . . Robinson or Carson in goal . . . Always the station, always the train. Leeds have reached three play-offs in four years – and choked in all of them . . . Woodgate, Garbutt, Kilgallon and Harte at the back . . . Two finals – Watford 2006, Doncaster 2007 – and now this semi-final, against Millwall. Elland Road is now owned by the city council. It has become a heritage site; the stadium that football forgot, a theatre of broken dreams, a stubborn survival of an irrecoverable past. It is a temple to the glory and the doom, the pride and the shame, the optimism and the pessimism of the self-appointed capital of God's Own Country . . . McPhail, Lennon, Milner and Delph in midfield . . . It was once a stage for the performance of heaven, a citadel of power, a shrine to modernity, a beacon guiding all the diverse tribes of Leeds to their predestined end; the pot of gold at the end of the rainbow. Now it is a time capsule, a nostalgia-drenched enclosure for a third-tier football team whose passionate and loyal fans continue to drift in and out every other week, shifting and mingling in stands, and drinking in bars named after old folk legends and warrior-kings . . . Kewell and Keogh, or maybe Smithy, up front . . . There is a Four Yorkshiremen-esque pining for the squalor and unrelieved bleakness of the good-old-bad-old-days. And, as the image, the soundbite, the idea that the civic boosters tried to convey to the world – of a busy, modern, thriving hub of commerce and industry – all collapse, and provincial urban renewal is exposed as a mirage and social mobility grinds to a halt, Leeds seeks solace in its past, takes refuge in its ugly-beautiful mists and embraces the relentless rain, the dark skies and the unending gloom of a mythical, vanishing north . . . Rose, Taiwo, Swan and Woods as subs . . .

Six weeks into Grayson's reign, Leeds lost 2-0 at Hereford and the fans turned on the team, singing 'You're not fit to wear the shirt'. After taking his new charges to see *The Damned United*, the manager joked to Bates that at least he had lasted longer than Clough. The chairman replied that it had been a close-run thing. Eventually, Grayson turned things around and United won their last 11 home games, matching a forty-year-old record from the Revie era, to qualify for the 2008–9 League One play-offs. And then, once again, they choked. After watching them being dumped out of the semi-final by Millwall at Elland Road, I decided to walk back to the station. It took about an hour and gave me a chance to wind down and reflect on a decade of shame and humiliation.

It had all started so promisingly. The glory days were coming back. O'Leary's freewheeling youngsters had, it seemed, finally released Leeds from the purgatory of their post-Paris decline. They were top of the Premier League, staring down at Manchester United and about to embark on a great big European adventure. They even made noises about supplanting Ferguson's team as English football's dominant force. And why not? Thorp Arch, their acclaimed – and envied – conveyor-belt of home-grown talent, was already producing the next generation of Woodgates, Smiths and Kewells.

During the course of the noughties, however, they had gone from threatening to win the Champions League to threatening to win the old third division. They had disappeared from the spotlight in a decade when English football had conquered the globe. When the world's richest league had lived it up. When broadcast contracts, transfer budgets and wages had all reached galactic levels. When the top flight had attracted some of the best footballers on the planet. When the top clubs, like the global economy, had lost all inhibitions about debt, becoming slicker both on and off the field. When Abramovich's takeover at Stamford Bridge, where he spent £700 million in six years, had opened the floodgates for other mega-rich owners – most notably Sheikh Mansour's Abu Dhabi United Group, who bought Manchester City and pumped £242 million into the transfer market. Thorp Arch had, indeed, produced a new generation of stars, but they had become part of a diaspora scattered across the far corners of the Premiership. Lennon, Milner and Fabian Delph had been snapped up by teams trying to break into the top four. Michael Woods, Danny Rose, Tom Taiwo, Luke Garbutt, George Swan and Louis Hutton had been poached before they had a chance to take their driving tests. They joined Smith, Harte, Robinson, Scott Carson, Woodgate, McPhail, Andy Keogh and Matthew Kilgallon – and a host of other former academy 'babies' – in the ultimate what-if fantasy football team of the noughties. Thorp Arch United: the team that never was.

There had been 37,000 people inside Elland Road for the Millwall game, 36,000 of whom were Leeds fans. The supporters' faith had endured through the darkest of times. The ground's average attendance had been around 23,000, astonishing for a third-tier team. Leeds had the largest away following of any of the 72 Football League clubs – 2,480 on average. The atmosphere against Millwall had been incredible. The noise, just like the old days, had been over-whelming. And yet, at the end of a decade when the Premier League had gone stratospheric, the club were about to spend a third successive season in a league whose name most fans still had trouble recalling.

As I walked out of the ground, to the inevitable strains of 'We are the champions, the champions of Europe', I looked up at the row of red-brick houses on top of Beeston Hill, starkly silhouetted against the night sky. 'We'll always have Paris,' I found myself muttering. As I made my way back to the glass-and-steel towers of the city centre, past the boarded-up houses, the enclaves of sheltered housing, the derelict warehouses and the abandoned shops, it seemed – just like in the wilderness years – that we would never escape our history; our fate. I was walking through *Billy Liar* land, the area Hoggart had grown up in; where he had absorbed the dying white working-class culture immortalised in *The Uses Of Literacy*. Back then, in the 1950s, it had been a slum district. Its inhabitants, he had written, were 'not climbing. They do not quarrel with their general level.' Fifty years later, while no longer a slum, it had become the land of the marginalised and the forgotten, a testament to

the failure of urban regeneration. It was completely
off the shiny new Leeds' compass, home to an under-
class which had little stake in the city and appeared
to be as spiritually deprived and detached from the
mainstream of society as the Victorian working classes
had been over a century ago, when Colonel Harding
unveiled the Black Prince.

Leeds, its mayor had insisted back then, must be at
the very epicentre of change, must rise above the
sordid and rejoice in the beautiful. It must be brought
out of its prickly isolation and engage with, become
part of, the modern world. It must be integrated into
the mainstream and reinvent itself as a forward-
looking, twentieth-century city. It must, like every
other northern city – and most other northern towns
– be represented at the national level by a football
team. And its football team must become part of the
elite. At the beginning of the twenty-first century, its
football team's thrilling assault on the citadels of
Manchester, Milan and Madrid appeared to provide
evidence that it had, indeed, reinvented itself; that it
could thrive in the fluid networks of global consumer
capitalism. Ten years on, however, it had become a
doughnut city: jam in the middle, unleavened dough
in the ring beyond.

United's training ground might have migrated to
the northern heights, but Elland Road, the club's spiritual home, remained in the doughy ring. On my last
visit to Thorp Arch, just a few months before the
living-the-dream meltdown, I had watched the players
clip-clop across the courtyard to a car park filled with
Ferraris and Porsches. Some of them lived in the neigh-

bouring picture-book villages, others had moved into the town centre's new penthouses, only a stone's throw away from the inner-city heartland. Beeston, Hunslet, Armley and Middleton, the cluster of estates that spawned writers like Waterhouse, Bennett, Taylor-Bradford, Phillips, Hall and Harrison, had been the engine room of the industrial revolution, the catalyst for Leeds' late-Victorian rise. In this lost decade, their plain terraced streets had become a byword for un-relenting misery. Leeds has always been a place of comers and goers, but the only people coming in and out of 'the ring' had been journalists, documentary-makers and film directors, all hungry for 'broken society' vignettes.

In her brilliant book *Estates* (2007), Lynsey Hanley examined the stigma that was still, fifty years after *The Uses Of Literacy*, attached to inner-city dwellers. Some young children from disadvantaged backgrounds, she noted, seemed to have walls in their heads. The phrase was first used by Germans to describe the East Berliners' reluctance to integrate with the western part of the city after the Berlin Wall had come down. The wall in your head is a barrier to knowledge and self-aware-ness. To breach the wall, wrote Hanley, you must 'find a crack in it and whittle out a little escape route . . . you believe yourself to be proud of having overcome the limitations of your environment . . . and yet you know that in some ways you will never escape.' To make her point, Hanley quoted a line from Penny Woolcock's TV drama *Tiny Goes Shopping*, which was set in Beeston: 'No one ever comes here − and no one ever leaves.'

During a decade in which Britain had undergone the biggest growth in inequality since Victorian times, a stream of storytellers had scratched beneath the glistening veneer of Barcelona-on-Aire to discover an unchanged world of deprivation and hopelessness. To the south and east of the city, only a mile or two from the glazed-over Victoria Quarter, were sprawling estates up to fourth-generation unemployment. Despite the apparent boom, something had gone wrong. The tone of these writers' work was far removed from the New Wave books and films of the late 1950s and early 1960s, lacking that belief in the essential decency of the working classes found in *Billy Liar*, *This Sporting Life* and other kitchen-sink classics. Their world was as gritty and realistic as the West Riding of, say, *Room At The Top* and *A Kind Of Loving* – but one totally devoid of hope.

In *The Dark Heart*, Nick Davies described how the street children, beggars, muggers and joy riders of Leeds all came creeping out at night. The *Observer* commissioned novelist Sue Townsend to visit the Gipton, my dad's old stamping ground and one of Jenkinson's brave new housing estates. The socialist vicar's plan had been for a socially mixed population to live in a garden city of trees, wide boulevards, great schools and open spaces. Townsend discovered high levels of unemployment, benefit-dependency and burglary. The Gipton had fallen into the bottom 3 per cent on the national index of deprivation. It was the home of the country's nineteenth worst street for crime. If a Martian landed on the estate, she wrote, 'it would surely conclude that it had stumbled on some primitive, emerging society. You could never suppose that the poverty of the people and the landscape were the consequence of any form of governance.'

Adrian Mole's creator stood on a recreation ground and watched as three wrecked, burned-out cars, set alight by joyriders, were winched on the back of a lorry. A community leader told her that no one wanted to live in its post-war, semi-detached houses. 'When I moved here,' he said, 'it was Utopia.' The government gave it £23 million for urban renewal and the money was spent on renovations, fortifications and anti-joyriding measures. But the 'twockers' regarded the concrete barriers and bollards as a new challenge. As David McKie wrote in *A Local History Of Britain* (2008): 'The enrichment of the richest duly took place. But where are the signs of trickledown on the Gipton estate? It was created with the very best of intentions for families who had previously lived in squalid slums . . . it is sad, but inescapably true – it has always been sad but inescapably true – that some communities reach a pitch of dejection from which they can never recover.'

Leeds, today, is a dual city. A city with two parallel existences. It contains some of the most affluent and deprived areas in England. In its twelve inner-city districts, which have a combined population of 227,000, one family in three lives below the official poverty line. After spending most of the last decade hyping its buzzing city centre, and dropping designer fashionable names like Harvey Nichols, Paul Smith, Louis Vuitton and Vivienne Westwood, the council now acknowledges the existence of a 'city within a city'. The economic growth of the nineties was tilted towards commuter areas rather than the urban core. The number of office staff increased by a quarter after 1991, but there was an 11 per cent fall in manufacturing jobs. The UK's 'fastest-growing city' offered few opportunities to the semi-skilled workers who'd lost their jobs during the Thatcher years. Most banks pulled out of the poorer districts, leaving residents vulnerable to extortionate interest rates from loan firms. Many of these districts, like Little London, Sheepscar, Beeston and East End Park – the subject of a Feargal Keane BBC documentary called Forgotten Britain – suffered high rates of deprivation, unemployment and drug use.

As I walked back to the station after the Millwall game, reciting The Team That Never Was to 'amuse' myself, I began to notice several big holes in the ground. The jam was slipping out of the doughnut. The nineties' dream was over. It had gone the way of all other Leeds dreams, from Brodrick's – through Revie's – to Ridsdale's. The iconic Clarence Dock resembled an urban desert. The city had squandered its boom money on insipid, gimmicky projects. Only one building, the Cloth Hall Street apartments, had made it into Kenneth Powell's *New Architecture of Britain* – whereas ten Manchester developments were included. 'Leeds,' wrote Powell, 'is an architecturally timid city.' Huge cranes still dominated the skyline, but several new shopping centres had been put on hold. Kevin Linfoot, the property tycoon responsible for reshaping the face of the town centre, had commissioned Ian Simpson – the designer of Manchester's Beetham Tower – to build a monument to the shiny new city's aspiration. He called it Lumiere Towers and claimed it would be western Europe's tallest residential building. It was mothballed in August 2007. When the

£85 million Bridgewater Place – a monstrous carbuncle known locally as 'the Dalek' – opened that year, twenty-two tall buildings were going through the planning process; two years later, they had all been shelved.

At the turn of the millennium, when the first of Linfoot's new wave high-rise buildings went up and Mandela opened Millennium Square, Goths mingled outside the Corn Exchange while small, independent market stalls did business within. Two years ago, Zurich Financial Services evicted all the small, independent traders from Brodrick's circular building and turned it into an upmarket food hall. Today, 15 per cent of the apartments built for young professionals are empty. Leeds has the highest number of vacant properties of any city outside London. High-rise blocks of flats bought by buy-to-let investors have become, as one architect sneered, 'slums in the sky'. In 2009, Linfoot's company was placed in administration.

Kaddish

2009. I meet my dad at the top of the hill. He is shortly to retire as secretary of the Leeds Jewish Workers Burial Society. One of the Jewish cemeteries is about to be closed down. As uncle Louis predicted just before he died, it's all down to subsidence. If we dig out the treasures from the rocks beneath, the rocks will react. Following the collapse of several graves, civil engineers classified Hilltop Cemetery as dangerous. As I watch a small group of mourners say a Kaddish, I look out across a huge circumference of inspiration and influence. When my dad arrives he tells me he'll miss his job. He got it a couple of years after being made redundant in the 1980s. He has to pick up the dead bodies, put them in a bag and take them to the Jewish mortuary in Chapeltown. And then – after they've been washed, prepared properly for burial and dressed in a plain shroud – he puts them in a coffin, drives them to the shul and then on to one of the two remaining cemeteries at the top of the hill. A mourners' car follows his hearse to the cemetery and when they get to the cemetery they take the coffin out of the hearse and put it on to a bogie, which is a kind of a handcart. His grandparents came to Leeds in a handcart, he smiles, and now his generation are leaving in a handcart. The coffin is wheeled into the prayer house and the mourners crowd in and the rabbi delivers a eulogy and the coffin is taken down to the grave.

Over the last fifty years, the Jewish population of Leeds has shrunk significantly. In the 1950s it numbered between 20,000 and 25,000. At the time of the last census it had dropped to 8,267. There has been a steady drift away from religious observance and, like the one-time thriving areas of Newcastle, Liverpool and Sunderland, my vanishing tribe has become part of a diminishing diaspora. My great-grandparents escaped oppression and sought refuge in the Leylands. My grandparents escaped the ghetto and moved into inner-city Chapeltown. My parents integrated into post-war, multicultural Leeds. But the forward march of Leeds Jewry has come to a halt with the fourth generation. Large numbers of this – my – generation have left the city, the football club, even the religion. Many of us now reside in 'London and the south' – where there are better opportunities, better lifestyles and, allegedly, better football clubs. The Leeds Jewish community has more than halved over the past thirty years. As a recent study concluded, it is 'provincial, ageing, and slow moving'. The death rate is higher than the birth rate and there has been an upsurge in marrying out. The trend-bucking strictly orthodox are still, as the Old Testament urged, going forth and multiplying. But while some have defected to Manchester and London, others have simply withdrawn from civil society. The ultra-frummers are isolationists not integrationists; they choose to live inside an imaginary ghetto wall of ritual and faith. 'The worry,' says Rabbi Anthony Gilbert, who was one of my neighbours when I was a boy, 'is that in the next ten to fifteen years we're going to see shrinkage again on the scale of the last twenty years. In a couple of generations there'll be no Jews left.' As a national newspaper asked in 2006: 'Is this the last generation of British Jews?'

In 1950, when my uncle wrote his play *They Came to Leeds*, Anglo-Jewry numbered 450,000. Today it is 270,000 – and falling. Rabbi Adin Steinsaltz, the world's leading Talmudic scholar, believes it is demographically unviable; 'a dying community', he called it. Leeds Jewry has returned to its original, late nineteenth-century size. Back then, in the squalid, low-lying ghetto, the Yiddish-speaking settlers came up against a brick wall of bigotry, but their sons and daughters – who grew up in the hungry thirties, lived through the war and moved upwards and outwards during the never-had-it-so-good

fifties and white-heat-of-technology sixties – had, as
Hoggart observed, an 'in-built sense of the need for
movement'. Their fifty-year journey, from the inner
city, up into the suburbs – and then into the market
towns nudging the dales, is almost identical to the one
taken by Leeds United players. Revie's rookies started
out in digs in Beeston; O'Leary's babies ended up in
what estate agents call the 'magic triangle' of Wetherby,
Ilkley and Harrogate on the northern edge of Leeds.

In *The Damned Utd*, referring to directors like Manny
Cussins, Albert Morris and Sydney Simon, Peace
wrote: 'Half Gentile, half Jew; a last, lost tribe of self-
made Yorkshiremen and Israelites. In search of the
promised land; of public recognition, of acceptance and
of gratitude.' This last, lost tribe's stewardship of the
club was a wastershed moment for the community,
confirmation that they belonged; like Leeds itself, they
were going places. In a documentary on the filming
of Peace's book, a Jewish season-ticket holder described
his 'love affair' with the Revie side. 'I knew them all
as young boys,' he sighed. 'I grew up with them.'

Following the club's financial collapse in 2003 there
was an expectation that, just as Cussins and Simon had
once ridden to the rescue, so the modern-day community would stop the club from going under; as Rob
Bagchi and Paul Rogerson recounted in *The Unforgiven*,
'after years of fatalistic inertia, one week of belated
action at the end of November 1961 can still be
described as the defining week in United's history.
Without it, it's arguable whether there would be a
professional football club in the city today.' In the early
eighties, Silver had to dig deep into his pockets to stave

off bankruptcy. And in 2004 the Krasner group, referred to in one newspaper as 'a consortium of Jewish property developers', made a brief, and none too popular, appearance. The chat rooms were flooded with anti-semitic comments. If the consortium had been Catholics, would their faith have been mentioned? I even heard a few comments in various press rooms about the return of the 'Leeds kosher nostra'. This was a time when the ethnic origins of various mega-rich foreign owners – Abramovich, the Glazers – had begun to attract comment. There was nothing particularly new in this. Silver told me that he had attracted 'a lot of anti-Semitic remarks when things started going wrong'.

The Jewish influence began to wane in the board-room after 1996, the year Silver sold up to Caspian. He was the last of a dying breed. Today, a huge gulf has emerged between the ever-shrinking, inward-turning community ensconced in the affluent north and the impoverished heartland marooned south of the river. It is hard not to contrast the Jews' successful integration in the sixties with the Asian community's present alienation. Unlike second- and third-generation Asians, my parents and grandparents eventually became part of a bigger tribe: the Tribe of Don. According to a well-known axiom of the time, Leeds Rugby had Lewis Jones and Leeds United had Jewish loans. It went a lot further than that, of course. I kicked footballs into the players' back gardens. They joined our golf clubs and opened our market stalls and made guest appearances at our charity events and we all marched on together, onwards and upwards, looking forwards not backwards; the children of the new industrial poor moving away from inner-city poverty — into, or at least it seemed so at the time, an inclusive, multicultural meritocracy. Don was always in Herbert's house and Herbert was always round Don's. On Saturday morning we were part of the rebbe's congregation, in the afternoon we were part of Revie's . . .

7. The Book of Leeds

'You shall count seven sabbaths of years for your-self, seven times seven years; and the time of the seven sabbaths of years shall be to you forty-nine years. Then you shall cause the trumpet of the Jubilee to sound on the tenth day of the seventh month; on the Day of Atonement you shall make the trumpet to sound throughout all your land. And you shall consecrate the fiftieth year, and proclaim liberty throughout all the land to all its inhabitants. It shall be a Jubilee for you'

Leviticus 25: 8–11

2010. Promotion to the Championship.The voice on the Elland Road Tannoy proclaims liberty throughout all the land – or at least all the city – but warns Loiners to 'keep off the pitch, please keep off the pitch.' Fat chance. Not after the relegations, administration and humiliation. Not after the nation-wide mockery. Not after three seasons trapped in the third division. Not after a half-century of rise and fall, success and failure, hope and hopelessness. Before the game that sealed promotion I took my dad to the Queen's Hotel, the high and unbreachable white fortress he used to call The Ritz of Leeds. The hotel, like Leeds United, has one foot in the past and one foot in the future.There are plaques on its walls commemorating the city's great and good and some of its suites are named after long-dead football heroes. I half expect to bump into Revie or Waterhouse or Eamonn Andrews – or some other ghosts from the past. Dad is eighty-one and I will soon be fifty. Fifty years, I tell him, since This Sporting Life *was published. What a book, what a movie; the last, and most experimental of the New Wave films. Its reverse chronology was very influential. It was way ahead of its time, coming years before Martin Amis's* Time's Arrow, *or Kurt Vonnegut's* Slaughterhouse 5 *where the anti-hero watches a backwards-run film of the American bombing of Germany and sees cities rebuilding themselves. Over the past fifty years Leeds has rebuilt itself from a provincial backwater to a European metropolis. It has tried to shed its insular, parochial, fatalistic mindset. But it has always been a schizophrenic city; a city with two parallel existences, two contradictory narratives.*

2000. Top of the Premiership on the first day of the year, third at the end of the season and UEFA Cup semi-finalists. Leeds is rebranding itself as a shiny new city, a twenty-four-hour continental hub, a vision of the post-industrial, postmodern, multicultural future. Nelson Mandela opens the new Millennium Square, introduced by Lucas Radebe. O'Leary's babies are the darlings of the media. The game is about to be blown away by the new cosmopolitanism as foreign owners, managers and players seize its commanding heights. An Asian student is left unconscious after an attack outside a Leeds nightclub. Criminal charges are pressed against two Leeds United players and the club begins to unravel. Peace publishes the first novel of his Red Riding quartet – a brutal, unsparing exploration of the region that spawned the Ripper. Leeds is about to sink or swim, Champions League or bust, vibrant European city or provincial backwater. It has some of the best nightclubs in the world and one of the best football clubs in Britain but to flourish in this commercial free-for-all, both the city and the team need to be in, and stay in, the promised land. Unlike Revie and Cussins, O'Leary and Ridsdale get the chequebook, and the club credit card, out. They spend, spend, spend their way into the world's most lucrative club competition. And they reinvent themselves as the go-getting, free-flowing, swashbuckling new kids on the block.

1990. Second Division champions. And the north will rise again. Revie is dead and Thatcherism has collapsed and Wilkinson, like Fukuyama, declares the end of history and locks up the ghost of old Don. The football world is in motion, spinning out of control and nobody knows what will happen next. The Iron Curtain and the Berlin Wall have been breached and Italia 90 puts the country in the grip of an incurable football fever. The Taylor Report, 'Nessun Dorma', Gascoigne's tears, Fever Pitch *pave the way for a new era of English foot-ball. Fukuyama thinks the grand narrative of Western cap-italism has reached its climax and that the movement towards the realisation of human potential has found its ultimate expres-sion in a neo-liberal, free-market, winner-takes-all globalisa-tion. Football comes home and the north is regenerated and Leeds reorganises itself to compete in a new global economy, created by multinational corporations, which has decimated much of the traditional manufacturing areas of Britain's industrial heartlands. And – a year after Revie, the man who changed everything for Leeds United, was cremated on the outskirts of Edinburgh, a victim of a terrible disease – the city will, once again, turn outwards to the world beyond, rise above the sordid and rejoice in the beautiful, shed its history, abolish the cate-gory of the impossible and soar into the future. Leeds United are on the move again, marching on together, coming from nowhere to terrorise the respectable.*

1980. Allan Clarke, one of Revie's favourite sons, takes over and, after five years of decline, there is a new mood of opti-mism, the sense of a new dawn. Clarke promises to deliver a trophy within three years. In his first season, Leeds finish ninth in the First Division. Then he signs Kenny Burns and Frank Worthington but the interest payments on the cash borrowed to pay for them leave the club on the verge of bankruptcy and they disappear in – into – a cloud of smoke; a fog which, once again, hangs over the city. Leeds, the West Riding, Yorkshire, all turn nasty and violent, unleashing a vicious parochialism. In response to the harrowing of the north, we, who are Leeds, close ranks, batten down the hatches, turn our backs on the outside world. Leeds fans demand a return to the past. They sing 'Bring back, bring back, bring back Don Revie to Leeds'. And, as United bring back the Revieites – Clarke, Gray and Bremner – the city slips back into isolation and out of the mainstream of British society. Thatcher is in power, Revie's character is assassinated and John Lennon is murdered. It's the end of an era; an age when the Billy Liar generation dreamed of being the first northerners to stand on the top of the earth and look out at the promised land. The great classless, utopian, meritocratic experiment has not brought a dynamic, energetic and upwardly mobile society. It has brought soulless concrete towns, brutalising architecture and the destruction of vital pieces of the country's history.

1970. Leeds are English champions and making a bid for the impossible Treble. They have seven players called up for the England squad. All their Scottish, Welsh and Irish players are full internationals. Revie says he won't be satisfied until his team have landed the world club championship. Eddie Gray waltzes past six Burnley defenders to score one of the goals of the century. Leeds is pedestrianising its town centre and building new monuments to its ambition, like the Yorkshire Post *headquarters and the International Pool. It will become the Motorway City of the Seventies. The M1 and the inner ring road connect it to the outside world as Revie lets the Lads off the leash, lets them play a more open, exhilarating brand of football. The sixties are over: the Beatles have split, England failed to defend their World Cup title and Wilson is out of office. Busby retires, Bestie keeps going* missing and Revie's Leeds and Shankly's Liverpool emerge as the powers of the English game. Manufacturing begins to disappear and a service-based, information economy begins to take its place. The Billy Liar generation accuses the old city of kneeling down before the god of poured concrete. A court hears that two Leeds police officers took a special interest in David Oluwale, who was found face down in the River Aire, urinating on him as he slept and making him perform 'penances', such as banging his head on the pavement. The disgraced Leeds architect John Poulson faces bankruptcy; his practice collapses, his habit of bribing local councillors is investigated and his shiny civic showpieces are exposed as hollow fantasies – monuments to blandness and brutality.

1960. *Relegation to the Second Division.* This Sporting Life *and* A Kind of Loving *are published,* Billy Liar *opens in the West End,* Room at the Top *is nominated for ten Oscars and Northern Man revolutionises British life. The New Wave films, adopting Joe Lampton's mantra 'I was going to the Top', tell stories about provincial ambition, about aspirational anti-heroes desperate to flee their grimy, industrial backwaters and climb up hills carved out of millstone grit, look out over exciting new vistas and dream of making something of their lives. Leeds, like the rest of the country, is moving from a blue-collar to a white-collar society. There is a feeling of hope, a sense of possibility, a desperation for change. Leeds has always been a place of exchange, of comers and goers, of appearances and disappearances. It has always been a cross-off point in the middle of Britain, equidistant between London and Edinburgh, halfway between Hull and

Liverpool. And it is now about to go to the Top, to take the great leap forward. The Tetley's empire expands, Leeds city council announces a system of urban motorways and Billy Bremner makes his debut. The promised land is there for the taking.

Conclusion

'At Elland Road, a sleeping giant is rousing itself for the journey back to the promised land.'

Oliver Kay, *The Times*, 2010

Liz: 'It's easy. You get on a train and, four hours later, there you are in London.'
Billy: 'The idea of being in London next Saturday, put down on paper and staring me in the face, filled my bowels with quick-flushing terror.'

1900. Mir Zanen Do. We are here. The train pulls into the station and the porters shout 'Leeds'. The doors are thrown open and, as my great-grandfather stares up at the black town hall tower, some touts try to seize his luggage. But he entrusts his bundles of belongings to a kind stranger, an Irishman who speaks a bit of Yiddish. The Irishman tells him that the Jewish ghetto is a filthy, overcrowded, stinking hell-hole. 'Welcome to Leeds,' he smiles. Still, he has made it, he is here, at last, at the threshold of a new life, a new beginning, a new world across the ocean. Now we are slaves; in the year ahead may we be free men.

2010. The train pulls into the station and my dad is waiting
for me on the platform. Always the station, always the train.
We have a cup of tea in the Queen's Hotel and he tells me
about the time he waited on Revie's table in the ballroom at
Manny Cussins' daughter's wedding. It's all over, he says
suddenly. Leeds will choke against Bristol Rovers. And then
they'll choke in the play-offs. They've been playing badly ever
since they beat Man United. They've gone, lost the plot. I
remind him that he wrote off the great Revie team back in
the early-1970s and they bounced back, stronger than ever,
winning the Cup and then the title.

Whoever wrote the script for the 2009-10 season will
have been keenly aware of the two contradictory narratives of the Book of Leeds: one, that we have a manifest destiny to triumph, and, two, that we never do. It
was a season of two halves. In the first half, Grayson's
team established themselves as runaway leaders, amassing
an incredible 56 points. For a while, even more incredibly, they stopped being The Club Everyone Loves To
Hate. In fact, after knocking Manchester United out
of the FA Cup at Old Trafford, they became English
football's feel-good story. Following a decade of billionaire ownership and Big Four dominance, the truculent
Yorkshiremen had not only restored the magic of the
Cup – 'a bit of romance filtered back into football's
ugly modern world and it was long overdue,' hymned
the *Daily Mail* – they had become an antidote to the
debt-loading investors who were sucking the life out
of the game.

Storming the home of their oldest foes raised expectations to preposterous, delusionary heights. The Mighty

Whites were certainties for automatic promotion. They would soon be going toe to toe with the big boys. Given their footballing pedigree, they would undoubtedly attract the attention of a billionaire benefactor – who would then throw money at a talented cast of players and propel them, once more, towards the promised land.

In the second half of the campaign, of course, Leeds stumbled. The pressure had a paralysing effect. Promotion began to slip away. Another classic choke seemed on the cards. This probably explained the gloom at half-time in the final game of the season. Elland Road was overcome by fatalism. Leeds had to beat Bristol Rovers to go up, but they were a goal behind and down to ten men. And they hadn't created a single chance. All was lost. In the press room, a Leeds-supporting colleague affected a Private Fraser demeanour. 'We're doomed to the play-offs,' he sighed. 'Which means we're stuck in this division for another season. We never win play-offs: Charlton 1987, Watford 2006, Doncaster 2007, Millwall 2008 . . .' Somewhat improbably, I found myself quoting Teddy Sheringham back at him. Sheringham once said that the greatest sight in football was Manchester United chasing a lead. For me, I pointed out, a far more thrilling sight had always been the Mighty Whites chasing a lead while handicapped by a four-match home ban (1971-2) or a fifteen-point deduction (2007-8) or a bent referee (1960-2010). Being one man down was grist for our mill.

And so it came to pass. Two goals in four minutes sent Leeds back into the Championship. When the final whistle sounded, thousands of delirious fans invaded the pitch. Dave Gaertner, the press officer of Leeds United Supporters Club, once explained what it felt like to be a Leeds fan. 'I once saw a cartoon of a mouse looking up as a huge eagle swoops down on it,' he told the *Guardian*. 'The mouse is holding up its middle finger at the eagle.' After a long period of inertia, of confinement – of absence – the club has, once again, emerged from the wilderness to stick its middle finger up at the football elite. The glacial pace of progress has suddenly accelerated and a lingering sense of inferiority has exploded in an instant of euphoria. An old world has disappeared and a new one has emerged to fill the gap; a new tribe, a new generation, is about to get its chance.

This time around, however, the new tribe are not trying to smash the glass ceiling. While we were away things have changed. The Premier League's world-conquering boom has created a chasm between the elite clubs and the rest. The English top flight, the world's richest league, has become a plutocratic competition, winnable only by a small handful of teams. Only four clubs have won it in 18 years: Man United, Chelsea, Arsenal and Blackburn. Four clubs – Man United, Chelsea, Arsenal and Liverpool – have won 16 out of the last 19 FA Cups. Portsmouth, last season's beaten Cup finalists, paid the price for their ambition by appearing in the companies' winding-up court and getting relegated. From time to time, unfashionable provincial teams like Portsmouth, Hull and Burnley manage to get into the Premier League. But their only ambition – a task which unsurprisingly proved beyond all three last season – is to stay in it.

Conclusion

Leeds United are different. They are based in the fourth biggest city in the country, have a fanatical support base and play in a world-famous stadium. But whereas previous new dawns – such as Wilkinson's banning of Revieite images and the O'Leary-Ridsdale dash for growth – were attempts to erase the past, this one is infused with the myth and mystique of the past. The Glory Days continue to cast a shadow over Elland Road, where visitors are greeted by a bronze statue of Billy Bremner, our Scottish warrior-king. Echoes of past glories ring around the ground. Most of the Revieites still live in Leeds or keep coming back for reunions, which are always packed out with hundreds of fans. They give after-dinner speeches, open supermarkets and act as ambassadors and matchday hosts. Their autobiographies do a roaring trade.

It is as if we are trying to hammer the old world of sideburned centre halves, sock tags and Smiley badges into the emptied scenes of our childhoods. The good-old-bad-old days are being revisited, and rewritten, by people who were children and teenagers in the seventies and are now curating exhibitions, writing books and commissioning dramas about their formative years. In January 2010, just as Leeds United made a brief return to public consciousness, *Red Riding* – a series set in the washed-out grey landscapes of mid-seventies Leeds – won a BAFTA and *The Damned United* DVD was released. 'I wanted to capture a disappearing world,' explained Tom Hooper, the film's director; a world of dark dressing rooms, half-time cups of tea, red-brick terraced houses and perpetually dull, leaden skies.

After saying goodbye to my dad at the Queen's, and before going off to Elland Road for the Bristol Rovers match, I revisited the old, disappearing world at Leeds City Museum, which is housed in one of Cuthbert Brodrick's three great Victorian buildings and was originally known as the Mechanics Institute, a place of 'self-improvement for the working man'. After the Second World War it reopened as an amateur theatre; my uncle Louis' play They Came To Leeds – about the east European Jews who escaped the pogroms – was staged there. In 2010, it had become a theatre of memory. On the ground floor, next to the final resting place of the 'Leeds Mummy', a film celebrating the city's great and good was playing on an endless loop. Alan Bennett was referred to as a 'national treasure' – although his national appeal, according to the film, lay in his parochialism, his provincialism and his equivocal relationship to change. On the first floor, several Jewish-themed stalls celebrated the community's heritage using religious artefacts and klezmer music. A copy of the *Jewish Telegraph* featured the fortieth anniversary of the Beth Hamidrash Hagadol Synagogue Choir. Over four decades, 160 choristers had sung in the choir. I was one of them, and I spotted myself in the 1973 photograph, in the front row with six other boys. In the two most recent photographs, the front row of sopranos had disappeared; most of the singers were in their seventies and eighties.

The main exhibition was on the top floor. It was entitled *A Game Of Two Halves* and showcased the history and memorabilia of Leeds United Football Club. It included a video of the hundred greatest Leeds goals of all time, including Lorimer's disallowed effort in the 1975 European Cup Final. Revie's great team, it seemed, were now just as much part of the city's heritage industry as Burtons tailoring, Waddingtons printers and Tetleys beer. Revie created Leeds United As We Know It. He found a crack in the wall and tried to whittle out an escape route. But, like these bastions of industry and real ale, his creation has been left for dead by the global giants. After a half-century in which the club, like the city, has tried to reinvent itself as a thrusting, forward-looking European force, it has somehow ended up as a symbol of a disappearing old Britain. It is forever associated with a pre-1992 world. A world before the Premier League and the Champions League transformed the footballing landscape. A world where tough, sometimes, brutal teams put side before self every time; where tempers flared, hatchet men went unpunished for taking out the opposition's star turn and fans – and sideburned players – kicked the shit out of each other. The Damned United.

Bremner's statue is about as close as modern Leeds gets to a signature piece of public art. In the mid-1980s, Anthony Gormley's Brick Man was denied planning permission in the face of trenchant opposition from the local press and Conservatives. There are no iconic, wow-factor buildings or Angel-of-the-North type sculptures to greet visitors arriving by rail. I didn't lose much sleep when KW Linfoot went into administration, but I lamented the decommissioning of its skycraper. Like Elland Road and the town hall, those two great monuments to metamorphosis, it would have put Leeds on the map again. In a decade when most

British cities managed to erect a statement building, the non-appearance of Leeds' first skyscraper seemed more of a metaphor for the city's – and its football team's – longstanding under-achievement. Like the disappearance of the 'Promised Land Delivered' sign, its absence spoke of thwarted ambition, a prophecy unfulfilled. As in the mid-seventies, it was the recession stupid. But there was also something very Leeds about Linfoot's demise. As Rod McPhee, a *Yorkshire Evening Post* columnist, commented: 'The truth is that a lot of people still don't like a winner, or only like a winner when they've lost everything.'

Leeds United lost pretty much everything in the last decade. They lost a fantasy football team of homegrown talent: Robinson, Woodgate, Kilgallon, Harte, Delph, McPhail, Lennon, Milner, Rose, Keogh, Smith. They lost ownership of their football stadium and training ground. And they lost membership of the Premier League, the flagship of world club football, missing out on the satellite TV bonanza of the noughties. As a result, somewhat perversely, some people grew to like them, and their own fan base grew larger and more fanatical. At the start of the decade they had tried to break into the European elite alongside Manchester United, Real Madrid, Barcelona and the two Milans. By the end of it, they were rubbing shoulders with Yeovil Town, Hartlepool, Southend and Wycombe. And yet, in recent seasons, only Manchester United, Liverpool and Arsenal have had more visits to their website.

In an anthology of writing edited by Nick Hornby, United fan Don Watson proudly described Leeds as 'the apotheosis of the seventies. After all it was here that the outdoor scenes of *A Clockwork Orange* were shot.' In *Pies And Prejudice*, Stuart Maconie recalled his youthful infatuation with Revie's team: 'The Nazis in Umbro, the Daleks dressed by Gola, a crack squad of inhuman automata with one purpose in mind, the ruthless subjugation of other life forms . . . I loved them.' I, too, loved the Revie side. The Don delivered. He set a template for all unfashionable teams hoping to barge into the ranks of the elite. He is the reason why, as the railway curves around Elland Road football ground, my heart always lifts. I was told that my great-grand-father, clutching his one-way ticket to the promised land, experienced a similar feeling when he spotted the black town hall tower at the turn of the last century. The Revie side were not so much a football team more a paradigm shift: a one-way ticket out of a life of provincial isolation. This book is, in part, a love letter to that side, to a lost, disappearing world, to the epoch of my childhood, to the way I grew up thinking and dreaming about football. I'll never forget the way Super Leeds tore into Bayern Munich in 1975. Paris is scorched in my mind. But what's the use of powerlessly mourning the mysterious promise such a moment held? It's time to let go of the legacy. To stop being a seventies revival act. To shed the past.

Before we do, we should accept that Revie was not 'the messiah'; neither was he 'a very naughty boy'. The Life Of Don was not about working miracles. Nor was it, as one revisionist account of the sixties and seventies claims, 'in part responsible for everything bad about British sport and sporting attitudes in those benighted decades.' It was about the vertiginous rise of an upwardly mobile, inwardly anxious, ultimately fatalistic Northern Man. His insecurity was a key facet of his, his club's – and his adopted city's – character. Like Keith Waterhouse, and my dad, he was motivated by a fear of returning to the poverty of his childhood. One of Waterhouse's obituarists noted that the writer never seemed to feel secure, 'even when his vast output and considerable royalties should have assured him that he would never lack money again.' Hoggart wrote about Northern Man's deep feeling of vulnerability in the last chapter of *The Uses Of Literacy*: 'He has left his class, at least in spirit, by being in certain ways unusual, and he is still unusual in another class, too tense and overwound.'

Age has caught up with Northern Man. Many of the angry young writers who stormed the citadels in 1960 – the year *Billy Liar* hit the West End, *Room at the Top* took Hollywood by storm and *This Sporting Life* and *A Kind Of Loving* appeared in bookshops – are now in their seventies and eighties. Waterhouse, Alan Sillitoe and John Braine are no longer with us. Lke Revie's Leeds, these prickly outsiders were part of a restless, meritocratic tide, their working-class anti-heroes – Billy Fisher, Joe Lampton, Frank Machin – redolent of a gritty, black-and-white past. Their stories were laced with hope, confidence and a sense of adventure. They were going to the Top. Sillitoe, who created the movement's archetype – Arthur Seaton – died as I was finishing this book, a week before the most socially unrepresentative parliament since the 1930s was voted in. 67 per cent of the new cabinet go to top private schools – compared with just 7 per cent of the total population – as do 75 per cent of judges, 70 per cent of finance directors and 45 per cent of top civil servants. 'More than ever, power belongs to an old boy network of public schoolboys and Oxford graduates,' wrote the historian Dominic Sandbrook. 'The dream of a genuinely fluid, open society, with opportunities for all regardless of background, seems more remote than ever.'

Leeds United's – and football's – golden age, like the era of social mobility, is over. Unfashionable, provincial teams now dream only of survival – not of transforming themselves into English, or even European, champions. During the last fifty years, United have often been portrayed as the dark heart of football. Under Revie's tense and overwound control, they were labelled Dirty Leeds. During Risdale's ambitious tenure they became known as Greedy Leeds. 'Doing a Leeds' is now shorthand for chasing the dream and suffering a spectacular fall from grace. But there was nothing inevitable, as the anti-Leeds brigade gleefully suggest, about these meltdowns. Nor, as the club's tribalists incessantly protest, is there a conspiracy against Leeds. At the most crucial moments in their history, just as they were about to close in on the pinnacle, they have, quite simply, blown it. According to the received view of their most recent self-immolation, it was Ridsdale's hubris which did for Leeds. But this is only part of the story. In 2001, just as in 1919, 1975 and 1992 – and on many other big, one-off, all-or-nothing occasions – there was a loss of nerve, a collective failure of will. O'Leary's kids, only ninety minutes away from a 're-match' with Bayern Munich in the European Cup final, went feral, froze and hit the buffers. We have often lacked the ruthlessness, the self-belief, to cross the threshold. Alex Ferguson would never have kept his big names on the pitch simply for old time's sake, like Jimmy Armfield did in Paris. Liverpool cast Bill Shankly adrift after his departure, even going so far as to ban their high priest from the training ground. The tribe of Leeds have never stopped pining for their high priest.

As Eddie Gray has pointed out, '(Revie's) era can be a noose around the necks of some managers'. In the 36 years since his departure there has only been one manager who, however briefly, escaped that noose. And, under Howard Wilkinson, Leeds won their only major trophy of that period. The past glories were 'crutches', argued the Sergeant, 'for people who basked in the reflected glory of those bygone days'. They still are. The hope is that Grayson – like Wilkinson, his old manager, steeped in the mythology of Leeds United – will now, also, break free of the double-edged legacy. That he will write a new chapter in the Book of Leeds, usher in a new era of reinvention. That in an ever-changing, corporate world of greed and excess, his side will become, once again, an irresistible force, a harbinger of an exciting future, launching another exhilarating assault on an all-powerful, self-serving, rapacious establishment. That Billy Liar will get on the train, the Israelites will cross over into the promised land and the name of Leeds United, as one of its founders once dreamed, will finally appear 'on the rolls of the Football Association as the city which passed through fire, was cleansed, and given a fair and sporting chance to rehabilitate itself'.

Bibliography

Kester Aspden, *The Hounding of David Oluwale*, Vintage, 2007

Philippe Auclair, *Cantona, The Rebel Who Would Be King*, Macmillan, 2009

Rob Bagchi and Paul Rogerson, *The Unforgiven: The Story of Don Revie's Leeds United*, Aurum, 2009

Alan Bennett, *Talking Heads*, BBC, 1988
                              Untold Stories, Faber, 2005

Mihir Bose, *Sporting Alien*, Mainstream, 1996

Billy Bremner, *You Get Nowt for Coming Second*, Souvenir Press Ltd, 1969

Jack Charlton. *The Autobiography*, Partridge Press, 1996

Tony Collins, *Rugby's Great Split*, Routledge, 2006

Tony Collins, *The Curious Rise and Fall of Leeds Parish Church, in 1895 & All That, Leeds*, 2009

Richard Coomber, *King John*, Leeds United Publishing Limited, 2000

Jason Cowley, *The Last Game*, Simon & Schuster, 2009

Hunter Davies, *The Glory Game*, Sphere, 1973

Anna Douglas and Janet Douglas, *A Lasting Moment: Marc Riboud, Photographs of Leeds*, 1954 & 2004, Leeds City Council, 2009

Rob Endeacott, *Dirty Leeds*, Tonto, 2009

Max Farrar, *The Struggle for 'Community' In A British Multi-Ethnic Inner-City Area: Paradise in the Making*, Edwin Mellen Press 2003

Murray Freedman, *Essays on Leeds and Anglo-Jewish History and Demography*, self-publication, 2003

Caroline Gall, *Service Crew: The Inside Story of Leeds United's Hooligan Gangs*, Milo Books, 2007

Johnny Giles, *Forward with Leeds*, Stanley Paul, 1970

Dan Goldstein, *The Rough Guide: English Football – A Fans' Handbook*, 1999–2000

Eddie Gray, *Marching On Together*, Hodder & Stoughton, 2001

Nigel Grizzard, *Leeds Jewry and the Great War 1914–1918*, Porton and Sons Ltd, 1981

Lynsey Hanley, *Estates*, Granta, 2007

Bernard Hare, *Urban Grimshaw And The Shed Crew*, Sceptre, 2006

Tony Harrison, *V*, Bloodaxe, 1985

Phil Hay, *Leeds United From Darkness Into White*, Mainstream, 2007

Richard Hoggart, *The Uses Of Literacy*, Pelican, 1957

Norman Hunter, *Biting Talk: My Autobiography*, Hodder & Stoughton, 2004

Simon Inglis, *League Football and the Men Who Made It*, Willow Books, 1988

Anthony C King, *The Problem of Identity and the Cult of Eric Cantona*, PhD Thesis, 1995

Ernest Krausz, *Leeds Jewry: Its History and Social Structure*, Cambridge: Jewish Historical Society of England, 1964

Irina Kudenko, *Negotiating Jewishness: Identity and Citizenship in the Leeds Jewish Community*, PhD Thesis, 2008

Bibliography

Simon Kuper and Stefan Szymanski, *Why England Lose*, HarperCollins, 2009

Peter Lorimer, *Leeds and Scotland Hero*, Mainstream, 2005

John Minnis with Trevor Mitchell, *Religion and Place in Leeds*, English Heritage, 2007

Stuart Maconie, *Pies And Prejudice*, Ebury, 2007

Andrew Mourant, *Don Revie – Portrait Of A Footballing Enigma*, Mainstream, 1990

The Essential History of Leeds United, Headline, 2000

Duncan McKenzie with David Saffer, *The Last Fancy Dan*, Vertical, 2009

David McKie, *A Local History of Britain*, Atlantic, 2008

Gregor Muir, *Lucky Kunst*, Aurum Press, 2009

WR Mitchell, *A History Of Leeds*, Phillimore, 2000

David O'Leary, *Leeds United On Trial*, Little, Brown, 2001

David Peace, *The Damned United*, Faber, 2006

             Nineteen Seventy-Four, Serpent's Tail, 1999

Tom Palmer, *If You're Proud to be a Leeds Fan*, Mainstream, 2002

Caryl Phillips, *Foreigners*, Harvill Secker, 2007

Peter Ridsdale, *United We Fall*, Macmillan, 2007

Barney Ronay, *The Manager*, Sphere, 2009

Phil Rostron, *Leeds United: Trials and Tribulations*, Mainstream, 2004

Dave Russell, *Looking North*, Manchester University Press, 2004

David Saffer & Howard Dapin, *Boys Of '72*, The History Press, 2006

Louis Saipe, *A History Of The Jews Of Leeds*, Leeds Jewish Representative Council, 1956

Dominic Sandbrook, *Never Had It So Good*, Abacus, 2005

Stuart Sprake and Tim Johnson, *The Forgotten Truth of Gary Sprake*, Tempus, 2006

David Storey, *This Sporting Life*, Macmillan, 1960

David Thornton, *Great Leeds Stories*, Fort, 2005

Alwyn W Turner, *Crisis? What Crisis?* Aurum, 2008

Stephen Wagg, 'Nowt For Being Second, Leeds, Leeds United and the Ghost of Don Revie', in *Sport, Leisure and Culture in the Postmodern City*, Ashgate, 2009

Martin Wainwright, *True North*, Guardian books, 2009

Leeds:Shaping The City, RIBA, 2009

Andrew Ward and John Williams, *Football Nation*, Bloomsbury, 2009

Keith Waterhouse, *Billy Liar*, Penguin, 1959

City Lights, Hodder & Stoughton, 1984

Don Watson, 'Pyscho Mike And The Phantom Ice Rink', in *My Favourite Year*, H F & G Witherby, 1993

John Wray, *Leeds United and a Life in the Press Box*, Vertical, 2008

Ken Worpole, *Scholarship Boy:The Poetry of Tony Harrison*, New Left Review, September/October 1985

Acknowledgements

This book would not have been possible without the support and enthusiasm of David Luxton, a literary agent, Leeds United fan and all-round-nice-guy. Thanks to my mum for being my research assistant, my dad for all those breakfasts and trips to the cemetery and Kester Aspden for showing me the way. Thanks to Tristan Jones and Rowan Yapp for their excellent editing skills and Richard Collins for his excellent copy-editing skills. Thanks to my family for putting up with me for the last two years. And thanks to the following for providing a quiet place to research and write: Marie Burns, Jason Coppell, Kevin Mitchell, David Saffer, Tom Taylor-Jones, The British Library, Leeds Central Library, The Leeds Library, The University Of Essex Library, The Leeds Jewish Telegraph, The Ellington Hotel, The Queens Hotel, The Radisson Hotel and 42, The Calls.

Knowledge, memories, inspiration and advice have been provided by the following people: John Aizelwood, Freddy Apfel, Rob Bagchi, Irena Bauman, James Brown, Will Buckley, Paul Chatterton, Allan Clarke, Elaine Clavane, Emile Clavane, Peter Clavane, Anita Cohen, Lennie Cohen, Tony Collins, David Conn, Robert Endeacott, Hayden Evans, Max Farrar, Ronnie

Feldman, Bill Fotherby, Murray Freedman, Duncan Hamilton, Bernard Hare, Sue Hollinraike, Tom Hooper, Neil Jeffries, Jeremy Krikler, Irina Kudenko, James Lawton, Ian Lee, Mike Levy, Rod McPhee, Jodie Matthews, Shakeel Meer, Blake Morrison, Hazel Mostyn, Tom Palmer, David Peace, Caryl Phillips, Ces Podd, Jeff Powell, Lucas Radebe, Dave Russell, David Saffer, Phil Shaw, Leslie Silver, Sheila Silver, Tony Stanley, Nick Stimson, Kate Storey, Gordon Strachan, Rachael Unsworth, Stephen Wagg, David Walker, Keith Warner, Jonathan Wilson.

And a final thanks to the three doyens of the Golden Age, Hugh McIlvanney, Brian Glanville and James Lawton, who made me want to stop playing football and start writing about it.

Index

Index

Brodrick, Cuthbert, 19, 21, 22–3, 36
Brolin, Tomas, 174
Brown, James, 160, 164–5, 166
Brown, Tony, 88, 94
Buchan, Charlie, 30
Buckley, Major Frank, 39
Burn, Gordon, 167
Burnley FC, 90, 148, 250, 256
Burns, Ken, 124
Burns, Kenny, 156, 249
Burton's, 36, 94, 183, 187, 259
Busby, Matt, 52, 65, 72–3, 78, 84, 112

Cantona, Eric
    at Leeds, 114, 151, 155, 160–1, 170–1, 174
    Leeds fans' homage to, 159, 171, 203
    sold to Manchester United, 168–75
Caplin, Bobby, 79
Cardiff City, 208, 219, 226
Carlisle United, 9
Carson, Scott, 225, 232
Carter, Raich, 40
Caspian media company, 183–5, 186, 191, 192
Celtic, 88, 123
Champions League: (2001), 4, 205–6
Channon, Mick, 110
Chapman, Herbert, 26, 29–31

Charity Shield: (1975), 119
Charles, John, 39–40, 57, 114
Charlie Bubbles (film), 111
Charlton, Jack
    award, 202
    background, 103
    on Collins, 66
    as hard man, 63, 64
    on Lambton, 40
    as later role model, 228
    matches, 86, 87
    perks, 76
    pre-match rituals, 89
    and Revie, 48–9, 54
    tactics, 83
Charlton Athletic, 10, 131, 156
Chelsea
    anti-Semitism, 147
    Bates at, 226
    finances, 163, 191, 232
    hard men, 63
    matches against Leeds, 84–7, 90, 161
    recent dominance, 256
    Service Crew riots at, 141
    team image, 84–5
City Lights (Waterhouse), 138
Clark, Alan (politician), 148–9
Clarke, Allan
    background, 103
    joins Leeds, 83
    as manager, 133, 157, 249
    matches, 1, 86, 95–6, 98

Index

Gormley, Anthony, 259

Graham, George, 185, 188, 189–91, 213

Gray, Eddie
background, 103
at Cussins' funeral, 147
on Leeds' popularity, 82
on Leeds' reputation as hard men, 63
as manager, 133, 157
as manager again, 225
matches, 83, 85, 87, 90, 95, 250
on Revie, 264

Grayson, Simon, 7, 8, 228, 229–30, 231, 254, 264

Greaves, Jimmy, 55, 173

Grimshaw, Atkinson, 138

Guinness scandal, 149

Haigh, Kenneth, 43, 69

Hall, Sir John, 183

Hall, Willis, 69

Halpern, Sir Ralph, 187

Hampson, Billy, 30, 39

Hanley, Lynsey, 235

Hardaker, Alan, 91

Harding, Colonel T. W., 26, 28–9, 36, 103, 234

Harris, Gabby, 80

Harris, Richard, 60, 70

Harris, Ron 'Chopper', 63, 87

Harrison, Stephen, 187

Harrison, Tony, 67, 68, 69, 105, 137, 139

Hart, Paul, 190

Harvey, David, 64, 67, 78

Harvey, Marcus, 167

Hasselbaink, Jimmy Floyd, 191, 204

Hateley, Mark, 132, 174

Heath, Edward, 107

Helm, John, 81

Hepworth, Barbara, 135

Hepworth, Norris, 29

Hereford United, 231

Heysel stadium disaster (1985), 130, 131

Hidegkuti, Nándor, 50

Higgins, Jack, 69, 70

Hilaire, Vince, 126, 145, 202, 203

Hillsborough disaster (1989), 131–2, 158–9

Hirst, Damien, 166, 167–8

Histon FC, 229

The History of Button Hill (Stowell novel), 142

Hoddle, Glenn, 132

Hoggart, Richard, 69, 233, 242, 262

Holbeck Rugby Club, 9

Hood, David, 184

Hooper, Tom, 257

Hornby, Nick, 159–60, 260–1

Houseman, Peter, 86

Howard, Michael, 149

Index

Index

Index

Sidique Khan, Mohammad, 215–16, 217
Silkin, Sam, 149
Sillitoe, Alan, 137, 262
Silver, Leslie, 80, 156–7, 182, 183, 185, 242–3
Simon, Sydney, 78, 242
Simpson, Ian, 238–9
Sing As We Go (film), 46
Singh, Harpal, 203–4, 212–13
Sky, 162, 197
Slaughterhouse 5 (Vonnegut novel), 247
Smiles, Samuel, 22
Smith, Alan, 190, 191, 203, 206, 208, 212, 224
Smith, Giles, 227
Smith, Harvey, 43
Smith, Tommy, 63
Snodin, Ian, 132
Southampton FC, 10, 95–6, 99
Southwell, Tim, 164–5
Sparta Prague, 90
Speed, Gary, 161, 169, 174
Speight, Kevin, 194
Spencer, David, 187
Sprake, Gary, 52, 64, 86, 89, 103
The Square Ball (fanzine), 172
Stein, Jock, 123, 133
Steinsaltz, Rabbi Adin, 241
Sterland, Mel, 170
Stiles, Nobby, 63

Storey, David, 46, 62–4, 67, 69, 135–6
Storey, Kate, 61–2, 135
Storey, Peter, 63
Stowell, Gordon, 34–5, 142
Strachan, Gordon, 157–8, 160, 161, 169, 170, 174
Stringer, Graham, 180
Stuttgart, 164, 169, 171
Sugar, Alan, 183
Suggett, Colin, 87–8, 94, 95
Sunderland AFC, 116, 123
Sutcliffe, Peter (Yorkshire Ripper), 119, 128, 219
Sutton FC, 90
Swan, George, 232
Swansea City, 58
Sykes, Paul, 184

Taiwo, Tom, 231, 232
Talking Heads (Bennett), 68, 137–8
Tanweer, Shehzad, 215–16
Tarbuck, Jimmy, 80
Taylor, Graham, 158
Taylor, Jack, 40–1
Taylor, Peter, 115
Taylor Report (1990), 158–9, 183
Tetley's beer, 178, 259
Thatcher, Margaret, 119, 125, 130, 132, 134, 149, 159

287

Index